OTHELLO

The RSC Shakespeare

Edited by Jonathan Bate and Eric Rasmussen

Chief Associate Editors: Héloïse Sénéchal and Jan Sewell

Associate Editors: Trey Jansen, Eleanor Lowe, Lucy Munro,
Dee Anna Phares

Othello

Textual editing: Dee Anna Phares

Introduction and "Shakespeare's Career in the Theater": Jonathan Bate

Commentary: Héloïse Sénéchal

Scene-by-Scene Analysis: Esme Miskimmin

In Performance: Karin Brown (RSC stagings), Jan Sewell (overview)

The Director's Cut (interviews by Jonathan Bate and Kevin Wright):
Trevor Nunn and Michael Attenborough

Playing Iago: Antony Sher

The RSC Shakespeare

William Shakespeare

OTHELLO

Edited by Jonathan Bate and Eric Rasmussen

Introduction by Jonathan Bate

The Modern Library
New York

CONTENTS

INTRODUCTION

VENICE

For Shakespeare's original audience, the title *The Tragedy of Othello, the Moor of Venice* would have instantly suggested a meeting of the familiar and the strange, of East and West. "Venice" was synonymous with European sophistication, "Moor" with the atmosphere of the Orient. Yet the short Italian novel on which the play is based makes little of the Moor's status as an outsider. Written by Giraldi Cinthio, it was one of a series of exemplary stories concerning marital infidelity. Its purpose was to show how "it sometimes happens that without any fault at all, a faithful and loving lady, through the insidious plots of a villainous mind, and the frailty of one who believes more than he need, is murdered by her faithful husband." In Venice, a Moor, dear to the Senate because he has served the interests of the republic in battle, marries a virtuous lady called Disdemona. The Venetian lords decide to change the guard in Cyprus and the Moor is chosen as commandant. Disdemona insists on going with him; they arrive safely in Cyprus (no storm, no Turks). The Moor's ensign or standard-bearer falls in love with Disdemona, who does not reciprocate. The ensign assumes that this is because she is in love with his superior, the corporal. His love for Disdemona turns to hate and he decides that if he cannot have her, nor should the Moor. He accordingly plots to make the Moor jealous of the corporal, thus destroying them both.

Venice was notorious for the number and openness of its courtesans, and the laxness of its wives. It was the pleasure capital of Europe, a city of sexual tourism. Cinthio's Disdemona, however, is "impelled not by female appetite but by the Moor's good qualities": she is an atypical Venetian woman. Shakespeare intends his Desdemona to be regarded in the same way, even as the men in the play exploit the stereotypical image of Venetian women. Iago pumps up

Rodorigo's desire on the quayside with talk of female lechery and he plays on Othello's fear that his wife might revert to type, reminding the Moor that Venetian women are habitual sexual deceivers:

> I know our country disposition well:
> In Venice they do let heaven see the pranks
> They dare not show their husbands: their best conscience
> Is not to leave't undone, but kept unknown.

Visiting Venice in the 1590s, Sir Henry Wotton remarked on the difficulty of distinguishing between whores and virtuous wives on the streets. The presence in the play of Bianca the courtesan ("A housewife that by selling her desires / Buys herself bread and cloth") is telling in this regard. In the overhearing scene, Othello fails to make exactly the distinction as to which woman, his wife or the courtesan, Iago and Cassio are talking about. Iago's seemingly casual references to Desdemona's "appetite" and "will," his view of Venetian women as sexual beasts, soon cause Othello to be convinced that his wife's hand is hot and moist, traditional signs of sexual license. The division between wife and whore is horribly dissolved in the fourth act, where home is turned to brothel, and Desdemona twice called "strumpet" and thrice "whore," culminating in the savage lines "I took you for that cunning whore of Venice / That married with Othello." Only when he has killed her does he rediscover the true coldness of her chastity—though just because Othello speaks of Desdemona thus, we should not regard her as the icy maiden of Petrarchan poetic tradition. In the scene before Othello's arrival in Cyprus she proves herself adept in feisty and sexually knowing banter with her male interlocutors. And at the very beginning of the play she has shown extraordinary strength of character in going against her father's will, eloping with Othello and then insisting on accompanying him to the frontier zone of Cyprus.

"THE MOOR"

Othello is ill at ease with Iago's language of double entendre because he is an "extravagant and wheeling stranger" who works within a very different poetic register. His verbal sphere is rich in allusion to an exotic other world filled with Arabian trees and turbaned Turks in Aleppo, not to mention "the Anthropophagi and men whose heads / Grew beneath their shoulders." "Valiant Othello, we must straight employ you / Against the general enemy Ottoman," says the Duke of Venice early in the play. The audience hears a consonance between the names of the captain-general "Othello" and the general enemy "Ottoman." This would have been especially apparent if, as is likely, the original pronunciation of the hero's name was Italianized as "Otello." Othman was the name of the founder of the mighty Ottoman or Turkish empire, the great rival civilization to Christianity. Othello's name suggests his origin in the Ottoman territories, against which he is now fighting. The clash of Christian against Turk was one of Shakespeare's major additions to his source.

To Shakespeare and his contemporaries, Turk, Arab, and Moor all represented the Islamic "other," but they were not necessarily homogenized into a single image of generic "barbarianism." Arabic culture was frequently associated with learning and civilization, in contrast to the prevailing images of Turk and Saracen. A Barbar could be "brave" rather than "barbarous": George Peele's *Battle of Alcazar in Barbary*, a play based on real recent historical events, has both "a barbarous Moor, / The negro Muly Hamet" and a "brave Barbarian Lord Muly Molocco." A Moor could help you out in your war against the Turk—or, for that matter, the Spaniard. How you judged the Islamic "other" depended not only on ideological stereotype but also on the particularities of diplomatic liaison and changing allegiance in a world of superpower rivalry. At the end of *Alcazar*, the evil Moor Muly Mahamet is defeated. The throne of Barbary goes to Abdelmelec's virtuous brother, who is also called Muly Mahamet and who was a real historical figure. His ambassador, Abd el-Oahed ben Messaoud, visited the Elizabethan court in 1600 in order to explore the possibility of forming an alliance to conquer Spain with a mixture of the English navy and African troops. Shakespeare's company played at court that Christmas, so he may have seen the Barbarian delegation in the flesh. The surviving portrait of the ambassador is perhaps the best image we have of what Shakespeare intended Othello to look like.

Peele's play mingled historical matter with a more general sense of the barbarian, the other, the devilish—bad Muly Mahamet surrounds himself with demonic and underworld associations. Audiences would have come to *The Moor of Venice* with the expectation of something similar, but witnessed a remarkable inversion whereby a

1. A noble Moor: the Barbary ambassador painted in London, 1600.

sophisticated Venetian is the one who comes to be associated with the devil and damnable actions. So evil is Iago's behavior that at the end of the play, Othello not only calls him a "demi-devil" but half expects him to have the cloven foot of Lucifer.

Othello is initially referred to (by Rodorigo and Iago) not by his name, but as "him" and then "his Moorship" and then "the Moor." Depriving someone of their name and referring to them solely in terms of their ethnic origin is a classic form of racism. In Shakespeare's other Venetian play, something similar happens with "the Jew." In early modern English, however, the primary usage of the term "Moor" was as a religious, not a racial, identification: Moor meant "Mohammedan," that is to say Muslim. The word was frequently used as a general term for "not one of us," non-Christian. To the play's original audience, the opposite of "the Moor" would have been not "the white man" but "the Christian."

One of the most striking things about the figure of Othello would accordingly have been that he is a committed Christian. The ground of the play is laid out in the first scene, when Iago trumpets his own military virtues, in contrast to Cassio's "theoretical" knowledge of the art of war (Cassio comes from Florence, home of such theorists of war as Machiavelli):

> And I — of whom his eyes had seen the proof
> At Rhodes, at Cyprus and on others' grounds,
> Christened and heathen . . .

These lines give an immediate sense of confrontation between Christian and heathen dominions, with Rhodes and Cyprus as pressure points. Startlingly, though, the Moor is fighting for the Christians, not the heathens.

Again, consider Othello's response to the drunken brawl in Cyprus:

> Are we turned Turks, and to ourselves do that
> Which heaven hath forbid the Ottomites?
> For Christian shame, put by this barbarous brawl!

Such Christian language in the mouth of a Moor, a Muslim, is inherently a paradox. It suggests that Othello would have been assumed to be a convert. The "baptism" that Iago says he will cause Othello to renounce would have taken place not at birth but at conversion. The action of the play reconverts Othello from Christianity, through the machinations of Iago. In this sense, it is fitting that Iago appeals to a "Divinity of hell" and that Othello acknowledges at the end of the play that he is bound for damnation.

The notion of conversion was crucial in the Elizabethan perception of the relationship between European Christianity and the Ottoman empire. The phrase to "turn Turk" entered the common lexicon. Islam was as powerful an alien force to Europeans in the sixteenth century as communism was to Americans in the twentieth. To turn Turk was to go over to the other side. It could happen in a number of different ways: some travelers converted by a process of cultural assimilation, others who had been captured and enslaved did so in the belief that they would then be released. It is easy to forget how many English privateers became Ottoman slaves—on one occasion, two thousand wives petitioned King James and Parliament for help in ransoming their husbands from Muslim captivity.

If Shakespeare read all the way through Richard Knolles' *General History of the Turks*, one of the books to which he seems to have turned during his preparation for the writing of *Othello*, he would have learned that once every three years the Turks levied a tax on the Christians living in the Balkans: it took the form of ten to twelve thousand children. They were deported and converted (circumcised), then trained up to become soldiers. They formed a highly feared cadre in the Turkish army known as the Janissaries—there is an elite guard of them in *The Battle of Alcazar*, while Bajazet's army in Christopher Marlowe's *Tamburlaine the Great* combines "circumcisèd Turks / And warlike bands of Christians renegade." Othello is a Janissary in reverse: not a Christian turned Muslim fighting against Christians, but a Muslim turned Christian fighting against Muslims. Although the captain-general of the Venetian army was always a "stranger," conversion in Othello's direction, from Muslim to Christian, was much rarer than the opposite turn.

The second Elizabethan sense of the word "Moor" was specifically racial and geographical: it referred to a native or inhabitant of Mauretania, a region of north Africa corresponding to parts of present-day Morocco and Algeria. This association is invoked when Iago falsely tells Rodorigo toward the end of the play that Othello "goes into Mauritania and taketh away with him the fair Desdemona." Ethnic Moors were members of a Muslim people of mixed Berber and Arab descent. In the eighth century they had conquered Spain. This may be the association suggested by Othello's second weapon, his sword of Spain.

Given that the Spanish empire was England's great enemy, there would have been a certain ambivalence about the Moors—they may have overthrown Christianity, but at least it was Spanish Catholic Christianity. Philip II's worst fear was an uprising of the remaining Moors in Granada synchronized with a Turkish invasion, just as Elizabeth I's worst fear was an uprising of the Irish synchronized with a Spanish invasion. As it was, the Turks took a different turn: in 1570, shortly after the end of the Morisco uprising and Philip's ethnic cleansing of Granada, they attacked Cyprus.

The alliance of European Christians against the Ottomans was uneasy because of post-Reformation divisions in Europe itself. Independent lesser powers such as Venice and England found themselves negotiating for footholds in the Mediterranean theater. Hence the diplomatic maneuvering that brought the Barbary ambassadors to London—and hence also the blow to Venice caused by the loss of Cyprus in 1571. Shakespeare changes history. He sees off the Turk and implies instead that the real danger to the isle comes from the internal collapse of civil society. Venice regarded Cyprus as a key Christian outpost against the Turk, but what happens in the play is that it is turned heathen from within rather than without. There is deep irony in Iago's "Nay, it is true, or else I am a Turk," for it *is* Iago who does the Turkish work of destroying the Christian community. All three major characters invert audience expectation: Othello is a counter-Janissary, Desdemona is—contrary to ethnic stereotyping—a Venetian lady who is not lascivious, and Christian Iago is a functional Turk.

Othello dies on a kiss, an embrace of black and white, perhaps a symbolic reconciliation of the virtues of West and East, Europe and

Orient, but the public image he wants to be remembered by in the letter back to Venice is of confrontation between Christian and Turk, with himself as the defender of Christianity in Aleppo, a point of eastern extremity in Syria. In smiting himself, Othello recognizes that he has now become the Turk. By killing Desdemona he has renounced his Christian civility and damned himself. He symbolically takes back upon himself the insignia of Islam—turban, circumcision—that he had renounced when he turned Christian. He has beaten a Venetian wife and traduced the state. He has been turned Turk. Not, however, by the general Ottoman but by the supersubtle Venetian, the "honest" Iago.

IAGO AND OTHELLO

As Shakespeare adds the Turkish context to the story that was his source, so he takes away the simple motivation of being in love with Disdemona that Cinthio gave the ensign. Jealousy over the matter of promotion is sufficient explanation for the first part of Iago's plot, whereby Cassio's weakness for the bottle leads to his being cashiered. But why does Iago then go so much further, utterly destroying the general on whose patronage he depends? Othello asks the question at the end of the play: "Will you, I pray, demand that demi-devil / Why he hath thus ensnared my soul and body?" But Iago refuses to answer: "Demand me nothing. What you know, you know. / From this time forth I never will speak word." It sounds like a deliberate challenge to the audience to work it out for themselves.

No one has risen to that challenge better than the early nineteenth-century critic William Hazlitt, who regarded the love of playacting as the key to Iago's procedure ("Othello," *Characters of Shakespear's Plays*, 1817):

> Iago in fact belongs to a class of character, common to Shakespeare and at the same time peculiar to him; whose heads are as acute and active as their hearts are hard and callous . . . [He] plots the ruin of his friends as an exercise for his ingenuity, and stabs men in the dark to prevent *ennui* . . . He is an amateur of tragedy in real life; and instead of employing his

invention on imaginary characters, or long-forgotten inci-
dents, he takes the bolder and more desperate course of getting
up his plot at home, casts the principal parts among his nearest
friends and connections, and rehearses it in downright
earnest, with steady nerves and unabated resolution.

Exactly because he is scriptwriter, director, and stage villain rolled
into one, Iago is an astonishingly compelling presence in the theater.
And he is given the largest part. It would have been easy for him to
dwarf the other characters, as the bad brother Edmund sometimes
seems to dwarf his good brother Edgar in *King Lear*. Shakespeare's
challenge was to make Othello rise far above Iago's other dupe,
Rodorigo. To be reduced to a gibbering idiot over the matter of a misplaced handkerchief is to be duped indeed. But the mesmerizing
effect of the poetic writing is such that we never think of Othello as
foolish or laughable, not even in the temptation scene of the third act
in which Iago twists every word, every detail, to the advantage of his
plot. Instead, we turn the Moor's own phrase back on to him: "But
yet the pity of it, Iago! O, Iago, the pity of it, Iago!"

Desdemona inspires our pity not because she is pitiful, but
because her courage in going against her father's will, in following
her husband to the far frontier of the Venetian empire in Cyprus, and
in generously speaking out for Cassio, becomes the cause of her
death. Othello inspires our pity because he also inspires our awe,
above all through his soaring language. For the Renaissance, the
twin powers of rational thought and persuasive language, *oratio* and
ratio, were what raised humankind above the level of the beasts. The
tragedy of *Othello* is that Iago's persuasive but specious reasoning
(you're black, you're getting on in years, Venetian women are noto-
riously fickle . . .) transforms Othello from great orator to savage
beast.

According to the critic A. C. Bradley, in his highly influential book
Shakespearean Tragedy (1904), Othello's description of himself as
"one not easily jealous, but being wrought, / Perplexed in the
extreme" is perfectly just: "His tragedy lies in this—that his whole
nature was indisposed to jealousy, and yet was such that he was
unusually open to deception, and, if once wrought to passion, likely

to act with little reflection, with no delay, and in the most decisive manner conceivable." This is not to say that susceptibility to manipulation is Othello's "tragic flaw." For Shakespeare and his contemporaries, to call a play "the tragedy of" such and such a character was to make a point about the direction of their journey, not the hardwiring of their psychology. "Tragedie," wrote Geoffrey Chaucer, father of English verse, "is to seyn a certeyn storie, / As olde bookes maken us memorie, / Of hym that stood in greet prosperitee, / And is yfallen out of heigh degree / Into myserie, and endeth wrecchedly." The higher they climb, the harder they fall: tragedy is traditionally about heroes and kings and generals, larger-than-life figures who rise to the top of fortune's wheel and are then toppled off.

It is a structure saturated with irony: the very quality that is the source of a character's greatness is also the cause of his downfall. This is why talk of a "tragic flaw" is misleading. The theory of the flaw arises from a misunderstanding of Aristotle's influential account of ancient Greek tragedy. For Aristotle, *hamartia*, the thing that precipitates tragedy, is not a psychological predisposition but an event—not a character trait but a fatal action. In several famous cases in Greek tragedy, the particular mistake is to kill a blood relative in ignorance of their identity. So too in Shakespeare, it is action (in Othello's case, over-precipitate action) that determines character, and not vice versa.

In Shakespearean tragedy, the time is out of joint and the lead character is out of his accustomed role. Hamlet the scholar is happy to be presented with an intellectual puzzle, but unsure how to proceed when presented with a demand to kill. Othello the courageous soldier, by contrast, relishes decisive action but is insecure among "the wealthy curlèd darlings" of the Venetian state. Imagine Othello in Hamlet's situation. He would have needed no second prompting. On hearing the ghost's story about his father's murder, he would have gone straight down from the battlements and throttled King Claudius with his bare hands. There would have been no tragedy. Now imagine Hamlet in Othello's situation. He would have questioned every witness, arranged for Desdemona to see a play about adultery and watched for a guilty reaction. Her innocence would have become obvious and, again, there would be no tragedy. The tragedy comes not from some inherent flaw but from the mismatch of character and situation.

The audience's sense of the reckless speed of Othello's action is heightened by the play's clever "double-time" scheme. Looked at from one point of view, the action is highly compressed. The first act takes place in a single night in Venice, as the Senate sits in emergency session upon hearing the news of the Turkish fleet's sailing toward Cyprus. There is then an imagined lapse of time to cover the sea voyage. The second act begins with the arrival in Cyprus and proceeds to the evening's celebration of the evaporation of the Turkish threat, during which Cassio gets disastrously drunk. Othello and Desdemona have their second interrupted night in the marital bedroom. The third and fourth acts, during which Cassio intercedes with Desdemona and Iago persuades Othello of his wife's infidelity, occupy another day, and then the fifth act brings the catastrophe on the third and last night. But looked at from another point of view, the action must take much longer: there has to be opportunity for the supposed adultery, for the business of the handkerchief, and for Lodovico's sea voyage from Venice. The audience watching a strong production in the theater does not, however, notice the inconsistency implied by this double-time scheme, such is their intense absorption in the rapid unfolding of the plot.

In an essay called "Shakespeare and Stoicism of Seneca," published in 1927, the poet and critic T. S. Eliot took a very different view of Othello from A. C. Bradley's:

I have always felt that I have never read a more terrible exposure of human weakness—of universal human weakness—than the last great speech of Othello . . . What Othello seems to me to be doing in this speech is cheering himself up. He is endeavouring to escape reality, he has ceased to think of Desdemona, and is thinking about himself. Humility is the most difficult of all virtues to achieve; nothing dies harder than the desire to think well of oneself. Othello succeeds in turning himself into a pathetic figure, by adopting an *aesthetic* rather than a moral attitude, dramatising himself against his environment. He takes in the spectator, but the human motive is primarily to take in himself.

In the classical tragedy of ancient Greece and Rome, the hero often reaches a state of supreme self-awareness just before the moment of his death. Aristotle called this *anagnorisis*, recognition. This final clarity brings a strange and unworldly sense of satisfaction to the protagonist as he or she faces the end. For Eliot, Othello by contrast remains deluded. His self-dramatization is an evasion that substitutes for the recognition that he has in fact been all too "easily jealous."

According to this view, Othello is the victim of the very linguistic facility that has won him Desdemona. A contemporary of Eliot's, the spiritually minded critic G. Wilson Knight, coined the phrase "the Othello music" to describe the unsurpassed lyricism of the Moor's language. "Rude am I in my speech," he says back in the first act as he launches into some of the least plain, most richly textured speeches in the English language. Far from being "round unvarnished," as he claims they are, Othello's poetic tales "Of moving accidents by flood and field, / Of hair-breadth scapes i'th'imminent deadly breach" constitute the very "witchcraft" that makes Desdemona fall in love with him. "I think this tale would win my daughter too," remarks the Duke admiringly. Iago's sinister art is to reduce Othello from this loquacity to the degenerate outbursts of invective that pollute his mouth in the fourth act ("Goats and monkeys! . . . Lie with her? Lie on her? . . . Pish! Noses, ears and lips! . . . Confess? Handkerchief? O devil!"). In the fifth act, however, Othello's language recovers its former beauty. It is in this sense that Eliot detected something disturbingly "aesthetic" about Othello's last speeches.

The forms of Shakespeare's verse loosened and became more flexible as he matured as a writer. His early plays have a higher proportion of rhyme and a greater regularity in rhythm, the essential pattern being that of iambic pentameter (ten syllables, five stresses, the stress on every second syllable). In the early plays, lines are very frequently end-stopped: punctuation marks a pause at the line ending, meaning that the movement of the syntax (the grammatical construction) falls in with that of the meter (the rhythmical construction). In the later plays, there are far fewer rhyming couplets (sometimes rhyme only features as a marker to indicate that a scene is ending) and the rhythmic movement has far greater variety, freedom, and flow. Mature Shakespearean blank (unrhymed) verse is typically not end-stopped but "run on" (a feature known as "enjambment"). Instead of pausing heavily at the line ending, the speaker hurries forward, the sense demanded by the grammar working in creative tension against the holding pattern of the meter. The heavier pauses migrate to the middle of the lines, where they are known as the "caesura" and where their placing varies. A single line of verse is shared between two speakers much more frequently than in the early plays. And the pentameter itself becomes a more subtle instrument. The iambic beat is broken up, there is often an extra ("redundant") unstressed eleventh syllable at the end of the line (this is known as a "feminine ending"). There are more modulations between verse and prose. Occasionally the verse is so loose that neither the original typesetters of the plays when they were first printed nor the modern editors of scholarly texts can be entirely certain whether verse or prose is intended. Iambic pentameter is the ideal medium for dramatic poetry in English because its rhythm and duration seem to fall in naturally with the speech patterns of the language. In its capacity to combine the ordinary variety of speech with the heightened precision of poetry, the supple mature Shakespearean "loose pentameter" is perhaps the most expressive vocal instrument ever given to the actor.

Othello's speech at the beginning of the murder scene offers a brilliant controlled combination of the patterns of repetition and variation that are typical of early Shakespearean rhetoric and the mellifluous imagistic invention, expanding from clause to clause, that is characteristic of his mature style:

It is the cause, it is the cause, my soul:
Let me not name it to you, you chaste stars:
It is the cause. Yet I'll not shed her blood,
Nor scar that whiter skin of hers than snow,
And smooth as monumental alabaster:
Yet she must die, else she'll betray more men.
Put out the light, and then put out the light.
If I quench thee, thou flaming minister,

I can again thy former light restore,
Should I repent me: but once put out thy light,
Thou cunning'st pattern of excelling nature,
I know not where is that Promethean heat
That can thy light relume. . . .

These beautiful words are being used to justify the ugly impending act of suffocation, the extirpation of that very thing—human breath—which makes beautiful speech possible. It is an extreme example of tragedy's troubling juxtaposition of violence and the aesthetic, made doubly painful by the cultural associations now attached to the image of a powerful and athletic black man killing his white wife out of sexual resentment.

Shakespeare's Venetian world is suffused with sexual as well as racial prejudice. Each of the three women in the play is viewed at some point—in Bianca's case, at all points—as a sexual commodity. And yet the female characters are never passive. They express themselves with vigor and take action into their own hands. Desdemona only becomes a victim when she lies vulnerably asleep. The play does not necessarily replicate the prejudices of its male characters. In a remarkable passage in the Folio text,* Emilia lucidly articulates an argument that skewers the double standard of her society:

. . . Let husbands know
Their wives have sense like them: they see and smell
And have their palates both for sweet and sour,
As husbands have. What is it that they do
When they change us for others? Is it sport?
I think it is. And doth affection breed it?
I think it doth. Is't frailty that thus errs?
It is so too. And have not we affections?
Desires for sport? And frailty, as men have?
Then let them use us well: else let them know,
The ills we do, their ills instruct us so.

*See discussion of Quarto/Folio variants in "About the Text," below.

In Gregory Doran's 2004 production for the Royal Shakespeare Company, Emilia appeared to have lived by what she preached. Desdemona describes Lodovico as a "proper" man. The adjective simultaneously suggests handsome, accomplished, and decent; Emilia responds by emphasizing the "handsome" and then says "I know a lady in Venice would have walked barefoot to Palestine for a touch of his nether lip." In rehearsal for Doran's production, the actors explored the possibility that the lady is Emilia herself. Could her words here and some part of Iago's behavior in the play be explained by the hypothesis that she has had an affair with Lodovico?

It is a matter of debate as to how seriously we should take Iago's claims that both Cassio and Othello have cuckolded him. For Samuel Taylor Coleridge, this was "the motive-hunting of motiveless malignity." But it was the convention in Shakespeare's theater that characters addressing the audience in soliloquy speak the truth. Iago is no respecter of convention, yet a sense of his own sexual insecurity may well be one of his driving motives. He says of Cassio, "He hath a daily beauty in his life / That makes me ugly." This is one of the keys to Iago's character: Cassio's good nature tortures him because it exposes his own moral and social deficiencies, just as the very beauty of Othello and Desdemona's love for each other is something that he cannot bear to witness and that he accordingly feels compelled to destroy.

His method of doing so is revealed in the linguistic echo chamber of the gripping temptation scene in the third act. "Alas," says Othello, "thou echo'st me, / As if there were some monster in thy thought / Too hideous to be shown": in the course of the dialogue, with its pattern of suggestion and repetition, the monster of envy that resides within Iago is transferred into the jealous fit that brings down Othello. It is an extraordinary performance on Iago's part, in which—A. C. Bradley's phrase again—"absolute evil [is] united with supreme intellectual power." Where Othello's poetry is one of the great embodiments of Shakespeare's lyrical art, Iago's prose and his plotting take us straight to his inventor's supreme intellectual power.

ABOUT THE TEXT

Shakespeare endures through history. He illuminates later times as well as his own. He helps us to understand the human condition. But he cannot do this without a good text of the plays. Without editions there would be no Shakespeare. That is why every twenty years or so throughout the last three centuries there has been a major new edition of his complete works. One aspect of editing is the process of keeping the texts up to date—modernizing the spelling, punctuation, and typography (though not, of course, the actual words), providing explanatory notes in the light of changing educational practices (a generation ago, most of Shakespeare's classical and biblical allusions could be assumed to be generally understood, but now they can't).

But because Shakespeare did not personally oversee the publication of his plays, editors also have to make decisions about the relative authority of the early printed editions. Half of the sum of his plays only appeared posthumously, in the elaborately produced First Folio text of 1623, the original "Complete Works" prepared for the press by Shakespeare's fellow actors, the people who knew the plays better than anyone else. The other half had appeared in print in his lifetime, in the more compact and cheaper form of "Quarto" editions, some of which reproduced good quality texts, others of which were to a greater or lesser degree garbled and error-strewn. In the case of a few plays there are hundreds of differences between the Quarto and Folio editions, some of them far from trivial.

Othello is a classic example of a "two text" Shakespeare play. The Folio includes about 150 lines that are not in the Quarto, and there are about a thousand verbal variants between the two texts. Even tiny variants can be dramatically telling: in Quarto, Desdemona asks Emilia to put "our" wedding sheets on the bed, whereas in Folio she asks for "my" wedding sheets. Though there is not a scholarly consensus on the matter, it seems that the extra 150 lines in Folio are theatrically purposeful additions to the original script. A minority of scholars believe, to the contrary, that the Quarto preserves a cut text.

The Folio seems closer to playhouse practice. Its additions include an extra expository speech in the opening scene concerning the Moor's marriage (1.1.128–47), which serves to clarify matters for the audience, and a new extended simile for Othello at the climax of the temptation scene ("Like to the Pontic Sea . . . "), which serves to convert Iago's oath to the stars and elements into a cruel parody of Othello's rhetoric. It is possible that the experience of symmetrical staging, with both characters kneeling, required a rewrite creating symmetrical speeches. Most interestingly, the Folio strengthens the female roles. The willow song is not in the original version; it is a Folio addition, which adds immeasurably to the pathos of Desdemona's tragedy. Three further passages (4.3.87–106, 5.2.176–79, 5.2.217–20) considerably flesh out the character of Emilia. Most powerful is the extraordinary defense of woman in Act 4 Scene 3:

> But I do think it is their husbands' faults
> If wives do fall . . .
> . . . And have not we affections?
> Desires for sport? And frailty, as men have?

The introduction of this plea for recognition of female bodily desire and for an end to the double standard over adultery makes an enormous difference to the play. That Shakespeare seems to have written it not in his first draft but in response to theatrical need is most revealing.

If you look at printers' handbooks from the age of Shakespeare, you quickly discover that one of the first rules was that, whenever possible, compositors were recommended to set their type from existing printed books rather than manuscripts. This was the age before mechanical typesetting, where each individual letter had to be picked out by hand from the compositor's case and placed on a stick (upside down and back to front) before being laid on the press. It was an age of murky rush-light and of manuscripts written in a secretary hand that had dozens of different, hard-to-decipher forms. Printers' lives were a lot easier when they were reprinting existing books rather than struggling with handwritten copy. Easily the quickest way to have created the First Folio would have been simply to reprint those eighteen plays that had already appeared in Quarto and only work from manuscript on the other eighteen.

But that is not what happened. Whenever Quartos were used, playhouse "promptbooks" were also consulted and stage directions copied in from them. And in the case of several major plays where a reasonably well-printed Quarto was available, the Folio printers were instructed to work from an alternative, playhouse-derived manuscript. This meant that the whole process of producing the first complete Shakespeare took months, even years, longer than it might have done. But for the men overseeing the project, John Hemings and Henry Condell, friends and fellow actors who had been remembered in Shakespeare's will, the additional labor and cost were worth the effort for the sake of producing an edition that was close to the practice of the theater. They wanted all the plays in print so that people could, as they wrote in their prefatory address to the reader, "read him and again and again," but they also wanted "the great variety of readers" to work from texts that were close to the theater life for which Shakespeare originally intended them. For this reason, the *RSC Shakespeare*, in both *Complete Works* and individual volumes, uses the Folio as base text wherever possible. Significant Quarto variants are, however, noted in the Textual Notes and Quarto-only passages are appended after the text of *Othello*.

The following notes highlight various aspects of the editorial process and indicate conventions used in the text of this edition:

Lists of Parts are supplied in the First Folio for only six plays, one of which is *Othello*, so the list at the beginning of the play is reproduced from the First Folio with minor editorial adjustments. Capitals indicate that part of the name which is used for speech headings in the script (thus OTHELLO, the Moor).

Locations are provided by the Folio for only two plays. Eighteenth-century editors, working in an age of elaborately realistic stage sets, were the first to provide detailed locations. Given that Shakespeare wrote for a bare stage and often an imprecise sense of place, we have relegated locations to the explanatory notes at the foot of the page, where they are given at the beginning of each scene where the imaginary location is different from the one before. We have emphasized broad geographical settings (Venice and Cyprus) rather than specifics of the kind that suggest anachronistically realistic staging. We have therefore avoided such niceties as "another room in the palace."

Act and Scene Divisions were provided in the Folio in a much more thoroughgoing way than in the Quartos. Sometimes, however, they were erroneous or omitted; corrections and additions supplied by editorial tradition are indicated by square brackets. Five-act division is based on a classical model, and act breaks provided the opportunity to replace the candles in the indoor Blackfriars playhouse which the King's Men used after 1608, but Shakespeare did not necessarily think in terms of a five-part structure of dramatic composition. The Folio convention is that a scene ends when the stage is empty. Nowadays, partly under the influence of film, we tend to consider a scene to be a dramatic unit that ends with either a change of imaginary location or a significant passage of time within the narrative. Shakespeare's fluidity of composition accords well with this convention, so in addition to act and scene numbers we provide a *running scene* count in the right margin at the beginning of each new scene, in the typeface used for editorial directions. Where there is a scene break caused by a momentary bare stage, but the location does not change and extra time does not pass, we use the convention *running scene continues.* There is inevitably a degree of editorial judgment in making such calls, but the system is very valuable in suggesting the pace of the plays.

Speakers' Names are often inconsistent in Folio. We have regularized speech headings, but retained an element of deliberate inconsistency in entry directions, in order to give the flavor of Folio.

Verse is indicated by lines that do not run to the right margin and by capitalization of each line. The Folio printers sometimes set verse as prose, and vice versa (either out of misunderstanding or for reasons of space). We have silently corrected in such cases, although in some instances there is ambiguity, in which case we have leaned toward the preservation of Folio layout. Folio sometimes uses contraction ("turnd" rather than "turned") to indicate whether or not the final "-ed" of a past participle is sounded, an area where there is variation for the sake of the five-beat iambic pentameter rhythm. We use the convention of a grave accent to indicate sounding (thus "turnèd" would be two syllables), but would urge actors not to overstress. In cases where one speaker ends with a verse half line and the next begins with the other half of the pentameter, editors since the late eighteenth century have indented the second line. We have abandoned this convention, since the Folio does not use it, nor did actors' cues in the Shakespearean theater. An exception is made when the second speaker actively interrupts or completes the first speaker's sentence.

Spelling is modernized, but older forms are occasionally maintained where necessary for rhythm or aural effect.

Punctuation in Shakespeare's time was as much rhetorical as grammatical. "Colon" was originally a term for a unit of thought in an argument. The semicolon was a new unit of punctuation (some of the Quartos lack them altogether). We have modernized punctuation throughout, but have given more weight to Folio punctuation than many editors, since, though not Shakespearean, it reflects the usage of his period. In particular, we have used the colon far more than many editors: it is exceptionally useful as a way of indicating how many Shakespearean speeches unfold clause by clause in a developing argument that gives the illusion of enacting the process of thinking in the moment. We have also kept in mind the origin of punctuation in classical times as a way of assisting the actor and orator: the comma suggests the briefest of pauses for breath, the colon a middling one, and a full stop or period a longer pause. Semicolons, by contrast, belong to an era of punctuation that was only just coming in during Shakespeare's time and that is coming to an end now: we have accordingly used them only where they occur in our copy texts (and not always then). Dashes are sometimes used for parenthetical interjections where the Folio has brackets. They are also used for interruptions and changes in train of thought. Where a change of addressee occurs within a speech, we have used a dash preceded by a period (or occasionally another form of punctuation). Often the identity of the respective addressees is obvious from the context. When it is not, this has been indicated in a marginal stage direction.

Entrances and Exits are fairly thorough in Folio, which has accordingly been followed as faithfully as possible. Where characters are omitted or corrections are necessary, this is indicated by square brackets (e.g. "[*and Attendants*]"). *Exit* is sometimes silently normalized to *Exeunt* and *Manet* anglicized to "remains." We trust Folio positioning of entrances and exits to a greater degree than most editors.

Editorial Stage Directions such as stage business, asides, indications of addressee and of characters' position on the gallery stage are only used sparingly in Folio. Other editions mingle directions of this kind with original Folio and Quarto directions, sometimes marking them by means of square brackets. We have sought to distinguish what could be described as *directorial* interventions of this kind from Folio-style directions (either original or supplied) by placing them in the right margin in a different typeface. There is a degree of subjectivity about which directions are of which kind, but the procedure is intended as a reminder to the reader and the actor that Shakespearean stage directions are often dependent upon editorial inference alone and are not set in stone. We also depart from editorial tradition in sometimes admitting uncertainty and thus printing permissive stage directions, such as an **Aside?** (often a line may be equally effective as an aside or a direct address—it is for each production or reading to make its own decision) or a **may exit** or a piece of business placed between arrows to indicate that it may occur at various different moments within a scene.

Line Numbers in the left margin are editorial, for reference and to key the explanatory and textual notes.

Explanatory Notes at the foot of each page explain allusions and gloss obsolete and difficult words, confusing phraseology, occasional major textual cruces, and so on. Particular attention is given to non-standard usage, bawdy innuendo, and technical terms (e.g. legal and military language). Where more than one sense is given, commas indicate shades of related meaning, slashes alternative or double meanings.

Textual Notes at the end of the play indicate major departures from the Folio. They take the following form: the reading of our text is given in bold and its source given after an equals sign, with "Q" indicating that it derives from the First Quarto of 1622, "Q2" from the Second Quarto of 1630, "F" from the First Folio of 1623, "F2" a reading that derives from the Second Folio of 1632, "F3" from the Third Folio of 1663–64, "F4" from the Fourth Folio of 1685, and "Ed" that it derives from the subsequent editorial tradition. The rejected Folio ("F") reading is then given. A selection of Quarto variants and plausible unadopted editorial readings is also included. Thus, for example: at "5.2.390, **Judean** = F. Q, F2 = Indian." This indicates that at Act 5 Scene 2 Line 390 we have retained the Folio reading "Judean" and that "Indian" is an interestingly different reading in the Quarto and Second Folio.

KEY FACTS

MAJOR PARTS: (*with percentage of lines/number of speeches/scenes on stage*) Iago (31%/272/12), Othello (25%/274/12), Desdemona (11%/165/9), Cassio (8%/110/9), Emilia (7%/103/8), Brabantio (4%/30/3), Rodorigo (3%/59/7), Lodovico (2%/33/4), Duke of Venice (2%/25/1), Montano (2%/24/3).

LINGUISTIC MEDIUM: 80% verse, 20% prose.

DATE: 1604. Performed at court, November 1604; apparently uses Knolles' *Historie of the Turkes*, published late 1603; probably post-dates the period when theaters were closed due to the plague from May 1603 to April 1604. The Turkish wars in the eastern Mediterranean were of interest to King James, who had written a poem about the 1571 naval battle of Lepanto, which was reprinted in 1603, the year of his accession to the English throne. Some scholars, however, argue for a slightly earlier date.

SOURCES: Based on a novella in Giovanni Battista Giraldi Cinthio's *Gli Hecatommithi* (1565), perhaps read in a 1584 French translation by Gabriel Chappuys. Context probably provided by Richard Knolles, *The Generall Historie of the Turkes* (1603), Sir Lewis Lewkenor's translation of Gasparo Contarini's *The Commonwealth and Government of Venice* (1599), and John Pory's translation of Leo Africanus' *Geographical Historie of Africa* (1600).

TEXT: There are two early texts, markedly different from each other: a Quarto published in 1622 and the First Folio of 1623. The Folio contains over 150 lines that are not in the Quarto. The Quarto has fuller stage directions, a handful of lines that are absent from the Folio, and a large number of oaths that were watered down or omitted in the Folio, as a result of the prohibition on stage swearing. In all, there are about a thousand verbal variants. The two texts seem to derive from different theatrical manuscripts, the Folio possibly having being set from a transcript by Ralph Crane, scribe to the King's Men. Scholars are divided as to whether the Folio-only passages, which include Othello's "Pontic sea" speech and Desdemona's willow song, are theatrically purposeful additions or theatrically pragmatic cuts. We respect the integrity of the Folio text, but in correcting its manifest errors—which are many, largely due to the presence of "Compositor E," the apprentice who was the poorest of the Folio's typesetters—we have been greatly helped by the existence of the Quarto.

THE TRAGEDY OF OTHELLO, THE MOOR OF VENICE

LIST OF PARTS

OTHELLO, the Moor (a general in the military service of Venice)

BRABANTIO (a senator) father to Desdemona

CASSIO, an honourable lieutenant

IAGO, a villain (Othello's flag-bearer)

RODORIGO, a gulled gentleman

DUKE of Venice

SENATORS

MONTANO, Governor of Cyprus

GENTLEMEN of Cyprus

LODOVICO } two noble Venetians
GRATIANO } (kinsmen of Brabantio)

SAILORS

CLOWN (servant to Othello)

DESDEMONA (daughter of Brabantio) wife to Othello

EMILIA, wife to Iago

BIANCA, a courtesan

(Officers, Messenger, Herald, Musicians and Attendants)

List of parts   gulled duped, deceived

Act 1 Scene 1

Enter Rodorigo and Iago

RODORIGO   Never tell me! I take it much unkindly

That thou, Iago, who hast had my purse

As if the strings were thine, shouldst know of this.

IAGO   But you'll not hear me: if ever I did dream

5   Of such a matter, abhor me.

RODORIGO   Thou told'st me

Thou didst hold him in thy hate.

IAGO   Despise me

If I do not. Three great ones of the city,

10   In personal suit to make me his lieutenant,

Off-capped to him, and by the faith of man,

I know my price, I am worth no worse a place:

But he, as loving his own pride and purposes,

Evades them with a bombast circumstance

15   Horribly stuffed with epithets of war,

Nonsuits my mediators. For 'Certes', says he,

'I have already chose my officer.'

And what was he?

Forsooth, a great arithmetician,

20   One Michael Cassio, a Florentine —

A fellow almost damned in a fair wife —

That never set a squadron in the field

1.1 *Location: Venice (street)*   **1 Never tell me!** expression of disbelief   **much unkindly** with great resentment/dissatisfaction   **3 this** i.e. Desdemona and Othello's elopement   **7 him** i.e. Othello   **9 great ones** i.e. noble, influential men/official dignitaries   **10 suit** formal request, entreaty   **11 Off-capped** removed their hats (a mark of respect)   **14 bombast circumstance** elaborate evasive talk, wordy circumlocution   **15 epithets of war** military terms   **16 Nonsuits my mediators** thwarts the request of my intermediaries (from the legal term "nonsuit" meaning the withdrawal of a lawsuit)   **'Certes'** certainly   **19 Forsooth** in truth   **arithmetician** i.e. mere theorist (in military matters)/mathematician (Florence was known for its bankers)   **20 Florentine** person from Florence (then a city-state in northern Italy)   **21 almost . . . wife** a man with a beautiful wife was **damned** because he was bound to be cuckolded; perhaps Shakespeare originally intended Cassio to be married, or else the line refers to an imminent or a narrowly avoided wedding (Bianca later claims that Cassio is going to marry her); but editors have struggled to make sense of the line, and a printer's error is possible; the most satisfactory emendation would be **limned** (depicted, portrayed), which fits with Iago's emphasis on Cassio's effeminacy, as he compares him first to a **wife** and then to a **spinster**   **22 squadron** group of soldiers in a square formation/small detachment of soldiers

Nor the division of a battle knows
More than a spinster, unless the bookish theoric,
25   Wherein the toga'd consuls can propose
As masterly as he. Mere prattle without practice
Is all his soldiership. But he, sir, had th'election;
And I — of whom his eyes had seen the proof
At Rhodes, at Cyprus and on others' grounds,
30   Christened and heathen — must be beleed and calmed
By debitor and creditor: this counter-caster,
He — in good time — must his lieutenant be,
And I — bless the mark! — his Moorship's ancient.

RODORIGO   By heaven, I rather would have been his hangman.
35   IAGO   Why, there's no remedy: 'tis the curse of service;
Preferment goes by letter and affection,
And not by old gradation, where each second
Stood heir to th'first. Now, sir, be judge yourself
Whether I in any just term am affined
40   To love the Moor.

RODORIGO   I would not follow him then.

IAGO   O, sir, content you:
I follow him to serve my turn upon him.
We cannot all be masters, nor all masters

---

23 division . . . battle disposition of a battalion   **24 spinster** woman who stays at home
spinning   **unless** except for   **theoric** theory   **25 toga'd consuls** toga-wearing councillors
toga garment worn by citizens of ancient Rome   **propose** discourse, hold forth   **26 prattle**
idle talk   **27 had th'election** was chosen   **28 his** i.e. Othello's   **29 Rhodes** island in the
Mediterranean Sea, between Cyprus and Greece   **Cyprus** Mediterranean island to the south
of Turkey   **30 Christened** converted to Christianity   **beleed** unable to move, as a ship is
without wind (the nautical metaphor continues with **calmed**)   **31 debitor and creditor**
i.e. bookkeeping/a bookkeeper (another dig at the **arithmetician** Cassio)   **counter-caster**
one who employs counters in making calculations, an accountant   **32 in good time**
opportunely (sarcastic)   **33 bless the mark** apologetic expression used to excuse the
mention of something unpleasant or profane   **his Moorship** a contemptuous reference to
Othello, varying "his worship" or "his lordship"; the term "moor" could be applied to a person
of either African or Middle Eastern origin, and was often used to refer to someone from
Barbary in north Africa; it was also used to mean "Muslim"   **ancient** ensign (i.e. soldier who
carries the military banner)   **35 service** being a servant/military duty   **36 Preferment**
promotion   **letter and affection** personal recommendation and favoritism   **37 old
gradation** the traditional way of advancing steadily up the ranks   **39 term** manner, way
affined bound   **41 follow** serve   **43 serve my turn** serve my own purposes (**serve** plays on
the notion of being a servant)

45 Cannot be truly followed. You shall mark
 Many a duteous and knee-crooking knave
 That — doting on his own obsequious bondage —
 Wears out his time, much like his master's ass,
 For nought but provender, and when he's old, cashiered:
50 Whip me such honest knaves. Others there are
 Who, trimmed in forms and visages of duty,
 Keep yet their hearts attending on themselves,
 And throwing but shows of service on their lords,
 Do well thrive by them,
55 And when they have lined their coats
 Do themselves homage: these fellows have some soul,
 And such a one do I profess myself. For, sir,
 It is as sure as you are Rodorigo,
 Were I the Moor, I would not be Iago:
60 In following him, I follow but myself.
 Heaven is my judge, not I for love and duty,
 But seeming so, for my peculiar end,
 For when my outward action doth demonstrate
 The native act and figure of my heart
65 In compliment extern, 'tis not long after
 But I will wear my heart upon my sleeve
 For daws to peck at: I am not what I am.

RODORIGO What a full fortune does the thick-lips owe
 If he can carry't thus!

70 **IAGO** Call up her father:
 Rouse him, make after him, poison his delight,
 Proclaim him in the streets, incense her kinsmen,

---

45 truly loyally **mark** note, observe **46 knee-crooking** bowing **48 time** lifetime/time as a servant **49 provender** food **cashiered** (he's) dismissed/discarded **50 Whip me** whip (**me** is emphatic) **51 trimmed** dressed up, adorned **visages** outward appearances **52 attending on** waiting on, serving **55 lined their coats** i.e. got all they can/lined their purses **56 Do themselves homage** serve their own interests exclusively **59 Were . . . Iago** if I were Othello I would not wish to be a servant like me/if I were in Othello's position I would not be fooled by a self-seeking servant **61 not I for** I am not one for, I do not serve out of **62 peculiar** personal **63 demonstrate** display, manifest **64 native** innate, natural **figure** form/appearance **65 compliment extern** external show **67 daws** jackdaws (small birds of the crow family, proverbially foolish)/fools **68 full** perfect, complete **owe** own **69 carry't** carry it off, manage it **71 make after** pursue **72 Proclaim** denounce

And though he in a fertile climate dwell,
Plague him with flies: though that his joy be joy,
75 Yet throw such chances of vexation on't
As it may lose some colour.

RODORIGO   Here is her father's house, I'll call aloud.

IAGO   Do, with like timorous accent and dire yell
As when, by night and negligence, the fire
80 Is spied in populous cities.

RODORIGO   What, ho, Brabantio! Signior Brabantio, ho!

IAGO   Awake! What, ho! Brabantio, thieves, thieves!
Look to your house, your daughter and your bags!
Thieves, thieves!

85 BRABANTIO   What is the reason of this   *Above*   *At a window*
terrible summons?
What is the matter there?

RODORIGO   Signior, is all your family within?

IAGO   Are your doors locked?

BRABANTIO   Why? Wherefore ask you this?

90 IAGO   Sir, you're robbed. For shame, put on your gown!
Your heart is burst, you have lost half your soul:
Even now, now, very now, an old black ram
Is tupping your white ewe. Arise, arise!
Awake the snorting citizens with the bell,
95 Or else the devil will make a grandsire of you.
Arise, I say!

BRABANTIO   What, have you lost your wits?

RODORIGO   Most reverend signior, do you know my voice?

BRABANTIO   Not I: what are you?

100 RODORIGO   My name is Rodorigo.

BRABANTIO   The worser welcome.

---

73 **though** even though   74 **though that** although   75 **chances** possibilities
76 **As it may** that may cause it to   78 **like timorous accent** such terrifying tones   83 **bags**
moneybags   85 ***Above*** i.e. on the upper staging level or gallery   89 **Wherefore** why
90 **gown** coat/senator's robes   92 **ram** a proverbially lustful beast   93 **tupping** mounting
sexually; the **ram** was proverbially lusty, hence slang for "lecher"   94 **snorting** snoring
(also picks up on the bestial imagery of the previous lines)   **bell** alarm bell   95 **devil**
i.e. Othello (the devil was popularly imaged as black)   **grandsire** grandfather   98 **reverend**
respected

I have charged thee not to haunt about my doors:
In honest plainness thou hast heard me say
My daughter is not for thee: and now in madness —
105   Being full of supper and distemp'ring draughts —
Upon malicious knavery dost thou come
To start my quiet.

RODORIGO   Sir, sir, sir—

BRABANTIO   But thou must needs be sure
110   My spirits and my place have in their power
To make this bitter to thee.

RODORIGO   Patience, good sir.

BRABANTIO   What tell'st thou me of robbing?
This is Venice: my house is not a grange.

115 RODORIGO   Most grave Brabantio,
In simple and pure soul I come to you.

IAGO   Sir, you are one of those that will not serve God if
the devil bid you. Because we come to do you service and you
think we are ruffians, you'll have your daughter covered
120   with a Barbary horse: you'll have your nephews neigh to
you: you'll have coursers for cousins and jennets for
germans.

BRABANTIO   What profane wretch art thou?

IAGO   I am one, sir, that comes to tell you your daughter
125   and the Moor are making the beast with two backs.

BRABANTIO   Thou art a villain.

IAGO   You are a senator.

BRABANTIO   This thou shalt answer. I know thee, Rodorigo.

RODORIGO   Sir, I will answer anything. But I beseech you
130   If't be your pleasure and most wise consent —
As partly I find it is — that your fair daughter,

---

102 **charged** ordered   **haunt** loiter, lurk   105 **distemp'ring draughts** intoxicating drinks
107 **start** startle, disrupt   110 **spirits . . . place** disposition and my position of authority
114 **grange** isolated house in the country   115 **grave** dignified, respected   116 **simple**
honest   119 **covered** a term for copulation between a stallion and a mare   120 **Barbary**
horse i.e. Othello   **Barbary** region in northern Africa including Morocco, Algiers, Tripoli, and
Tunis   **nephews** grandsons   121 **coursers** large powerful horses   **jennets** small Spanish
horses   122 **germans** close relatives   123 **profane** irreverent/foulmouthed   125 **making . . .**
backs i.e. having sex   128 **answer** answer for, be held responsible for   130 **pleasure** wish

At this odd-even and dull watch o'th'night,
Transported with no worse nor better guard
But with a knave of common hire, a gondolier,
135 To the gross clasps of a lascivious Moor:
If this be known to you and your allowance
We then have done you bold and saucy wrongs:
But if you know not this, my manners tell me
We have your wrong rebuke. Do not believe
140 That, from the sense of all civility,
I thus would play and trifle with your reverence.
Your daughter — if you have not given her leave —
I say again, hath made a gross revolt,
Tying her duty, beauty, wit and fortunes
145 In an extravagant and wheeling stranger
Of here and everywhere. Straight satisfy yourself:
If she be in her chamber or your house,
Let loose on me the justice of the state
For thus deluding you.

150 **BRABANTIO**   Strike on the tinder, ho!
Give me a taper! Call up all my people!
This accident is not unlike my dream:
Belief of it oppresses me already.
Light, I say, light!   *Exit [above]*

155 **IAGO**   Farewell, for I must leave you:
It seems not meet nor wholesome to my place
To be producted — as, if I stay, I shall —
Against the Moor, for I do know the state,
However this may gall him with some check,

---

132 odd-even time that is neither day nor night—i.e. around midnight   **133 Transported with** be transported by   **134 But with** i.e. than   **knave** servant, lackey   **135 gross** lustful/vile   **136 allowance** permission   **137 saucy** insolent   **140 from** contrary to   **civility** civilized behavior   **141 your reverence** the respect due to you/you, a respected person   **142 leave** permission   **143 gross** monstrous, flagrant/indecent   **144 wit** intelligence, good sense   **145 In** i.e. to   **extravagant and wheeling** roaming and roving   **stranger** foreigner   **146 Straight** immediately   **150 Strike . . . tinder** i.e. strike a light   **151 taper** candle   **152 accident** event   **156 meet** appropriate   **wholesome** beneficial, conducive   **place** position (as Othello's ensign)   **157 producted** produced as a witness   **159 gall** annoy   **check** reprimand

160   Cannot with safety cast him, for he's embarked
        With such loud reason to the Cyprus wars,
        Which even now stands in act, that, for their souls,
        Another of his fathom they have none,
        To lead their business: in which regard,
165   Though I do hate him as I do hell-pains.
        Yet for necessity of present life
        I must show out a flag and sign of love,
        Which is indeed but sign. That you shall surely find him,
        Lead to the Sagittary the raisèd search,
170   And there will I be with him. So farewell.   *Exit*

Enter Brabantio with Servants and torches

BRABANTIO   It is too true an evil: gone she is,
        And what's to come of my despisèd time
        Is nought but bitterness. Now, Rodorigo,
        Where didst thou see her?— O, unhappy girl!—
175   With the Moor, say'st thou?— Who would be a father?—
        How didst thou know 'twas she?— O, she deceives me
        Past thought!— What said she to you?— Get more tapers:
        Raise all my kindred.— Are they married, think you?

RODORIGO   Truly, I think they are.

180 **BRABANTIO**   O heaven! How got she out? O treason of the blood!
        Fathers, from hence trust not your daughters' minds
        By what you see them act. Is there not charms
        By which the property of youth and maidhood
        May be abused? Have you not read, Rodorigo,
185   Of some such thing?

RODORIGO   Yes, sir, I have indeed.

---

160 cast cast off, dismiss   **embarked** engaged, committed   **161 loud reason** resounding support   **162 stands in act** are under way   **for** i.e. to save   **163 fathom** ability   **166 life** livelihood   **167 sign** show, display (plays on the sense of "military flag")   **168 That** in order that   **169 Sagittary** inn or house named after Sagittarius, a centaur (half-man, half-horse) famed for his archery; centaurs were associated with lust, so Sagittarius, always depicted with bow and arrow, may be seen as a type of bestial Cupid   **raisèd search** search party roused from sleep   **172 my despisèd time** the miserable remainder of my life/the remainder of my life in which I will be scorned for what has happened   **174 unhappy** misfortune-causing/ill-fated   **177 Past thought** beyond belief (or "understanding")   **180 treason . . . blood** rebellion against her family/revolt of the (sexual) passions   **182 charms** spells, enchantments **183 property** rightful nature   **maidhood** girlhood, virginity

BRABANTIO   Call up my brother.—

                O, would you had had her!—   *To Rodorigo*

Some one way, some another.— Do you know

Where we may apprehend her and the Moor?

190   RODORIGO   I think I can discover him, if you please

To get good guard and go along with me.

BRABANTIO   Pray you lead on. At every house I'll call:

I may command at most.— Get weapons, ho!

And raise some special officers of might.—

195   On, good Rodorigo: I will deserve your pains.   *Exeunt*

Act 1 Scene 2

Enter Othello, Iago, Attendants with torches

IAGO   Though in the trade of war I have slain men,

Yet do I hold it very stuff o'th'conscience

To do no contrived murder: I lack iniquity

Sometime to do me service. Nine or ten times

5   I had thought t'have yerked him here under the ribs.

OTHELLO   'Tis better as it is.

IAGO   Nay, but he prated

And spoke such scurvy and provoking terms

Against your honour

10   That with the little godliness I have

I did full hard forbear him. But I pray you, sir,

Are you fast married? Be assured of this,

That the magnifico is much beloved,

And hath in his effect a voice potential

15   As double as the duke's: he will divorce you,

190 **discover** reveal   193 **may command** have the authority to demand aid   195 **deserve your pains** reward you for your trouble   **1.2   *Location: Venice (outside the Sagittary)*** 1 **trade** (mercantile) dealings/craft   2 **very stuff** fundamental material (**stuff** maintains the metaphor of **trade** with its senses of "fabric or goods for exchange/materials for manufacture") 3 **contrived** premeditated   **iniquity** wickedness   5 **yerked** stabbed with a sudden movement **him** i.e. Rodorigo   7 **prated** spoke insolently/told tales, blabbed   8 **scurvy** contemptible 11 **I . . . him** I restrained myself with great difficulty from attacking him/I tolerated him with great difficulty   12 **fast** firmly   13 **magnifico** i.e. Brabantio, one of the foremost noblemen, or Magnifici, in Venice   14 **in his effect** at his disposal   **a . . . duke's** a powerful influence/an influence that is potentially double that of the duke **voice** influence/vote

Or put upon you what restraint or grievance
The law — with all his might to enforce it on —
Will give him cable.

OTHELLO   Let him do his spite;
20   My services which I have done the signiory
Shall out-tongue his complaints. 'Tis yet to know —
Which, when I know that boasting is an honour,
I shall promulgate — I fetch my life and being
From men of royal siege, and my demerits
25   May speak, unbonneted, to as proud a fortune
As this that I have reached. For know, Iago,
But that I love the gentle Desdemona,
I would not my unhousèd free condition
Put into circumscription and confine
30   For the sea's worth. But look, what lights come yond?

Enter Cassio [and Officers] with torches

IAGO   Those are the raisèd father and his friends:
You were best go in.

OTHELLO   Not I: I must be found.
My parts, my title and my perfect soul
35   Shall manifest me rightly. Is it they?

IAGO   By Janus, I think no.

OTHELLO   The servants of the duke's? And my lieutenant?—
The goodness of the night upon you, friends!
What is the news?

40   CASSIO   The duke does greet you, general,
And he requires your haste-post-haste appearance
Even on the instant.

---

16 **what** whatever   **grievance** hardship, oppression   18 **cable** rope, i.e. scope   20 **signiory** Venetian governing body   21 **'Tis . . . know** it is not yet known   23 **promulgate** declare publicly   24 **siege** throne, i.e. rank   **demerits** merits, deserts   25 **unbonneted** with my hat off (i.e. respectfully, modestly)/without removing my hat (i.e. on terms of equality)   **proud** great, splendid   28 **unhousèd** unconfined   29 **circumscription and confine** enclosure and confinement   30 **sea's worth** i.e. treasure lying under the sea   **yond** yonder, over there   31 **raisèd** roused from sleep/angered   34 **parts** personal qualities   **title** legal rights as a husband/high military rank   **perfect** unblemished, guiltless   36 **Janus** Roman god with two faces   41 **haste-post-haste** speedy, urgent

OTHELLO	What is the matter, think you?
CASSIO	Something from Cyprus, as I may divine.

45 It is a business of some heat: the galleys
Have sent a dozen sequent messengers
This very night at one another's heels,
And many of the consuls, raised and met,
Are at the duke's already. You have been hotly called for:
50 When, being not at your lodging to be found,
The senate hath sent about three several quests
To search you out.

OTHELLO   'Tis well I am found by you.
I will but spend a word here in the house
55 And go with you.   [*Exit*]

CASSIO   Ancient, what makes he here?

IAGO   Faith, he tonight hath boarded a land caract:
If it prove lawful prize, he's made for ever.

CASSIO   I do not understand.

60 IAGO   He's married.

CASSIO   To who?

IAGO   Marry, to—
[*Enter Othello*]
Come, captain, will you go?

OTHELLO   Have with you.

CASSIO   Here comes another troop to seek for you.

Enter Brabantio, Rodorigo, with Officers and torches   *And weapons*

65 IAGO   It is Brabantio. General, be advised:
He comes to bad intent.

OTHELLO   Holla, stand there!

RODORIGO   Signior, it is the Moor.

BRABANTIO   Down with him, thief!   *They draw*

---

43 matter business   **44 divine** guess   **45 heat** urgency   **46 sequent** successive   **51 several quests** separate search parties   **56 makes he** is he doing   **57 Faith** truly   **boarded** seized (a vessel) by force/had sex with   **caract** carrack, large Spanish ship used in war or as a merchant vessel (implicitly loaded with "treasure" a euphemism for "vagina" or "chastity")   **62 Marry** by the Virgin Mary (a common oath; puns on **married**)   **63 Have with you** I'll join you   **65 advised** warned   **66 to** with   **67 Holla** whoa, stop

70	IAGO	You, Rodorigo? Come, sir, I am for you.
	OTHELLO	Keep up your bright swords, for the dew will rust

them.
　　　Good signior, you shall more command with years
　　　Than with your weapons.

BRABANTIO　O thou foul thief,

75　　Where hast thou stowed my daughter?
　　　Damned as thou art, thou hast enchanted her,
　　　For I'll refer me to all things of sense —
　　　If she in chains of magic were not bound —
　　　Whether a maid so tender, fair and happy,
80　　So opposite to marriage that she shunned
　　　The wealthy curlèd dearling of our nation,
　　　Would ever have — t'incur a general mock —
　　　Run from her guardage to the sooty bosom
　　　Of such a thing as thou: to fear, not to delight.
85　　Judge me the world if 'tis not gross in sense
　　　That thou hast practised on her with foul charms,
　　　Abused her delicate youth with drugs or minerals
　　　That weakens motion: I'll have't disputed on:
　　　'Tis probable and palpable to thinking.
90　　I therefore apprehend and do attach thee
　　　For an abuser of the world, a practiser
　　　Of arts inhibited and out of warrant.—
　　　Lay hold upon him: if he do resist,
　　　Subdue him at his peril.

95　　OTHELLO　　Hold your hands,
　　　Both you of my inclining and the rest:
　　　Were it my cue to fight, I should have known it

---

71 up i.e. in their sheaths   74 foul abhorrent/wicked/ugly/dirty, black   75 stowed Brabantio
unwittingly continues the nautical imagery: "to stow" is to store cargo on a ship or in a sexual
sense "fill with the penis"   77 refer me to entrust myself to (the authority of)   79 tender
young/gentle/meek   fair beautiful/unstained/pale-complexioned, white   80 opposite
opposed   81 curlèd i.e. with elegantly styled hair   dearling darlings, favorites   82 a general
mock universal scorn   83 her guardage the guardianship of her father   85 Judge . . . world
let the world judge   gross in sense blatantly obvious   86 practised on worked cunningly on,
deceived   87 minerals mineral potions or poisons   88 motion normal faculties/perceptions
disputed on debated formally   90 attach arrest   92 arts . . . warrant magical practices that
are forbidden and illegal   95 Hold hold back, halt   96 of my inclining on my side

Without a prompter.— Whither will you that I go
To answer this your charge?

100 BRABANTIO   To prison, till fit time
Of law and course of direct session
Call thee to answer.

OTHELLO   What if I do obey?
How may the duke be therewith satisfied,
105 Whose messengers are here about my side
Upon some present business of the state
To bring me to him?

OFFICER   'Tis true, most worthy signior:
The duke's in council and your noble self,
110 I am sure, is sent for.

BRABANTIO   How? The duke in council?
In this time of the night? Bring him away;
Mine's not an idle cause: the duke himself,
Or any of my brothers of the state,
115 Cannot but feel this wrong as 'twere their own:
For if such actions may have passage free,
Bond-slaves and pagans shall our statesmen be.   *Exeunt*

Act 1 Scene 3
running scene 3

Enter Duke, Senators and Officers   *With torches*

DUKE   There's no composition in this news   *They sit at a table*
That gives them credit.

FIRST SENATOR   Indeed, they are disproportioned;
My letters say a hundred and seven galleys.

5 DUKE   And mine a hundred forty.

SECOND SENATOR   And mine two hundred:
But though they jump not on a just account —

---

98 Whither . . . I where do you want me to   101 course . . . session the proper process
of a judicial hearing (or " . . . of an immediate judicial hearing")   106 present immediate,
urgent/current   114 brothers . . . state fellow senators   116 have passage free i.e. go
unrestrained   1.3   *Location: Venice (duke's residence/council chamber)*
1 composition consistency   2 them i.e. the news   3 disproportioned inconsistent
7 jump agree, coincide   just account exact amount

As in these cases where the aim reports,
'Tis oft with difference — yet do they all confirm
10   A Turkish fleet, and bearing up to Cyprus.
DUKE   Nay, it is possible enough to judgement:
I do not so secure me in the error
But the main article I do approve
In fearful sense.
15   SAILOR   What ho, what ho, what ho!   *Within*

Enter Sailor

OFFICER   A messenger from the galleys.
DUKE   Now? What's the business?
SAILOR   The Turkish preparation makes for Rhodes:
So was I bid report here to the state
20   By Signior Angelo.   [*Exit Sailor*]
DUKE   How say you by this change?
FIRST SENATOR   This cannot be
By no assay of reason: 'tis a pageant,
To keep us in false gaze. When we consider
25   Th'importancy of Cyprus to the Turk,
And let ourselves again but understand
That as it more concerns the Turk than Rhodes,
So may he with more facile question bear it,
For that it stands not in such warlike brace,
30   But altogether lacks th'abilities
That Rhodes is dressed in: if we make thought of this,
We must not think the Turk is so unskilful
To leave that latest which concerns him first,
Neglecting an attempt of ease and gain
35   To wake and wage a danger profitless.
DUKE   Nay, in all confidence, he's not for Rhodes.

---

8 **aim** guess   12 **I . . . sense** this discrepancy does not make me so overconfident that I fail to recognize and fear the main point (i.e. that the Turkish fleet is making for Cyprus)
18 **preparation** force prepared for war   21 **How . . . by** what do you make of   23 **assay** test/endeavor   **pageant** show, spectacle/trick   24 **in false gaze** looking in the wrong direction/deluded   25 **Th'importancy** the importance   28 **So . . . it** so can he (**the Turk**) win it (**Cyprus**) with less arduous conflict   29 **For that** because   **brace** state of defensive readiness   30 **th'abilities** the strength/resources   31 **dressed in** equipped with   33 **latest** last   34 **attempt** undertaking/attack   35 **wage** risk

OFFICER   Here is more news.

Enter a Messenger

MESSENGER   The Ottomites, reverend and gracious,
Steering with due course toward the isle of Rhodes,
40   Have there injointed them with an after fleet.

FIRST SENATOR   Ay, so I thought. How many, as you guess?

MESSENGER   Of thirty sail: and now they do restem
Their backward course, bearing with frank appearance
Their purposes toward Cyprus. Signior Montano,
45   Your trusty and most valiant servitor,
With his free duty recommends you thus,
And prays you to believe him.   [*Exit Messenger*]

DUKE   'Tis certain then for Cyprus.
Marcus Luccicos, is not he in town?

50   FIRST SENATOR   He's now in Florence.

DUKE   Write from us to him: post-post-haste, dispatch!

FIRST SENATOR   Here comes Brabantio and the valiant Moor.

Enter Brabantio, Othello, Cassio, Iago, Rodorigo and Officers

DUKE   Valiant Othello, we must straight employ you
Against the general enemy Ottoman.—
55   I did not see you: welcome, gentle signior,   *To Brabantio*
We lacked your counsel and your help tonight.

BRABANTIO   So did I yours. Good your grace, pardon me:
Neither my place nor aught I heard of business
Hath raised me from my bed, nor doth the general care
60   Take hold on me, for my particular grief
Is of so floodgate and o'erbearing nature
That it engluts and swallows other sorrows
And it is still itself.

---

38 **Ottomites** members of the Ottoman Empire—i.e. Turks   **reverend and gracious**
i.e. senators   **40 injointed them** joined themselves   **after** following (in the rear; nautical
term)   **42 restem . . . course** hold once again to their former course   **43 frank** open
45 servitor servant   **46 free** unconstrained, willing   **recommends** informs/commends
himself to   **51 post-post-haste** immediately/speedily   **54 general enemy Ottoman** i.e.
universal enemy to all Christians   **55 gentle** noble   **58 place** position (as a senator)   **aught**
anything   **59 the general care** concern for the public interest/widespread anxiety at current
events   **60 particular** personal   **61 floodgate** i.e. torrential (like water released when a
floodgate is opened)   **62 engluts** consumes   **63 is still itself** i.e. is unchanged or
undiminished by other **sorrows**

DUKE	Why? What's the matter?	
65	BRABANTIO	My daughter! O, my daughter!
	SENATORS	Dead?
	BRABANTIO	Ay, to me:

She is abused, stol'n from me and corrupted
By spells and medicines bought of mountebanks;
70 For nature so prepost'rously to err —
Being not deficient, blind, or lame of sense —
Sans witchcraft could not.

DUKE   Whoe'er he be that in this foul proceeding
Hath thus beguiled your daughter of herself,
75 And you of her, the bloody book of law
You shall yourself read in the bitter letter
After your own sense: yea, though our proper son
Stood in your action.

BRABANTIO   Humbly I thank your grace.
80 Here is the man: this Moor, whom now it seems
Your special mandate for the state affairs
Hath hither brought.

ALL   We are very sorry for't.

DUKE   What, in your own part, can you say   *To Othello*
to this?

85 BRABANTIO   Nothing, but this is so.

OTHELLO   Most potent, grave and reverend signiors,
My very noble and approved good masters:
That I have ta'en away this old man's daughter,
It is most true: true I have married her;
90 The very head and front of my offending
Hath this extent, no more. Rude am I in my speech,
And little blessed with the soft phrase of peace;

---

68 abused wronged/misused/deceived   **69 mountebanks** charlatans/quack doctors
70 prepost'rously unnaturally   **err** stray/blunder/sin   **71 sense** perception, discernment,
reason   **72 Sans** without   **73 proceeding** manner of behaving/course of action
74 beguiled cheated/deprived/bewitched   **75 bloody** death-dealing (witchcraft was punishable
by death)   **77 After . . . sense** according to your own interpretation (however harsh)   **our
proper** my own   **78 Stood . . . action** were the accused party in your lawsuit   **85 but** except
86 grave respected, wise, dignified   **87 approved** proven/esteemed   **90 head and front**
highest extent (literally, "head and forehead")   **91 Rude** uncultivated/rough

For since these arms of mine had seven years' pith,
Till now some nine moons wasted, they have used
95   Their dearest action in the tented field,
And little of this great world can I speak
More than pertains to feats of broils and battle,
And therefore little shall I grace my cause
In speaking for myself. Yet, by your gracious patience,
100 I will a round unvarnished tale deliver
Of my whole course of love: what drugs, what charms,
What conjuration and what mighty magic —
For such proceeding I am charged withal —
I won his daughter.

105 **BRABANTIO**   A maiden never bold,
Of spirit so still and quiet that her motion
Blushed at herself: and she, in spite of nature,
Of years, of country, credit, everything,
To fall in love with what she feared to look on!
110 It is a judgement maimed and most imperfect
That will confess perfection so could err
Against all rules of nature, and must be driven
To find out practices of cunning hell
Why this should be. I therefore vouch again
115 That with some mixtures pow'rful o'er the blood,
Or with some dram, conjured to this effect,
He wrought upon her.

DUKE   To vouch this is no proof,
Without more wider and more overt test
120 Than these thin habits and poor likelihoods
Of modern seeming do prefer against him.

---

93 since . . . pith i.e. since I was seven years old   **pith** strength   **94 Till . . . wasted** i.e. until nine months ago   **wasted** passed away/waned/squandered   **95 dearest** worthiest, most valuable/best-loved   **tented** covered with military tents   **97 broils** turmoil, conflict   **100 round** blunt, plain   **102 conjuration** invocation of spirits/spells   **103 withal** with   **106 motion** natural inner impulses/physical movement   **108 years** age (Othello is older than Desdemona)   **credit** reputation   **113 practices** tricks/treachery/schemes   **114 vouch** assert, affirm   **115 mixtures** potions, medicines (perhaps with connotations of "unlawful sexual intercourse")   **blood** passions/sexual appetite   **116 dram** small draught, dose   **117 wrought** worked   **119 test** evidence/trial   **120 habits** clothes (i.e. appearances)   **121 modern seeming** commonplace appearance   **prefer** put forward

FIRST SENATOR   But, Othello, speak:
    Did you by indirect and forcèd courses
    Subdue and poison this young maid's affections?
125   Or came it by request and such fair question
    As soul to soul affordeth?
OTHELLO   I do beseech you,
    Send for the lady to the Sagittary
    And let her speak of me before her father:
130   If you do find me foul in her report,
    The trust, the office I do hold of you
    Not only take away, but let your sentence
    Even fall upon my life.
DUKE   Fetch Desdemona hither.
135 OTHELLO   Ancient, conduct them: you best know   *To Iago*
    the place.—   *[Exeunt Iago and Attendants]*
    And, till she come, as truly as to heaven
    I do confess the vices of my blood,
    So justly to your grave ears I'll present
    How I did thrive in this fair lady's love,
140   And she in mine.
DUKE   Say it, Othello.
OTHELLO   Her father loved me, oft invited me,
    Still questioned me the story of my life
    From year to year: the battle, sieges, fortune,
145   That I have passed.
    I ran it through, even from my boyish days
    To th'very moment that he bade me tell it,
    Wherein I spoke of most disastrous chances,
    Of moving accidents by flood and field,
150   Of hair-breadth scapes i'th'imminent deadly breach,

---

123 indirect devious, deceitful   **forcèd courses** forcible means   **125 question** conversation
126 affordeth grants, yields naturally   **131 office** official position   **137 blood** nature/
passions/anger   **138 justly** exactly/truthfully   **present** legal term meaning "to lay before
a court"   **143 Still** continually   **145 passed** experienced/got through   **148 disastrous**
unlucky/calamitous   **149 moving** changeable/emotionally stirring   **accidents** events
flood and field water and land/sea and battlefield   **150 scapes** escapes   **i'th'imminent
deadly breach** in the gap in a fortification (made by a battery), which presents an imminent
danger of death

Of being taken by the insolent foe
And sold to slavery, of my redemption thence,
And portance in my traveller's history,
Wherein of antres vast and deserts idle,
155 Rough quarries, rocks, hills whose head touch heaven,
It was my hint to speak: such was my process.
And of the cannibals that each other eat,
The Anthropophagi and men whose heads
Grew beneath their shoulders: these things to hear
160 Would Desdemona seriously incline,
But still the house-affairs would draw her thence,
Which ever as she could with haste dispatch,
She'd come again, and with a greedy ear
Devour up my discourse: which I observing,
165 Took once a pliant hour, and found good means
To draw from her a prayer of earnest heart
That I would all my pilgrimage dilate,
Whereof by parcels she had something heard,
But not intentively. I did consent,
170 And often did beguile her of her tears,
When I did speak of some distressful stroke
That my youth suffered. My story being done,
She gave me for my pains a world of kisses:
She swore, 'In faith 'twas strange, 'twas passing strange,
175 'Twas pitiful, 'twas wondrous pitiful!'
She wished she had not heard it, yet she wished
That heaven had made her such a man. She thanked me,
And bade me, if I had a friend that loved her,
I should but teach him how to tell my story,

---

151 **insolent** proud, overbearing   153 **portance** bearing/conduct   154 **antres** caves
deserts idle empty wildernesses   156 **hint** occasion/opportunity   **process** story,
account   158 **Anthropophagi** man-eaters   159 **these . . . hear** in order to hear these
things   160 **seriously** earnestly   **incline** be disposed mentally/lean in physically   165 **pliant**
suitable, accommodating   167 **pilgrimage** i.e. his life's journey and its adventures   **dilate**
relate/expand upon   168 **parcels** small parts   169 **intentively** intently, with close attention
170 **beguile her of** coax from her (perhaps a deliberate shift from the sense of "cheat"
employed by the duke in line 74)   171 **stroke** blow   173 **kisses** could mean "gentle touches"
174 **passing** surpassingly, exceedingly   177 **made her** created her to be/made for her

180   And that would woo her. Upon this hint I spake:
    She loved me for the dangers I had passed,
    And I loved her that she did pity them.
    This only is the witchcraft I have used.
    Here comes the lady: let her witness it.
    Enter Desdemona, Iago, Attendants

185   **DUKE**   I think this tale would win my daughter too.
    Good Brabantio,
    Take up this mangled matter at the best:
    Men do their broken weapons rather use
    Than their bare hands.

190   **BRABANTIO** I pray you hear her speak:
    If she confess that she was half the wooer,
    Destruction on my head if my bad blame
    Light on the man!— Come hither, gentle   *To Desdemona*
      mistress.
    Do you perceive in all this noble company

195   Where most you owe obedience?
  DESDEMONA My noble father,
    I do perceive here a divided duty.
    To you I am bound for life and education:
    My life and education both do learn me

200   How to respect you. You are the lord of duty,
    I am hitherto your daughter. But here's my husband,
    And so much duty as my mother showed
    To you, preferring you before her father,
    So much I challenge that I may profess

205   Due to the Moor my lord.
  BRABANTIO   God be with you! I have done.
    Please it your grace, on to the state affairs.
    I had rather to adopt a child than get it.
    Come hither, Moor:

---

180 hint opportunity/indication   **184 witness** testify to   **187 Take . . . best** i.e. make the best of a bad situation   **192 bad** mistaken/wrongful   **198 education** upbringing   **199 learn** teach   **201 hitherto** thus far   **203 preferring** promoting/esteeming   **204 challenge** claim, assert as a right   **207 Please it** if it please   **208 get** beget, conceive

210   I here do give thee that with all my heart
       Which but thou hast already, with all my heart
       I would keep from thee.— For your sake, jewel,   *To Desdemona*
       I am glad at soul I have no other child,
       For thy escape would teach me tyranny,
215   To hang clogs on them.— I have done, my lord.   *To the Duke*

DUKE   Let me speak like yourself, and lay a sentence
       Which, as a grise or step, may help these lovers.
       When remedies are past, the griefs are ended
       By seeing the worst, which late on hopes depended.
220   To mourn a mischief that is past and gone
       Is the next way to draw new mischief on.
       What cannot be preserved when fortune takes,
       Patience her injury a mock'ry makes.
       The robbed that smiles steals something from the thief:
225   He robs himself that spends a bootless grief.

BRABANTIO   So let the Turk of Cyprus us beguile,
       We lose it not, so long as we can smile.
       He bears the sentence well that nothing bears
       But the free comfort which from thence he hears:
230   But he bears both the sentence and the sorrow
       That, to pay grief, must of poor patience borrow.
       These sentences, to sugar or to gall,
       Being strong on both sides, are equivocal.
       But words are words: I never yet did hear

---

211 but were it not that   **212 For your sake** because of you   **214 escape** transgression/
elopement   **215 clogs** blocks of wood attached to the neck or leg to prevent escape
216 like yourself on your behalf/as you would speak if you were calm   **lay** apply   **sentence**
opinion/saying, maxim   **217 grise** flight of stairs/single step   **218 remedies are past** it
is too late for remedies   **griefs** hardships, suffering/distress   **219 late** recently   **220 mischief**
misfortune/wicked action   **221 next** nearest   **222 takes** takes away/seizes hold/strikes
223 Patience . . . makes enduring it patiently enables one to make light of the **injury** inflicted
by **fortune**   **225 spends** engages in/exhausts/expends (perhaps with the suggestion of tears)
bootless pointless/incurable   **226 beguile** cheat/deprive   **228 He . . . hears** he who derives
only the easy comfort of such a saying certainly bears out your maxim (**bears the sentence**
plays on the sense of "undergoes judicial sentence")   **229 free** easy/unrestrained/costless
231 to . . . borrow must try to abate his grief with the scant resources of patience   **poor**
unfortunate/feeble/impecunious   **232 These . . . equivocal** i.e. such maxims are just as
sweet as they are bitter, so they are equally valid in whichever fashion they are applied

235   That the bruisèd heart was pierced through the ears.

I humbly beseech you proceed to th'affairs of state.

DUKE   The Turk with a most mighty preparation makes for
Cyprus. Othello, the fortitude of the place is best known to
you, and though we have there a substitute of most allowed
240   sufficiency, yet opinion, a more sovereign mistress of effects,
throws a more safer voice on you: you must therefore be
content to slubber the gloss of your new fortunes with this
more stubborn and boisterous expedition.

OTHELLO   The tyrant custom, most grave senators,
245   Hath made the flinty and steel couch of war

My thrice-driven bed of down: I do agnize

A natural and prompt alacrity

I find in hardness, and do undertake

This present wars against the Ottomites.
250   Most humbly therefore bending to your state,

I crave fit disposition for my wife,

Due reference of place and exhibition,

With such accommodation and besort

As levels with her breeding.
255   DUKE   Why, at her fathers.

BRABANTIO   I will not have it so.

OTHELLO   Nor I.

DESDEMONA   Nor would I there reside,

To put my father in impatient thoughts
260   By being in his eye. Most gracious duke,

---

235 bruisèd crushed, battered   **pierced** affected, moved (i.e. soothed)   **through the ears**
i.e. by words   **238 fortitude** strength   **239 allowed sufficiency** acknowledged ability,
demonstrable competence   **240 opinion** public opinion   **effects** events/outcomes
241 throws . . . you votes for you as the more secure choice   **242 slubber** soil, smear
243 stubborn difficult/unyielding   **boisterous** rough, violent   **245 flinty** hard, stony
couch bed (in addition to the nature of **war** in general, Othello also refers to having to sleep
on the ground in one's armor)   **246 thrice-driven** i.e. extremely soft, having had the lightest
feathers separated from the rest three times over   **down** fine feathers of young birds   **agnize**
acknowledge   **247 alacrity** readiness   **248 hardness** hardship/a hard bed   **250 bending . . .
state** submitting (possibly bowing) to your authority as duke   **251 fit disposition** suitable
arrangements   **252 reference . . . exhibition** assignment of lodgings and financial
maintenance   **253 accommodation** provision/lodgings   **besort** suitable company
254 levels with equals/befits   **260 eye** sight

To my unfolding lend your prosperous ear,
And let me find a charter in your voice
T'assist my simpleness.

DUKE   What would you, Desdemona?

265 DESDEMONA That I love the Moor to live with him,
My downright violence and storm of fortunes
May trumpet to the world. My heart's subdued
Even to the very quality of my lord.
I saw Othello's visage in his mind,
270 And to his honours and his valiant parts
Did I my soul and fortunes consecrate:
So that, dear lords, if I be left behind
A moth of peace, and he go to the war,
The rites for why I love him are bereft me,
275 And I a heavy interim shall support
By his dear absence. Let me go with him.

OTHELLO   Let her have your voice.
Vouch with me, heaven, I therefore beg it not
To please the palate of my appetite,
280 Nor to comply with heat — the young affects
In my defunct and proper satisfaction —
But to be free and bounteous to her mind:
And heaven defend your good souls that you think
I will your serious and great business scant
285 When she is with me. No, when light-winged toys
Of feathered Cupid seel with wanton dullness

261 unfolding ensuing speech/explanation   prosperous favorable   262 charter permission/
privilege   263 simpleness unassuming disposition/guilelessness/foolishness   266 violence
violation of convention/extreme strength of feeling   storm of fortunes the tempestuous
nature of my lot/the disruption of my privileged life   267 subdued Even to entirely
submissive to/wholly conquered by   268 very quality fundamental nature   270 parts
qualities   271 consecrate dedicate solemnly, devote   273 moth i.e. insignificant creature/
creature that hovers idly/source of expense   274 rites rites of love/rights, privileges
276 dear heartfelt/costly   277 voice support, consent   278 Vouch witness   280 comply
with heat submit to sexual desire   young affects youthful passions   281 defunct . . .
satisfaction no longer active (defunct, dead) desire for sexual satisfaction   282 free generous
283 heaven may heaven   that if   284 scant neglect/diminish   285 toys trifles/Cupid's
arrows   286 feathered alludes either to Cupid's wings or to his arrows   Cupid Roman god
of love (traditionally depicted as a blind boy with wings)   seel blind (literally to sew up the
eyes of a young hawk for training purposes)   wanton dullness postcoital lethargy

My speculative and officed instrument,
That my disports corrupt and taint my business,
Let housewives make a skillet of my helm,
290   And all indign and base adversities
Make head against my estimation!

DUKE   Be it as you shall privately determine,
Either for her stay or going: th'affair cries haste,
And speed must answer it.

295   A SENATOR   You must away tonight.

OTHELLO   With all my heart.

DUKE   At nine i'th'morning here we'll meet again.
Othello, leave some officer behind,
And he shall our commission bring to you,
300   And such things else of quality and respect
As doth import you.

OTHELLO   So please your grace, my ancient:
A man he is of honesty and trust:
To his conveyance I assign my wife,
305   With what else needful your good grace shall think
To be sent after me.

DUKE   Let it be so.
Goodnight to everyone.— And, noble signior,   *To Brabantio*
If virtue no delighted beauty lack,
310   Your son-in-law is far more fair than black.

A SENATOR   Adieu, brave Moor: use Desdemona well.

BRABANTIO   Look to her, Moor, if thou hast eyes to see:
She has deceived her father, and may thee.

                Exeunt [Duke, Senators and Officers]

OTHELLO   My life upon her faith! Honest Iago,
315   My Desdemona must I leave to thee:
I prithee let thy wife attend on her,

---

287 speculative . . . instrument i.e. eyes, official faculties of vision   **288 That** so that
disports (sexual) entertainments   **289 skillet** cooking pot   **helm** helmet   **290 indign**
unworthy, dishonorable   **291 Make head** advance/raise troops   **estimation** reputation
293 cries calls for   **300 quality and respect** significance and relevance   **301 import** concern
304 conveyance escorting   **309 delighted** delightful   **310 fair** beautiful/pale/virtuous
black ugly/dark-complexioned/wicked   **314 Honest** honorable/virtuous/truthful

And bring them after in the best advantage.
Come, Desdemona, I have but an hour
Of love, of worldly matter and direction
320   To spend with thee: we must obey the time.

Exeunt [Othello and Desdemona]

RODORIGO   Iago—

IAGO   What say'st thou, noble heart?

RODORIGO   What will I do, think'st thou?

IAGO   Why, go to bed and sleep.

325   RODORIGO   I will incontinently drown myself.

IAGO   If thou dost, I shall never love thee after. Why, thou
silly gentleman?

RODORIGO   It is silliness to live when to live is torment: and then
have we a prescription to die when death is our physician.

330   IAGO   O villainous! I have looked upon the world for four
times seven years, and since I could distinguish betwixt a
benefit and an injury, I never found man that knew how to
love himself. Ere I would say I would drown myself for the
love of a guinea-hen, I would change my humanity with a
335   baboon.

RODORIGO   What should I do? I confess it is my shame to be so
fond, but it is not in my virtue to amend it.

IAGO   Virtue? A fig! 'Tis in ourselves that we are thus or
thus. Our bodies are our gardens, to the which our wills are
340   gardeners: so that if we will plant nettles or sow lettuce, set
hyssop and weed up thyme, supply it with one gender of
herbs or distract it with many, either to have it sterile with
idleness or manured with industry, why, the power and

---

317 in . . . advantage at the most favorable opportunity   319 direction instruction
320 time i.e. current urgency of affairs   322 heart friend   325 incontinently immediately/
loosely, unchastely   329 prescription ancient right/doctor's prescription   333 Ere before
334 guinea-hen female turkey or guinea-fowl/prostitute   change exchange   335 baboon
i.e. an idiot (monkeys were also associated with lechery)   337 fond doting, infatuated/foolish
virtue nature/power/moral strength   338 A fig! coarse exclamation of dismissive contempt,
often accompanied by the thrusting of the thumb between the index and middle fingers
340 set plant   341 hyssop an aromatic herb   gender type   342 distract divide   sterile
with idleness unproductive as a result of neglect

corrigible authority of this lies in our wills. If the beam of
our lives had not one scale of reason to poise another of
sensuality, the blood and baseness of our natures would
conduct us to most preposterous conclusions: but we have
reason to cool our raging motions, our carnal stings, our
unbitted lusts, whereof I take this that you call love to be a
sect or scion.

RODORIGO   It cannot be.

IAGO   It is merely a lust of the blood and a permission of
the will. Come, be a man. Drown thyself? Drown cats and
blind puppies. I have professed me thy friend and I confess
me knit to thy deserving with cables of perdurable
toughness: I could never better stead thee than now. Put
money in thy purse: follow thou the wars: defeat thy favour
with an usurped beard: I say, put money in thy purse. It
cannot be long that Desdemona should continue her love to
the Moor. Put money in thy purse. Nor he his to her: it was a
violent commencement in her, and thou shalt see an
answerable sequestration. Put but money in thy purse.
These Moors are changeable in their wills. Fill thy purse with
money. The food that to him now is as luscious as locusts
shall be to him shortly as bitter as coloquintida. She must
change for youth: when she is sated with his body, she will
find the errors of her choice: therefore put money in thy
purse. If thou wilt needs damn thyself, do it a more delicate
way than drowning. Make all the money thou canst. If
sanctimony and a frail vow betwixt an erring barbarian and

345
350
355
360
365
370

---

344 **corrigible authority** power to correct   **beam** bar from which the scales of a balance
are suspended/the balance itself   345 **poise** counterbalance   346 **blood** passions
347 **preposterous** perverse/illogical/monstrous   **conclusions** outcomes   348 **motions**
impulses, emotions   **carnal stings** sexual urges (with phallic connotations)   349 **unbitted**
unbridled, unrestrained   350 **sect or scion** cutting or shoot   353 **will** personal inclination/
sexual desire   355 **knit** tied firmly, committed   **perdurable** indestructible   356 **stead** help,
support   357 **defeat . . . beard** disfigure your face with a false beard (or perhaps "by growing
a beard")   362 **answerable sequestration** corresponding separation   364 **locusts** fruit of
the carob tree   365 **coloquintida** colocynth, a **bitter** apple   366 **change for youth** exchange
Othello for a younger man/because she's young (and therefore changeable)   368 **delicate**
enjoyable/elegant/ingenious   369 **Make** raise   370 **sanctimony** holiness   **erring**
roving/blundering/sinful   **barbarian** person from Barbary/uncivilized savage

supersubtle Venetian be not too hard for my wits and all the tribe of hell, thou shalt enjoy her. Therefore make money. A pox of drowning thyself! It is clean out of the way: seek thou rather to be hanged in compassing thy joy than to be

375   drowned and go without her.

RODORIGO   Wilt thou be fast to my hopes if I depend on the issue?

IAGO   Thou art sure of me. Go, make money. I have told thee often, and I re-tell thee again and again, I hate the

380   Moor: my cause is hearted; thine hath no less reason. Let us be conjunctive in our revenge against him: if thou canst cuckold him, thou dost thyself a pleasure, me a sport. There are many events in the womb of time which will be delivered. Traverse, go, provide thy money. We will have more of this

385   tomorrow. Adieu.

RODORIGO   Where shall we meet i'th'morning?

IAGO   At my lodging.

RODORIGO   I'll be with thee betimes.

IAGO   Go to, farewell. Do you hear,   *As Rodorigo leaves*
Rodorigo?

390   RODORIGO   I'll sell all my land.   *Exit*

IAGO   Thus do I ever make my fool my purse,
For I mine own gained knowledge should profane,
If I would time expend with such a snipe
But for my sport and profit. I hate the Moor:

395   And it is thought abroad that 'twixt my sheets
He has done my office: I know not if't be true,
But I, for mere suspicion in that kind,
Will do as if for surety. He holds me well,

---

371 supersubtle extremely refined/supremely cunning   **373 pox of** plague on   **pox** plague, venereal disease   **clean . . . way** entirely the wrong measure to take   **374 in** for **compassing** achieving/sexually embracing   **joy** sexual pleasure/Desdemona   **376 fast** reliable/constant   **377 issue** outcome   **378 art** i.e. may be   **380 hearted** grounded in the heart   **381 conjunctive** united   **382 cuckold him** make him a cuckold (i.e. a man with an unfaithful wife)   **384 Traverse** move (a military command)   **388 betimes** early   **389 Go to** expression of dismissive impatience   **392 profane** abuse/treat irreverently   **393 snipe** fool, dupe/type of bird   **394 But** except   **395 abroad** i.e. widely   **396 done my office** performed my role (i.e. had sex with my wife)   **397 in that kind** of that nature   **398 do . . . surety** proceed as if it were a certainty   **holds me well** has a good opinion of me

The better shall my purpose work on him.
400　Cassio's a proper man. Let me see now:
To get his place and to plume up my will
In double knavery. How, how? Let's see:
After some time, to abuse Othello's ears
That he is too familiar with his wife.
405　He hath a person and a smooth dispose
To be suspected, framed to make women false.
The Moor is of a free and open nature,
That thinks men honest that but seem to be so,
And will as tenderly be led by th'nose
410　As asses are.
I have't: it is engend'red: hell and night
Must bring this monstrous birth to the world's light.　[*Exit*]

Act 2 Scene 1

running scene 4

Enter Montano and two Gentlemen

MONTANO　What from the cape can you discern at sea?
FIRST GENTLEMAN　Nothing at all: it is a high-wrought flood:
I cannot, 'twixt the heaven and the main,
Descry a sail.
5　MONTANO　Methinks the wind hath spoke aloud at land:
A fuller blast ne'er shook our battlements.
If it hath ruffianed so upon the sea,
What ribs of oak, when mountains melt on them,
Can hold the mortise? What shall we hear of this?
10　SECOND GENTLEMAN　A segregation of the Turkish fleet:
For do but stand upon the foaming shore,

---

400 proper handsome/fine/accomplished　**401 plume up** glorify/put a feather in the cap of　**404 he** i.e. Cassio　**405 person** presence/appearance　**dispose** disposition/manner
406 framed formed　**false** unfaithful (to their husbands)　**407 free** frank/generous
409 tenderly easily　**411 engend'red** conceived　**412 monstrous** unnatural, deformed
2.1 *Location: a port in Cyprus*　**1 cape** headland　**2 high-wrought flood** agitated sea
3 main sea　**4 Descry** catch sight of　**7 ruffianed** behaved as a ruffian, i.e. raged　**8 ribs** strengthening timbers in the framework of a ship　**mountains** mountainous waves　**9 hold the mortise** keep their joints secure　**10 segregation** dispersal

The chidden billow seems to pelt the clouds:
The wind-shaked surge, with high and monstrous mane,
Seems to cast water on the burning bear
15   And quench the guards of th'ever-fixèd pole.
I never did like molestation view
On the enchafèd flood.

MONTANO   If that the Turkish fleet
Be not ensheltered and embayed, they are drowned:
20   It is impossible to bear it out.

Enter a [Third] Gentleman

THIRD GENTLEMAN   News, lads! Our wars are done:
The desperate tempest hath so banged the Turks
That their designment halts. A noble ship of Venice
Hath seen a grievous wreck and sufferance
25   On most part of their fleet.

MONTANO   How? Is this true?

THIRD GENTLEMAN   The ship is here put in,
A Veronesa. Michael Cassio,
Lieutenant to the warlike Moor Othello,
30   Is come on shore: the Moor himself at sea,
And is in full commission here for Cyprus.

MONTANO   I am glad on't: 'tis a worthy governor.

THIRD GENTLEMAN   But this same Cassio, though he speak of
comfort
Touching the Turkish loss, yet he looks sadly
35   And pray the Moor be safe; for they were parted
With foul and violent tempest.

MONTANO   Pray heavens he be,
For I have served him, and the man commands
Like a full soldier. Let's to the seaside, ho!

---

12 chidden rebuked, repelled (by the shore)   **billow** ocean swell   **13 mane** puns on "main"
(i.e. sea)   **14 burning bear** the constellation Ursa Minor (used for navigation)   **15 guards** the
two stars in Ursa Minor that were second in brightness to the Pole Star   **pole** the Pole Star or
North Star   **16 like molestation** similar turbulence   **17 enchafèd** furious, roused
19 embayed sheltered in a bay   **23 designment** enterprise   **24 sufferance** damage
28 Veronesa ship from or built in Verona (city in northern Italy)   **31 in . . . here** on his way
here with full delegated authority   **34 Touching** regarding   **sadly** serious, grave   **35 pray**
i.e. prays   **39 full** complete, perfect

40   As well to see the vessel that's come in
        As to throw out our eyes for brave Othello,
        Even till we make the main and th'aerial blue
        An indistinct regard.

THIRD GENTLEMAN   Come, let's do so;
45   For every minute is expectancy
        Of more arrivancy.

Enter Cassio

CASSIO   Thanks, you the valiant of the warlike isle,
        That so approve the Moor. O, let the heavens
        Give him defence against the elements,
50   For I have lost him on a dangerous sea.

MONTANO   Is he well shipped?

CASSIO   His bark is stoutly timbered, and his pilot
        Of very expert and approved allowance;
        Therefore my hopes, not surfeited to death,
55   Stand in bold cure.

[VOICES]   A sail, a sail, a sail!   *Within*

CASSIO   What noise?

GENTLEMAN   The town is empty: on the brow o'th'sea
        Stand ranks of people, and they cry 'A sail!'

60   CASSIO   My hopes do shape him for the
            governor.   *A shot is heard*

GENTLEMAN   They do discharge their shot of courtesy:
        Our friends at least.

CASSIO   I pray you, sir, go forth
        And give us truth who 'tis that is arrived.

65   GENTLEMAN   I shall.   *Exit*

MONTANO   But, good lieutenant, is your general wived?

---

42 **the . . . regard** the blueness of the sea and the sky one indistinguishable sight
46 **arrivancy** people arriving   48 **approve** praise, testify to the worth of   52 **bark** ship
pilot ship's captain   53 **Of . . . allowance** acknowledged to be a man of proven expertise
54 **not . . . cure** not being fatally overindulged, remain confident of a good outcome (medical
metaphor: "surfeit" refers to the gastrointestinal problems that result from too much food and
drink)   58 **brow o'th'sea** i.e. a cliff top   60 **shape him for** imagine it to be   61 **shot of**
courtesy welcoming cannon shot

CASSIO   Most fortunately: he hath achieved a maid
          That paragons description and wild fame,
          One that excels the quirks of blazoning pens,
70   And in th'essential vesture of creation
          Does tire the engineer.

Enter Gentleman

          How now? Who has put in?

GENTLEMAN   'Tis one Iago, ancient to the general.

CASSIO   He's had most favourable and happy speed:
75   Tempests themselves, high seas and howling winds,
          The guttered rocks and congregated sands,
          Traitors ensteeped to enclog the guiltless keel,
          As having sense of beauty, do omit
          Their mortal natures, letting go safely by
80   The divine Desdemona.

MONTANO   What is she?

CASSIO   She that I spake of, our great captain's captain,
          Left in the conduct of the bold Iago,
          Whose footing here anticipates our thoughts
85   A sennight's speed. Great Jove, Othello guard,
          And swell his sail with thine own powerful breath,
          That he may bless this bay with his tall ship,
          Make love's quick pants in Desdemona's arms,
          Give renewed fire to our extincted spirits—

Enter Desdemona, Iago, Rodorigo and Emilia [with Attendants]

90   O, behold,
          The riches of the ship is come on shore!   *Kneels*
          You men of Cyprus, let her have your knees.—

---

67 achieved won   **68 paragons** excels   **wild** unrestrained/excited   **fame** report   **69 quirks** clever conceits/verbal tricks   **blazoning** praising/proclaiming/vividly descriptive
70 th'essential . . . creation the innate God-given beauty of body or soul   **vesture** clothing
71 tire the engineer exhaust the writer trying to describe her (**tire**, picking up on **vesture**, puns on "attire")   **engineer** author   **72 put in** i.e. arrived at the harbor   **74 speed** haste/good fortune   **76 guttered** jagged   **congregated sands** massed sands, i.e. sandbanks
77 ensteeped immersed in water   **enclog** obstruct   **78 As** as if   **omit** neglect   **79 mortal** deadly   **83 in . . . of** to be escorted by   **84 footing** landing   **anticipates . . . speed** occurs a week earlier than we had expected   **85 sennight's** week's   **Jove** supreme Roman god
87 tall brave/fine/tall-masted   **88 quick** lively/rapid/burning   **89 extincted** extinguished

Hail to thee, lady! And the grace of heaven,
Before, behind thee, and on every hand
95   Enwheel thee round!   *Rises*

DESDEMONA   I thank you, valiant Cassio.
What tidings can you tell of my lord?

CASSIO   He is not yet arrived, nor know I aught
But that he's well and will be shortly here.

100   DESDEMONA   O, but I fear. How lost you company?

CASSIO   The great contention of sea and skies
Parted our fellowship.— But, hark! A sail.

[VOICES]   A sail, a sail!   *Within*   *A shot is heard*

GENTLEMAN   They give this greeting to the citadel:
105   This likewise is a friend.

CASSIO   See for the news.   [*Exit Gentleman*]
Good ancient, you are welcome.— Welcome, mistress.—
Let it not gall your patience, good Iago,
That I extend my manners: 'tis my breeding
110   That gives me this bold show of courtesy.   *Kisses Emilia*

IAGO   Sir, would she give you so much of her lips
As of her tongue she oft bestows on me,
You would have enough.

DESDEMONA   Alas, she has no speech.

115   IAGO   In faith, too much:
I find it still, when I have leave to sleep.
Marry, before your ladyship, I grant,
She puts her tongue a little in her heart
And chides with thinking.

120   EMILIA   You have little cause to say so.

IAGO   Come on, come on: you are pictures out of door,
bells in your parlours, wild-cats in your kitchens, saints in

---

95 Enwheel encircle   **102 fellowship** company, i.e. group of ships   **104 citadel** fortress
(where a garrison would have been stationed)   **108 gall** vex, irritate   **109 breeding**
upbringing   **112 tongue** i.e. in speaking incessantly/in kissing   **114 has no speech** is not a
great talker/has been rendered silent with embarrassment at Iago's words   **116 still** always
leave a free moment/permission   **117 before** in the presence of   **119 chides** scolds
121 pictures i.e. silent/attractive in appearance   **122 bells** i.e. noisy and jangling   **parlours**
nods at the original meaning of the word: "room set aside for conversation"

your injuries, devils being offended, players in your
housewifery, and housewives in your beds.

125 DESDEMONA O, fie upon thee, slanderer!

IAGO Nay, it is true, or else I am a Turk:
You rise to play and go to bed to work.

EMILIA You shall not write my praise.

IAGO No, let me not.

130 DESDEMONA What wouldst write of me, if thou shouldst praise
me?

IAGO O gentle lady, do not put me to't,
For I am nothing if not critical.

DESDEMONA Come on assay. There's one gone to the harbour?

IAGO Ay, madam.

135 DESDEMONA I am not merry, but I do beguile
The thing I am by seeming otherwise.
Come, how wouldst thou praise me?

IAGO I am about it, but indeed my invention
Comes from my pate as birdlime does from frieze,

140 It plucks out brains and all. But my muse labours,
And thus she is delivered:
'If she be fair and wise, fairness and wit,
The one's for use, the other useth it.'

DESDEMONA Well praised! How if she be black and witty?

145 IAGO 'If she be black, and thereto have a wit,
She'll find a white that shall her blackness fit.'

DESDEMONA Worse and worse.

EMILIA How if fair and foolish?

---

123 players triflers as opposed to serious workers   **124 housewifery** housekeeping
housewives hussies, whores   **126 Turk** i.e. an infidel, not to be trusted   **127 play** with sexual
connotations   **work** do chores/have sex   **133 assay** try/put me to the test   **135 beguile**
divert attention from   **138 invention** inventiveness   **139 pate** head/brains   **birdlime** sticky
substance spread on twigs to catch birds   **frieze** coarse woolen cloth   **140 muse** inspiring
goddess   **labours** toils/is in the process of giving birth (a sense continued with **delivered**)
142 fair beautiful/fair-haired   **wit** intelligence, perhaps playing on a "genital" sense   **143 The**
. . . it i.e. wisdom will make use of fairness; **use** plays on sense of "sexual employment"
144 black dark-haired and/or complexioned   **145 thereto** in addition   **146 white** fair-
complexioned person (puns on "wight," meaning "person," and possibly "wit," witty fellow)
blackness plays on sense of "vagina"   **fit** suit/fit into during sex

IAGO   'She never yet was foolish that was fair,
150   For even her folly helped her to an heir.'

DESDEMONA   These are old fond paradoxes to make fools laugh
i'th'ale-house. What miserable praise hast thou for her
that's foul and foolish?

IAGO   'There's none so foul and foolish thereunto,
155   But does foul pranks which fair and wise ones do.'

DESDEMONA   O heavy ignorance! Thou praisest the worst best.
But what praise couldst thou bestow on a deserving woman
indeed, one that, in the authority of her merit, did justly put
on the vouch of very malice itself?

160   IAGO   'She that was ever fair and never proud,
Had tongue at will and yet was never loud,
Never lacked gold and yet went never gay,
Fled from her wish and yet said "Now I may",
She that being ang'red, her revenge being nigh,
165   Bade her wrong stay and her displeasure fly,
She that in wisdom never was so frail
To change the cod's head for the salmon's tail,
She that could think and ne'er disclose her mind,
See suitors following and not look behind,
170   She was a wight, if ever such wights were—'

DESDEMONA   To do what?

IAGO   'To suckle fools and chronicle small beer.'

DESDEMONA   O, most lame and impotent conclusion! Do not
learn of him, Emilia, though he be thy husband. How say
175   you, Cassio? Is he not a most profane and liberal counsellor?

---

150 folly foolishness/lewdness   **to an heir** to marry an heir/get pregnant   **151 fond** foolish
153 foul ugly/black   **154 thereunto** in addition   **155 foul pranks** lewd acts   **156 heavy**
grievous/burdensome   **158 one . . . itself** one whose virtue is so powerful that it rightfully
compels the approving testimony of malice itself   **161 tongue** i.e. speech, plays on sense of
"oral sex"   **at will** when she wanted, plays on sense of "will"—carnal desire/penis   **162 gay**
showily dressed   **163 Fled . . . may** denied her own wishes even when she knew she might
indulge them/denied her lover until she chose   **167 change . . . tail** i.e. have (adulterous) sex
cod's head penis   **salmon's tail** vagina   **170 wight** person, plays on "white" meaning
"target" (vagina)   **172 suckle** breastfeed   **chronicle small beer** concern herself with trivial
matters   **175 liberal** freely spoken/licentious

CASSIO   He speaks home, madam: you may relish him more
in the soldier than in the scholar.   *Cassio takes Desdemona's*

hand and they converse apart

IAGO   He takes her by the palm: ay, well said,   *Aside*
whisper. With as little a web as this will I ensnare as great a
180   fly as Cassio. Ay, smile upon her, do: I will gyve thee in thine
own courtship. You say true, 'tis so, indeed: if such tricks as
these strip you out of your lieutenantry, it had been better
you had not kissed your three fingers so oft, which now
again you are most apt to play the sir in. Very good: well
185   kissed, and excellent courtesy! 'Tis so, indeed. Yet again your
fingers to your lips? Would they were clyster-pipes for your
sake!—The Moor! I know his trumpet.   *Trumpet within*

CASSIO   'Tis truly so.

DESDEMONA   Let's meet him and receive him.

190   CASSIO   Lo, where he comes!

Enter Othello and Attendants

OTHELLO   O my fair warrior!

DESDEMONA   My dear Othello!

OTHELLO   It gives me wonder great as my content
To see you here before me. O my soul's joy!
195   If after every tempest come such calms,
May the winds blow till they have wakened death!
And let the labouring bark climb hills of seas
Olympus-high and duck again as low
As hell's from heaven! If it were now to die,
200   'Twere now to be most happy, for I fear
My soul hath her content so absolute
That not another comfort like to this
Succeeds in unknown fate.

---

176 home directly   **177 in the** in the role of a   **180 gyve** shackle   **181 courtship** courtly
manners (plays on sense of "wooing")   **You . . . indeed** Iago mockingly pretends to speak to
Cassio   **tricks** fashionable mannerisms, courtly practices   **183 kissed . . . fingers** a gesture of
courtesy to a lady   **184 sir** i.e. well-bred gentleman   **185 courtesy** bow, courteous gesture
186 clyster-pipes tubes used for anal administration of medicine or enemas   **190 Lo** look
197 bark sailing ship   **198 Olympus-high** as high as Mount Olympus, the home of the Greek
gods   **199 to die** my time to die   **203 Succeeds** can follow

DESDEMONA   The heavens forbid
205   But that our loves and comforts should increase,
Even as our days do grow!

OTHELLO   Amen to that, sweet powers!
I cannot speak enough of this content:
It stops me here: it is too much of joy.
210   And this, and this, the greatest discords be   *Kisses her*
That e'er our hearts shall make!

IAGO   O, you are well tuned now!   *Aside*
But I'll set down the pegs that make this music,
As honest as I am.

215   OTHELLO   Come, let us to the castle.—   *To Desdemona*
News, friends: our wars are done, the Turks are drowned.
How does my old acquaintance of this isle?—
Honey, you shall be well desired in Cyprus:
I have found great love amongst them. O my sweet,
220   I prattle out of fashion, and I dote
In mine own comforts. I prithee, good Iago,
Go to the bay and disembark my coffers.
Bring thou the master to the citadel:
He is a good one, and his worthiness
225   Does challenge much respect.— Come, Desdemona,
Once more, well met at Cyprus.

Exeunt Othello and Desdemona
[*with Attendants. Iago and Rodorigo remain*]

IAGO   Do thou meet me presently at the   *To an Attendant*
harbour.—   *as he exits*

Come hither. If thou be'st valiant — as they say   *To Rodorigo*
base men being in love have then a nobility in their natures
230   more than is native to them — list me: the lieutenant tonight
watches on the court of guard. First, I must tell thee this:
Desdemona is directly in love with him.

---

209 stops arrests/chokes   **here** at this very moment/in my heart or throat   **213 set down**
loosen   **220 prattle** chatter   **out of fashion** contrary to my usual manner/unfashionably
dote behave foolishly/indulge   **221 comforts** happiness   **222 coffers** boxes, trunks
223 master ship's captain   **225 challenge** claim, require   **229 base** lowborn/unworthy
230 list listen to   **231 watches . . . guard** is on duty at the guardhouse   **232 directly**
completely

RODORIGO   With him? Why, 'tis not possible.

IAGO   Lay thy finger thus, and let thy soul be instructed.
235   Mark me with what violence she first loved the Moor, but for
bragging and telling her fantastical lies. To love him still for
prating? Let not thy discreet heart think it. Her eye must be
fed: and what delight shall she have to look on the devil?
When the blood is made dull with the act of sport, there
240   should be a game to inflame it and to give satiety a fresh
appetite, loveliness in favour, sympathy in years, manners
and beauties, all which the Moor is defective in. Now,
for want of these required conveniences, her delicate
tenderness will find itself abused, begin to heave the gorge,
245   disrelish and abhor the Moor: very nature will instruct her in
it and compel her to some second choice. Now, sir, this
granted — as it is a most pregnant and unforced position—
who stands so eminent in the degree of this fortune as Cassio
does? A knave very voluble, no further conscionable than
250   in putting on the mere form of civil and humane seeming
for the better compass of his salt and most hidden loose
affection? Why, none, why, none. A slipper and subtle knave,
a finder of occasion, that has an eye can stamp and
counterfeit advantages, though true advantage never
255   present itself: a devilish knave. Besides, the knave is
handsome, young, and hath all those requisites in him that
folly and green minds look after. A pestilent complete knave,
and the woman hath found him already.

---

234 thus i.e. on the lips   **235 Mark me** note, recollect   **but** only   **237 prating** chattering
discreet discerning, prudent   **239 dull** sluggish   **act of sport** sex   **240 a game** sexual
play/a new quarry   **241 favour** appearance   **sympathy** similarity   **243 required**
conveniences necessary correspondences (or "advantages")   **244 heave the gorge** retch
245 disrelish find distasteful   **247 pregnant** evident   **position** proposition, assertion
248 eminent . . . degree i.e. first in line   **eminent** high/conspicuous   **degree** step
249 voluble inconstant/glib   **conscionable** ruled by conscience   **250 humane**
courteous/kindly   **seeming** appearance   **251 compass** achievement   **salt** lecherous
252 slipper slippery   **subtle** cunning   **253 occasion** opportunity   **stamp** coin
254 advantages opportunities   **true** genuine/honest   **257 folly** foolishness/lewdness
green young/inexperienced   **after** out for   **pestilent** poisonous/confounded   **complete**
perfect, consummate

RODORIGO   I cannot believe that in her: she's full of most
260   blessed condition.

IAGO   Blessed fig's-end! The wine she drinks is made of
grapes. If she had been blessed, she would never have loved
the Moor. Blessed pudding! Didst thou not see her paddle
with the palm of his hand? Didst not mark that?

265   RODORIGO   Yes, that I did, but that was but courtesy.

IAGO   Lechery, by this hand: an index and obscure
prologue to the history of lust and foul thoughts. They met
so near with their lips that their breaths embraced together.
Villainous thoughts, Rodorigo! When these mutabilities so
270   marshal the way, hard at hand comes the master and main
exercise, th'incorporate conclusion. Pish! But, sir, be you
ruled by me: I have brought you from Venice. Watch you
tonight: for the command, I'll lay't upon you. Cassio knows
you not. I'll not be far from you. Do you find some occasion
275   to anger Cassio, either by speaking too loud, or tainting his
discipline, or from what other course you please, which the
time shall more favourably minister.

RODORIGO   Well.

IAGO   Sir, he's rash and very sudden in choler, and haply
280   may strike at you: provoke him that he may, for even out
of that will I cause these of Cyprus to mutiny, whose
qualification shall come into no true taste again but by the
displanting of Cassio. So shall you have a shorter journey to
your desires by the means I shall then have to prefer them,
285   and the impediment most profitably removed, without the
which there were no expectation of our prosperity.

260 condition disposition   261 Blessed fig's-end! exclamation of dismissive contempt
fig's-end vagina   261 The . . . grapes i.e. she's as mortal (and open to desire) as the next
person   263 pudding sausage/penis   paddle stroke/play with her fingers   266 index table
of contents/preface (plays on the sense of the pointing "forefinger")   obscure hidden
269 mutabilities changes, signs of sexual fickleness   270 hard close   main may contribute
to the language of hands and fingers with a play on the French *main* ("hand")   271 exercise
action/sexual act   incorporate carnal, united in one body   272 Watch you remain alert,
be on the lookout   273 for . . . you I'll bestow on you the leading role in carrying out our
plan/I'll give you instructions about what to do   275 tainting his discipline casting aspersions
on his military skill   277 minister provide   279 choler anger   haply perhaps/with any luck
281 these i.e. the people   whose . . . again i.e. who will not be appeased   283 displanting
uprooting, supplanting   284 prefer promote, advance   286 prosperity success

RODORIGO   I will do this, if you can bring it to any opportunity.

IAGO   I warrant thee. Meet me by and by at the citadel: I
must fetch his necessaries ashore. Farewell.

290 RODORIGO   Adieu.   *Exit*

IAGO   That Cassio loves her, I do well believe't:
That she loves him, 'tis apt and of great credit.
The Moor — howbeit that I endure him not —
Is of a constant, loving, noble nature,
295 And I dare think he'll prove to Desdemona
A most dear husband. Now, I do love her too,
Not out of absolute lust — though peradventure
I stand accountant for as great a sin —
But partly led to diet my revenge,
300 For that I do suspect the lusty Moor
Hath leaped into my seat, the thought whereof
Doth — like a poisonous mineral — gnaw my inwards:
And nothing can or shall content my soul
Till I am evened with him, wife for wife,
305 Or failing so, yet that I put the Moor
At least into a jealousy so strong
That judgement cannot cure. Which thing to do,
If this poor trash of Venice, whom I trace
For his quick hunting, stand the putting on,
310 I'll have our Michael Cassio on the hip,
Abuse him to the Moor in the right garb —
For I fear Cassio with my night-cap too —
Make the Moor thank me, love me and reward me
For making him egregiously an ass

---

287 I . . . opportunity it will bring about any opportunity for me   288 warrant assure
289 his i.e. Othello's   292 apt likely/appropriate   of great credit very believable
293 howbeit . . . not although I cannot bear him   296 dear beloved, precious (with grim play
on the sense of "costly")   297 peradventure perhaps/probably   298 accountant accountable
299 diet feed   300 For that because   301 leaped into plays on the sense of "mounted
sexually"   seat official place/saddle/(wife's) vagina   308 poor . . . Venice i.e. Rodorigo
trace follow   309 For on account of   stand . . . on continues to respond to my incitements
(suggestive of urging dogs on in a hunt)   310 on the hip at a disadvantage   311 right garb
way I plan/most effective manner   312 night-cap wife/(wife's) vagina; Iago suspects Cassio of
having sex with Emilia   314 egregiously monstrously, shamefully

315   And practising upon his peace and quiet
Even to madness. 'Tis here, but yet confused:
Knavery's plain face is never seen till used.   *Exit*

Act 2 Scene 2   *running scene 5*

Enter Othello's Herald with a proclamation

HERALD   It is Othello's pleasure, our noble and valiant
general, that upon certain tidings now arrived, importing
the mere perdition of the Turkish fleet, every man put
himself into triumph: some to dance, some to make bonfires,
5   each man to what sport and revels his addition leads him, for
besides these beneficial news, it is the celebration of his
nuptial. So much was his pleasure should be proclaimed. All
offices are open, and there is full liberty of feasting from this
present hour of five till the bell have told eleven. Bless the isle
10   of Cyprus and our noble general Othello!   *Exit*

[Act 2 Scene 3]   *running scene 6*

Enter Othello, Desdemona, Cassio and Attendants

OTHELLO   Good Michael, look you to the guard tonight:
Let's teach ourselves that honourable stop
Not to outsport discretion.
CASSIO   Iago hath direction what to do,
5   But notwithstanding, with my personal eye
Will I look to't.
OTHELLO   Iago is most honest.
Michael, goodnight: tomorrow with your earliest
Let me have speech with you.—
                    Come, my dear love,   *To Desdemona*

---

315 **practising upon** scheming against   316 **'Tis here** i.e. the plan exists/the plan is in my
head   **2.2 Location: Cyprus   3 mere perdition** total destruction   **4 triumph** public
celebration of victory   **5 addition** rank/occupation   **7 nuptial** marriage   **8 offices** kitchens,
pantries   **9 told** counted, struck   **2.3 Location: Cyprus (the citadel)   2 stop** restraint
3 outsport discretion make merry beyond the bounds of prudence   **8 with your earliest** at
your earliest convenience

10   The purchase made, the fruits are to ensue:
        That profit's yet to come 'tween me and you.—
        Goodnight.   *Exeunt [Othello, Desdemona and Attendants]*
        Enter Iago

CASSIO   Welcome, Iago: we must to the watch.

IAGO   Not this hour, lieutenant: 'tis not yet ten o'th'clock.
15   Our general cast us thus early for the love of his Desdemona,
          who let us not therefore blame: he hath not yet made
          wanton the night with her, and she is sport for Jove.

CASSIO   She's a most exquisite lady.

IAGO   And, I'll warrant her, full of game.

20 CASSIO   Indeed, she's a most fresh and delicate creature.

IAGO   What an eye she has! Methinks it sounds a parley to
          provocation.

CASSIO   An inviting eye, and yet methinks right modest.

IAGO   And when she speaks, is it not an alarum to love?

CASSIO   She is indeed perfection.

25 IAGO   Well, happiness to their sheets! Come, lieutenant, I
          have a stoup of wine, and here without are a brace of Cyprus
          gallants that would fain have a measure to the health of
          black Othello.

CASSIO   Not tonight, good Iago: I have very poor and
30   unhappy brains for drinking: I could well wish courtesy
          would invent some other custom of entertainment.

IAGO   O, they are our friends. But one cup: I'll drink for
          you.

CASSIO   I have drunk but one cup tonight, and that was
          craftily qualified too, and behold what innovation it makes
35   here: I am infortunate in the infirmity and dare not task my
          weakness with any more.

---

10 the . . . ensue i.e. though married, Othello and Desdemona have yet to consummate their
union   **15 cast** dismissed   **17 wanton** sportive/amorous/lascivious   **Jove** the supreme
Roman god was known for his amorous encounters with beautiful women   **18 exquisite**
accomplished, perfect   **19 full of game** sexually sportive, lustful   **20 delicate** charming/
dainty/elegant   **21 sounds a parley** issues a summons (literally, to military negotiations)
23 alarum call to arms   **26 stoup** cup, tankard   **without** outside   **brace** pair   **27 gallants**
fine young men disposed to pleasure   **fain** gladly   **have a measure** i.e. drink a toast
30 unhappy unfortunate   **34 craftily qualified** skillfully diluted   **innovation** alteration/
revolution   **35 infortunate** unfortunate, unlucky

IAGO   What, man? 'Tis a night of revels: the gallants
      desire it.

CASSIO   Where are they?

IAGO   Here at the door. I pray you call them in.

40 CASSIO   I'll do't, but it dislikes me.   *Exit*

IAGO   If I can fasten but one cup upon him,
      With that which he hath drunk tonight already,
      He'll be as full of quarrel and offence
      As my young mistress' dog. Now, my sick fool Rodorigo,
45   Whom love hath turned almost the wrong side out,
      To Desdemona hath tonight caroused
      Potations pottle-deep; and he's to watch:
      Three else of Cyprus, noble swelling spirits —
      That hold their honours in a wary distance,
50   The very elements of this warlike isle —
      Have I tonight flustered with flowing cups,
      And they watch too. Now, 'mongst this flock of drunkards
      Am I to put our Cassio in some action
      That may offend the isle.— But here they come:

Enter Cassio, Montano and Gentlemen   *Servants following with wine*

55   If consequence do but approve my dream,
      My boat sails freely, both with wind and stream.

CASSIO   'Fore heaven, they have given me a rouse already.

MONTANO   Good faith, a little one, not past a pint, as I am a
      soldier.

IAGO   Some wine, ho!

60   And let me the cannikin clink, clink,   *Sings*
      And let me the cannikin clink.
      A soldier's a man,

---

40 it dislikes me it displeases me/I do it reluctantly   **43 offence** aggression, readiness
to take offense   **44 my . . . dog** the overindulged lapdog of a young lady   **sick** lovesick
46 caroused drunk as a toast   **47 Potations pottle-deep** half-gallon draughts   **watch**
remain alert, be on the lookout (for a chance to provoke Cassio)   **48 swelling** proud
49 That . . . distance who are very conscious of protecting their honors (and thus quick to
take offense)   **50 elements** essence, typical constituents   **51 flustered** made drunkenly
excitable   **52 watch** are awake   **53 action** deed/fight   **55 approve** prove, bear out
56 stream current   **57 rouse** large quantity of drink   **60 cannikin** small drinking
vessel

O, man's life's but a span:
Why, then, let a soldier drink.

65 Some wine, boys!

CASSIO   'Fore heaven, an excellent song.

IAGO   I learned it in England, where indeed they are most
potent in potting: your Dane, your German, and your swag-
bellied Hollander— Drink, ho!— are nothing to your
70 English.

CASSIO   Is your Englishman so exquisite in his drinking?

IAGO   Why, he drinks you with facility, your Dane dead
drunk: he sweats not to overthrow your Almain: he gives
your Hollander a vomit ere the next pottle can be filled.

75 CASSIO   To the health of our general!

MONTANO   I am for it, lieutenant, and I'll do you justice.

IAGO   O sweet England!

King Stephen was and-a worthy peer,   *Sings*
His breeches cost him but a crown:
80 He held them sixpence all too dear,
With that he called the tailor lown.
He was a wight of high renown,
And thou art but of low degree:
'Tis pride that pulls the country down:
85 Then take thy auld cloak about thee.
Some wine, ho!

CASSIO   Why, this is a more exquisite song than the other.

IAGO   Will you hear't again?

CASSIO   No, for I hold him to be unworthy of his place that
90 does those things. Well, heav'n's above all, and there be souls
must be saved, and there be souls must not be saved.

IAGO   It's true, good lieutenant.

CASSIO   For mine own part — no offence to the general, nor
any man of quality — I hope to be saved.

---

63 span brief period (literally, span of the hand)   **67 most . . . potting** big drinkers
68 swag-bellied with a belly that sags heavily   **72 drinks you** drinks (**you** is emphatic)
73 Almain German   **74 pottle** half-gallon drinking vessel   **76 do you justice** i.e. match you
in the amount you drink   **78 King Stephen** twelfth-century king of England   **and-a** a
79 crown gold coin of varying value in different countries   **80 held** considered   **81 lown**
loon, rascal, base person   **85 auld** old   **94 quality** rank

95   IAGO   And so do I too, lieutenant.

      CASSIO   Ay, but, by your leave, not before me: the lieutenant
      is to be saved before the ancient. Let's have no more of this:
      let's to our affairs. Forgive us our sins! Gentlemen, let's look
      to our business. Do not think, gentlemen, I am drunk: this is
100   my ancient, this is my right hand, and this is my left. I am not
      drunk now: I can stand well enough, and I speak well
      enough.

      GENTLEMEN   Excellent well.

      CASSIO   Why, very well then: you must not think then, that I
105   am drunk.   Exit

      MONTANO   To th'platform, masters. Come, let's set   Starts to leave
      the watch.   [Exeunt Gentlemen?]

      IAGO   You see this fellow that is gone before: To Montano
      He's a soldier fit to stand by Caesar
      And give direction. And do but see his vice:
110   'Tis to his virtue a just equinox,
      The one as long as th'other. 'Tis pity of him.
      I fear the trust Othello puts him in
      On some odd time of his infirmity
      Will shake this island.

115   MONTANO   But is he often thus?

      IAGO   'Tis evermore his prologue to his sleep:
      He'll watch the horologe a double set,
      If drink rock not his cradle.

      MONTANO   It were well
120   The general were put in mind of it.
      Perhaps he sees it not, or his good nature
      Prizes the virtue that appears in Cassio
      And looks not on his evils: is not this true?

      Enter Rodorigo

      IAGO   How now, Rodorigo?   Aside to Rodorigo
125   I pray you, after the lieutenant, go.   [Exit Rodorigo]

---

106 th'platform the terrace on which guns were mounted and where the night watch stood
guard   **set the watch** mount the guard   **110 just equinox** exact equal   **equinox** moment
when day and night are of equal length   **111 pity of** a pity about   **117 watch . . . set** remain
awake during two revolutions of the clock (**horologe**)

MONTANO   And 'tis great pity that the noble Moor
           Should hazard such a place as his own second
           With one of an ingraft infirmity:
           It were an honest action to say so
130   To the Moor.

IAGO   Not I, for this fair island:
           I do love Cassio well and would do much
           To cure him of this evil.—   *Cry within*

                              But, hark! What noise?

Enter Cassio pursuing Rodorigo

CASSIO   You rogue! You rascal!

135 MONTANO   What's the matter, lieutenant?

CASSIO   A knave teach me my duty?
           I'll beat the knave into a twiggen bottle.

RODORIGO   Beat me?

CASSIO   Dost thou prate, rogue?   *Strikes Rodorigo*

140 MONTANO   Nay, good lieutenant: *Stops him*
           I pray you, sir, hold your hand.

CASSIO   Let me go, sir,
           Or I'll knock you o'er the mazzard.

MONTANO   Come, come, you're drunk.

145 CASSIO   Drunk?   *They fight*

IAGO   Away, I say: go out and cry a   *Aside to Rodorigo*
           mutiny.—   *[Exit Rodorigo]*
           Nay, good lieutenant— Alas, gentlemen—
           Help, ho!— Lieutenant— Sir Montano— Sir—
           Help, masters!— Here's a goodly watch indeed!   *Bell rings*
150   Who's that which rings the bell?— *Diablo*, ho!
           The town will rise. Fie, fie, lieutenant!
           You'll be ashamed for ever.

Enter Othello and Attendants   *With weapons*

OTHELLO   What is the matter here?

---

127 hazard . . . second risk as important a place as lieutenant   128 ingraft engrained
136 knave rogue/servant, low-ranking person   137 twiggen bottle wicker basket
(i.e. Rodorigo's body will be crisscrossed with wounds and bruises)   141 hold hold back
143 mazzard head   149 masters sirs   150 bell town alarm bell   *Diablo* devil (Spanish)
151 rise rise up/riot   152 ashamed filled with shame/dishonored

MONTANO   I bleed still: I am hurt to th'death. He   *Attacks Cassio?*
dies!

155 OTHELLO   Hold, for your lives!

IAGO   Hold, ho! Lieutenant— Sir Montano— Gentlemen,
Have you forgot all sense of place and duty?
Hold! The general speaks to you. Hold, for shame!

OTHELLO   Why, how now, ho! From whence ariseth this?
160 Are we turned Turks, and to ourselves do that
Which heaven hath forbid the Ottomites?
For Christian shame, put by this barbarous brawl!
He that stirs next to carve for his own rage
Holds his soul light: he dies upon his motion.—
165 Silence that dreadful bell: it frights the isle
From her propriety.— What is the matter, masters?
Honest Iago, that looks dead with grieving,
Speak: who began this? On thy love, I charge thee.

IAGO   I do not know. Friends all but now, even now,
170 In quarter and in terms like bride and groom
Devesting them for bed: and then, but now —
As if some planet had unwitted men —
Swords out, and tilting one at other's breasts
In opposition bloody. I cannot speak
175 Any beginning to this peevish odds,
And would in action glorious I had lost
Those legs that brought me to a part of it!

OTHELLO   How comes it, Michael, you are thus forgot?

CASSIO   I pray you pardon me: I cannot speak.

180 OTHELLO   Worthy Montano, you were wont to be civil:

---

157 place (your) official positions   **160 turned Turks** converted to Islam/betrayed ourselves
that . . . Ottomites attack each other, which the heaven-sent storm prevented the Turks from
doing to us; may also allude to Islamic prohibitions against alcohol/internecine strife
163 carve i.e. with his sword   **164 light** of small value   **he dies** i.e. I'll kill him
165 dreadful inspiring dread and terror   **166 From her propriety** out of its rightful ordered
state   **167 grieving** distress, sorrow   **168 love** loyal affection for me   **170 quarter** conduct
toward one another   **terms** speech/relations with one another   **171 Devesting them**
undressing themselves   **172 unwitted men** deprived men of their senses   **173 tilting**
thrusting   **175 peevish odds** senseless quarrel/headstrong conflict   **176 would** wish
178 are thus forgot have forgotten yourself in this way   **180 wont** accustomed

The gravity and stillness of your youth
The world hath noted, and your name is great
In mouths of wisest censure. What's the matter
That you unlace your reputation thus

185 And spend your rich opinion for the name
Of a night-brawler? Give me answer to it.

MONTANO   Worthy Othello, I am hurt to danger:
Your officer, Iago, can inform you —
While I spare speech, which something now offends me —

190 Of all that I do know, nor know I aught
By me that's said or done amiss this night,
Unless self-charity be sometimes a vice,
And to defend ourselves it be a sin
When violence assails us.

195 OTHELLO   Now, by heaven,
My blood begins my safer guides to rule,
And passion — having my best judgement collied —
Assays to lead the way: if I once stir,
Or do but lift this arm, the best of you

200 Shall sink in my rebuke. Give me to know
How this foul rout began, who set it on,
And he that is approved in this offence,
Though he had twinned with me, both at a birth,
Shall lose me. What, in a town of war

205 Yet wild, the people's hearts brim-full of fear,
To manage private and domestic quarrel?
In night, and on the court and guard of safety?
'Tis monstrous. Iago, who began't?

MONTANO   If partially affined, or leagued in office,   *To Iago*

181 **stillness** calmness/sobriety   183 **censure** judgment   184 **unlace** undo (the strings of a purse in order to **spend** the contents)   185 **opinion** reputation   189 **offends** hurts   190 **aught** anything   196 **blood** passion/anger   **safer guides** i.e. reason, judgment   197 **collied** blackened, obscured   198 **Assays** attempts   201 **rout** brawl   202 **approved** proved (guilty)   203 **twinned . . . birth** been my twin   204 **town of war** garrison town   205 **wild** excitable, unruly, not entirely under control   206 **manage** conduct   207 **on . . . safety** at the guardhouse and while on duty protecting public safety   208 **monstrous** unnatural, outrageous (ironically, a mere period stands in the way of the answer to Othello's question)   209 **partially . . . office** if, being personally predisposed (to Cassio) or allied (to him) because of your official roles

210   Thou dost deliver more or less than truth,
        Thou art no soldier.

IAGO   Touch me not so near:
        I had rather have this tongue cut from my mouth
        Than it should do offence to Michael Cassio,
215   Yet, I persuade myself, to speak the truth
        Shall nothing wrong him. This it is, general:
        Montano and myself being in speech,
        There comes a fellow crying out for help,
        And Cassio following him with determined sword
220   To execute upon him. Sir, this gentleman   *Indicates Montano*
        Steps in to Cassio and entreats his pause:
        Myself the crying fellow did pursue,
        Lest by his clamour — as it so fell out —
        The town might fall in fright: he, swift of foot,
225   Outran my purpose, and I returned then rather
        For that I heard the clink and fall of swords
        And Cassio high in oath, which till tonight
        I ne'er might say before. When I came back —
        For this was brief — I found them close together
230   At blow and thrust, even as again they were
        When you yourself did part them.
        More of this matter cannot I report.
        But men are men: the best sometimes forget:
        Though Cassio did some little wrong to him,
235   As men in rage strike those that wish them best,
        Yet surely Cassio, I believe, received
        From him that fled some strange indignity,
        Which patience could not pass.

OTHELLO   I know, Iago,
240   Thy honesty and love doth mince this matter,

---

212 Touch test/accuse/provoke   **near** intimately/closely   **219 with . . . him** determined to use his sword upon him (**execute** plays on sense of "put to death")   **221 his pause** him to stop   **225 rather For that** the more rapidly because   **227 high in oath** cursing loudly   **233 forget** forget themselves   **234 him** i.e. Montano   **237 indignity** insult, affront   **238 pass** let pass   **240 mince** make light of

Making it light to Cassio. Cassio, I love thee,
But never more be officer of mine.

Enter Desdemona, attended

Look, if my gentle love be not raised up.
I'll make thee an example.

245 DESDEMONA   What is the matter, dear?

OTHELLO   All's well, sweeting:
Come away to bed.— Sir, for your hurts,   *To Montano*
Myself will be your surgeon.— Lead him off.

[*Exeunt some with Montano*]

Iago, look with care about the town
250 And silence those whom this vile brawl distracted.—
Come, Desdemona: 'tis the soldiers' life
To have their balmy slumbers waked with strife.

Exeunt [all but Iago and Cassio]

IAGO   What, are you hurt, lieutenant?

CASSIO   Ay, past all surgery.

255 IAGO   Marry, heaven forbid!

CASSIO   Reputation, reputation, reputation! O, I have lost
my reputation! I have lost the immortal part of myself, and
what remains is bestial. My reputation, Iago, my reputation!

IAGO   As I am an honest man, I had thought you had
260 received some bodily wound; there is more sense in that
than in reputation. Reputation is an idle and most false
imposition: oft got without merit and lost without deserving:
you have lost no reputation at all, unless you repute yourself
such a loser. What, man, there are more ways to recover
265 the general again: you are but now cast in his mood — a
punishment more in policy than in malice — even so as one
would beat his offenceless dog to affright an imperious lion.
Sue to him again and he's yours.

CASSIO   I will rather sue to be despised than to deceive

---

246 **sweeting** sweetheart, darling   248 **Myself . . . surgeon** i.e. I will ensure that you receive good medical care/dress your wounds   250 **distracted** confused/caused disorder among
252 **balmy** soothing   260 **sense** physical feeling, i.e. pain   261 **idle** useless/empty
262 **imposition** thing imposed on one by others   264 **recover** regain (the favor of)
265 **cast . . . mood** dismissed in his fit of anger   268 **Sue to** petition, entreat

270   so good a commander with so slight, so drunken and
so indiscreet an officer. Drunk? And speak parrot? And
squabble? Swagger? Swear? And discourse fustian with one's
own shadow? O thou invisible spirit of wine, if thou hast no
name to be known by, let us call thee devil!

275   IAGO   What was he that you followed with your sword?
What had he done to you?

CASSIO   I know not.

IAGO   Is't possible?

CASSIO   I remember a mass of things, but nothing distinctly:
280   a quarrel, but nothing wherefore. O, that men should put an
enemy in their mouths to steal away their brains! That we
should, with joy, pleasance, revel and applause transform
ourselves into beasts!

IAGO   Why, but you are now well enough: how came you
285   thus recovered?

CASSIO   It hath pleased the devil drunkenness to give place
to the devil wrath: one unperfectness shows me another, to
make me frankly despise myself.

IAGO   Come, you are too severe a moraler. As the time, the
290   place and the condition of this country stands, I could
heartily wish this had not befallen: but since it is as it is,
mend it for your own good.

CASSIO   I will ask him for my place again: he shall tell me I
am a drunkard! Had I as many mouths as Hydra, such an
295   answer would stop them all. To be now a sensible man, by
and by a fool, and presently a beast! O, strange! Every
inordinate cup is unblessed, and the ingredient is a devil.

IAGO   Come, come, good wine is a good familiar creature,

---

270 **slight** worthless   271 **indiscreet** foolish, lacking sound judgment   **speak parrot**
babble repetitively/speak rubbish   272 **discourse fustian** speak elaborate nonsense
275 **What** who   280 **nothing wherefore** no reason for it   282 **pleasance** pleasure
288 **frankly** openly, unreservedly   289 **moraler** moralizer   292 **mend it** improve
matters   294 **Hydra** in Greek mythology, the many-headed snake that regrew two
heads for every one that was cut off   295 **stop** stop up, silence   297 **inordinate**
immoderate   298 **familiar** friendly (but quibbles on the sense of "malign attendant
spirit")

if it be well used: exclaim no more against it. And, good
300 lieutenant, I think you think I love you.

CASSIO   I have well approved it, sir. I drunk?

IAGO   You or any man living may be drunk at a time,
man. I tell you what you shall do. Our general's wife is now
the general: I may say so in this respect, for that he hath
305 devoted and given up himself to the contemplation, mark,
and denotement of her parts and graces: confess yourself
freely to her, importune her help to put you in your place
again. She is of so free, so kind, so apt, so blessed a
disposition, she holds it a vice in her goodness not to do more
310 than she is requested. This broken joint between you and her
husband entreat her to splinter, and, my fortunes against
any lay worth naming, this crack of your love shall grow
stronger than it was before.

CASSIO   You advise me well.

315 IAGO   I protest, in the sincerity of love and honest
kindness.

CASSIO   I think it freely, and betimes in the morning I will
beseech the virtuous Desdemona to undertake for me: I am
desperate of my fortunes if they check me.

320 IAGO   You are in the right. Goodnight, lieutenant: I must
to the watch.

CASSIO   Goodnight, honest Iago.   *Exit Cassio*

IAGO   And what's he then that says I play the villain?
When this advice is free I give, and honest,
325 Probal to thinking, and indeed the course
To win the Moor again? For 'tis most easy
Th'inclining Desdemona to subdue

301 approved it found it to be so through experience   **302 a time** some time   **304 for that**
(namely) that   **305 mark, and denotement** observation   **306 parts** personal qualities
307 importune crave, entreat; plays on negative senses of "pester, annoy/solicit for purposes of
prostitution"   **308 free** generous, but plays ambiguously on secondary sense of "sexually
available"; Iago's speech is open to a negative construction throughout   **apt** ready, willing
311 splinter set with a splint   **312 lay** wager/laying down a woman (for sex)   **crack** damage
(with sexual, anatomical overtones)   **315 protest** declare, avow   **317 think it freely** believe so
unreservedly   **betimes** early   **318 undertake** take on the matter/vouch   **319 desperate of**
hopeless about   **check** halt   **324 free** freely given/generous/frank   **325 Probal** probable,
credible, reasonable   **327 Th'inclining** disposed to be sympathetic/yielding   **subdue** win over

In any honest suit: she's framed as fruitful
As the free elements. And then for her
330   To win the Moor — were't to renounce his baptism,
All seals and symbols of redeemèd sin —
His soul is so enfettered to her love
That she may make, unmake, do what she list,
Even as her appetite shall play the god
335   With his weak function. How am I then a villain
To counsel Cassio to this parallel course
Directly to his good? Divinity of hell!
When devils will the blackest sins put on,
They do suggest at first with heavenly shows,
340   As I do now. For whiles this honest fool
Plies Desdemona to repair his fortune,
And she for him pleads strongly to the Moor,
I'll pour this pestilence into his ear,
That she repeals him for her body's lust,
345   And by how much she strives to do him good,
She shall undo her credit with the Moor.
So will I turn her virtue into pitch,
And out of her own goodness make the net
That shall enmesh them all.—

Enter Rodorigo

How now, Rodorigo?

350   **RODORIGO**   I do follow here in the chase, not like a hound that
hunts, but one that fills up the cry. My money is almost
spent; I have been tonight exceedingly well cudgelled, and I
think the issue will be I shall have so much experience for my
pains, and so, with no money at all and a little more wit,
355   return again to Venice.

---

328 framed as fruitful created as generous   **331 seals** pledges/tokens   **332 enfettered**
shackled, enslaved   **333 list** desires   **334 appetite** inclination/sexual desire   **335 function**
capabilities, intellectual faculties (**weak** because he is so enamored of her); possible play on
the sense of "sexual potency"   **336 parallel** i.e. to Iago's scheming intentions   **337 Divinity**
theology   **338 put on** urge, incite (men to commit)   **339 suggest** tempt   **341 Plies** solicits,
works on   **343 pestilence** plague/wickedness   **344 repeals him** tries to get him reinstated
346 credit trust/reputation   **347 pitch** sticky black tar-like substance   **350 chase** hunt
351 fills . . . cry makes up one of the pack   **352 cudgelled** beaten   **353 issue** outcome
354 wit sense

IAGO   How poor are they that have not patience!
What wound did ever heal but by degrees?
Thou know'st we work by wit, and not by witchcraft,
And wit depends on dilatory time.
360   Does't not go well? Cassio hath beaten thee,
And thou, by that small hurt, hath cashiered Cassio.
Though other things grow fair against the sun,
Yet fruits that blossom first will first be ripe.
Content thyself awhile. In troth, 'tis morning;
365   Pleasure and action make the hours seem short.
Retire thee: go where thou art billeted.
Away, I say! Thou shalt know more hereafter.
Nay, get thee gone.   *Exit Rodorigo*
Two things are to be done:
370   My wife must move for Cassio to her mistress:
I'll set her on:
Myself the while to draw the Moor apart
And bring him jump when he may Cassio find
Soliciting his wife: ay, that's the way.
375   Dull not device by coldness and delay.   *Exit*

Act 3 Scene 1   *running scene 7*

Enter Cassio, Musicians, Clown

CASSIO   Masters, play here: I will content your pains:
Something that's brief, and bid 'Good morrow,   *Music*
    general.'

CLOWN   Why masters, have your instruments been in
Naples, that they speak i'th'nose thus?

---

359 dilatory slow/delaying   **361 cashiered** (got) dismissed   **362 against** exposed to
363 Yet . . . ripe i.e. the dismissal of Cassio demonstrates that our plan is blossoming and will
ensure that the eventual outcome (fruit) of our schemes is successful   **364 troth** truth
370 move entreat, solicit   **372 the while** meanwhile   **373 jump** precisely   **375 device**
scheming   **3.1   *Location: Cyprus (governor's residence/citadel)   Musicians* music**
was traditionally played outside a bridal bedroom at dawn   **1 content your pains** pay for your
efforts   **4 Naples** southwestern Italian city   **i'th'nose** with a nasal twang like that of the
Neapolitan accent/like one whose nasal tissue has been damaged by syphilis, of which there
was a high incidence in Naples

5	MUSICIAN	How, sir? How?
	CLOWN	Are these, I pray you, wind instruments?
	MUSICIAN	Ay, marry, are they, sir.
	CLOWN	O, thereby hangs a tail.
	MUSICIAN	Whereby hangs a tale, sir?
10	CLOWN	Marry, sir, by many a wind instrument that I know. But, masters, here's money for you: and the *Gives money* general so likes your music that he desires you, for love's sake, to make no more noise with it.
	MUSICIAN	Well, sir, we will not.
15	CLOWN	If you have any music that may not be heard, to't again: but, as they say, to hear music the general does not greatly care.
	MUSICIAN	We have none such, sir.
	CLOWN	Then put up your pipes in your bag, for I'll away: go,
20		vanish into air, away! *Exeunt Musicians*
	CASSIO	Dost thou hear me, mine honest friend?
	CLOWN	No, I hear not your honest friend: I hear you.
	CASSIO	Prithee keep up thy quillets. There's a *Gives money* poor piece of gold for thee: if the gentlewoman that attends
25		the general be stirring, tell her there's one Cassio entreats her a little favour of speech: wilt thou do this?
	CLOWN	She is stirring, sir: if she will stir hither, I shall seem to notify unto her. *Exit Clown*

Enter Iago

	CASSIO	In happy time, Iago.
30	IAGO	You have not been a-bed, then?
	CASSIO	Why, no: the day had broke
		Before we parted. I have made bold, Iago,
		To send in to your wife: my suit to her
		Is that she will to virtuous Desdemona
35		Procure me some access.

---

5 **How** what   8 **tail** penis (though the Musician hears "tale," i.e. story)   10 **wind instrument** sense has now shifted to "flatulent anus"   12 **love's** the love you bear him/Othello's lovemaking with Desdemona   13 **noise** plays on nose   19 **up** away   23 **keep . . . quillets** hold back your quibbles   24 **gentlewoman** female attendant   25 **stirring** up and about (but in his response the Clown shifts the sense to "sexually arousing")   27 **seem** arrange, contrive 29 **In happy time** (you have come at) an opportune moment

IAGO   I'll send her to you presently,
And I'll devise a mean to draw the Moor
Out of the way, that your converse and business
May be more free.   *Exit*

40 CASSIO   I humbly thank you for't.— I never knew
A Florentine more kind and honest.

Enter Emilia

EMILIA   Good morrow, good Lieutenant: I am sorry
For your displeasure, but all will sure be well.
The general and his wife are talking of it,
45 And she speaks for you stoutly: the Moor replies
That he you hurt is of great fame in Cyprus
And great affinity, and that in wholesome wisdom
He might not but refuse you: but he protests he loves you
And needs no other suitor but his likings
50 To bring you in again.

CASSIO   Yet, I beseech you,
If you think fit, or that it may be done,
Give me advantage of some brief discourse
With Desdemon alone.

55 EMILIA   Pray you come in:
I will bestow you where you shall have time
To speak your bosom freely.

CASSIO   I am much bound to you.   *[Exeunt]*

Act 3 Scene 2
running scene 7 continues

Enter Othello, Iago and Gentlemen

OTHELLO   These letters give, Iago, to the pilot,   *Gives him letters*
And by him do my duties to the senate:
That done, I will be walking on the works.
Repair there to me.

36 presently immediately   **37 mean** method   **41 A Florentine** i.e. even a Florentine (one
of Cassio's own countrymen)   **43 displeasure** being out of favor   **46 fame** reputation
47 affinity family/connections   **wholesome** sound, beneficial   **49 suitor** petitioner
53 advantage of a favorable opportunity for   **57 bosom** heart, inmost thoughts   **3.2**   **2 do
my duties** convey my respects   **3 works** fortifications   **4 Repair** return/make your way

5	IAGO	Well, my good lord, I'll do't.
	OTHELLO	This fortification, gentlemen, shall we see't?
	GENTLEMEN	We'll wait upon your lordship. *Exeunt*

Act 3 Scene 3

Enter Desdemona, Cassio and Emilia

DESDEMONA   Be thou assured, good Cassio, I will do
All my abilities in thy behalf.

EMILIA   Good madam, do: I warrant it grieves my husband
As if the cause were his.

5   DESDEMONA   O, that's an honest fellow. Do not doubt, Cassio,
But I will have my lord and you again
As friendly as you were.

CASSIO   Bounteous madam,
Whatever shall become of Michael Cassio,
10   He's never anything but your true servant.

DESDEMONA   I know't: I thank you. You do love my lord:
You have known him long, and be you well assured
He shall in strangeness stand no further off
Than in a politic distance.

15   CASSIO   Ay, but, lady,
That policy may either last so long,
Or feed upon such nice and waterish diet,
Or breed itself so out of circumstances,
That I being absent and my place supplied,
20   My general will forget my love and service.

DESDEMONA   Do not doubt that: before Emilia here
I give thee warrant of thy place. Assure thee,
If I do vow a friendship, I'll perform it
To the last article: my lord shall never rest,
25   I'll watch him tame and talk him out of patience;

3.3   3 I warrant I'm sure   **13 strangeness** aloofness, unfriendliness   **14 politic**
discreet/expedient   **17 nice and waterish** insubstantial and thin (or possibly "luxurious and
succulent")   **18 breed . . . circumstances** renew itself out of various events/generate so few
opportunities (for my reinstatement)   **19 supplied** filled   **21 doubt** fear   **22 warrant**
assurance, guarantee   **25 watch him tame** tame him by preventing him from sleeping (a
method for training hawks)

His bed shall seem a school, his board a shrift:
I'll intermingle everything he does
With Cassio's suit. Therefore be merry, Cassio,
For thy solicitor shall rather die
30   Than give thy cause away.

Enter Othello and Iago

EMILIA   Madam, here comes my lord.

CASSIO   Madam, I'll take my leave.

DESDEMONA   Why, stay and hear me speak.

CASSIO   Madam, not now: I am very ill at ease,
35   Unfit for mine own purposes.

DESDEMONA   Well, do your discretion.   *Exit Cassio*

IAGO   Ha? I like not that.

OTHELLO   What dost thou say?

IAGO   Nothing, my lord; or if — I know not what.

40 OTHELLO Was not that Cassio parted from my wife?

IAGO   Cassio, my lord? No, sure, I cannot think it,
That he would steal away so guilty-like,
Seeing your coming.

OTHELLO   I do believe 'twas he.

45 DESDEMONA How now, my lord?
I have been talking with a suitor here,
A man that languishes in your displeasure.

OTHELLO   Who is't you mean?

DESDEMONA   Why, your lieutenant, Cassio. Good my lord,
50   If I have any grace or power to move you,
His present reconciliation take,
For if he be not one that truly loves you,
That errs in ignorance and not in cunning,
I have no judgement in an honest face.
55   I prithee call him back.

OTHELLO   Went he hence now?

---

26 board a shrift table (shall seem) a confessional   **29 solicitor** pleader/representative/
lawyer (legal language continues with **cause**)   **30 away** up   **36 do your discretion** obey your
own judgment   **46 suitor** petitioner (Desdemona unconsciously puns on the sense of "lover")
50 grace virtue/favor with you   **51 present reconciliation take** restore him to your favor
immediately/accept the reconciliation he now seeks   **53 in cunning** deliberately

DESDEMONA   Ay, sooth; so humbled
　　　　　That he hath left part of his grief with me
　　　　　To suffer with him. Good love, call him back.
60   OTHELLO   Not now, sweet Desdemon: some other time.
DESDEMONA   But shall't be shortly?
OTHELLO   The sooner, sweet, for you.
DESDEMONA   Shall't be tonight at supper?
OTHELLO   No, not tonight.
65   DESDEMONA   Tomorrow dinner, then?
OTHELLO   I shall not dine at home:
　　　　　I meet the captains at the citadel.
DESDEMONA   Why then, tomorrow night, on Tuesday morn,
　　　　　On Tuesday noon, or night; on Wednesday morn:
70   I prithee name the time, but let it not
　　　　　Exceed three days. In faith, he's penitent:
　　　　　And yet his trespass, in our common reason —
　　　　　Save that they say the wars must make example
　　　　　Out of her best — is not almost a fault
75   T'incur a private check. When shall he come?
　　　　　Tell me, Othello: I wonder in my soul
　　　　　What you would ask me that I should deny,
　　　　　Or stand so mamm'ring on. What? Michael Cassio,
　　　　　That came a-wooing with you, and so many a time —
80   When I have spoke of you dispraisingly —
　　　　　Hath ta'en your part: to have so much to do
　　　　　To bring him in! Trust me, I could do much—
OTHELLO   Prithee, no more: let him come when he will:
　　　　　I will deny thee nothing.
85   DESDEMONA   Why, this is not a boon:
　　　　　'Tis as I should entreat you wear your gloves,
　　　　　Or feed on nourishing dishes, or keep you warm,
　　　　　Or sue to you to do a peculiar profit
　　　　　To your own person: nay, when I have a suit

---

57 **sooth** truly   65 **dinner** lunch   72 **trespass** fault, offense   **common reason** everyday
judgment   74 **best** best men   **not almost** hardly even   75 **check** reprimand
78 **mamm'ring** stammering hesitantly   82 **in** i.e. into favor   85 **boon** favor graciously
granted   88 **peculiar** particular, personal

90   Wherein I mean to touch your love indeed,
      It shall be full of poise and difficult weight,
      And fearful to be granted.

OTHELLO   I will deny thee nothing:
      Whereon, I do beseech thee, grant me this,
95   To leave me but a little to myself.

DESDEMONA   Shall I deny you? No. Farewell, my lord.

OTHELLO   Farewell, my Desdemona, I'll come to thee straight.

DESDEMONA   Emilia, come.— Be as your fancies teach you:
      Whate'er you be, I am obedient.

                              Exeunt [Desdemona and Emilia]

100   OTHELLO   Excellent wretch! Perdition catch my soul,
      But I do love thee! And when I love thee not,
      Chaos is come again.

IAGO   My noble lord—

OTHELLO   What dost thou say, Iago?

105   IAGO   Did Michael Cassio, when you wooed my lady,
      Know of your love?

OTHELLO   He did, from first to last: why dost thou ask?

IAGO   But for a satisfaction of my thought,
      No further harm.

110   OTHELLO   Why of thy thought, Iago?

IAGO   I did not think he had been acquainted with her.

OTHELLO   O, yes, and went between us very oft.

IAGO   Indeed?

OTHELLO   Indeed? Ay, indeed. Discern'st thou aught in that?
115   Is he not honest?

IAGO   Honest, my lord?

OTHELLO   Honest, ay, honest.

IAGO   My lord, for aught I know.

OTHELLO   What dost thou think?

120   IAGO   Think, my lord?

OTHELLO   'Think, my lord?' Alas, thou echo'st me,

---

90 touch test   **91 poise** heaviness, importance/balance, equipoise (making choice hard)
difficult weight hard to assess or weigh   **94 Whereon** as a result of which   **97 straight**
straightaway, very soon   **98 fancies** inclinations, whims   **100 Perdition** destruction/
damnation   **catch** seize   **114 aught** anything

As if there were some monster in thy thought
Too hideous to be shown. Thou dost mean something.
I heard thee say even now, thou lik'st not that,
125   When Cassio left my wife: what didst not like?
And when I told thee he was of my counsel
Of my whole course of wooing, thou cried'st 'Indeed?'
And didst contract and purse thy brow together
As if thou then hadst shut up in thy brain
130   Some horrible conceit: if thou dost love me,
Show me thy thought.

IAGO   My lord, you know I love you.

OTHELLO   I think thou dost,
And for I know thou'rt full of love and honesty,
135   And weigh'st thy words before thou giv'st them breath,
Therefore these stops of thine fright me the more,
For such things in a false disloyal knave
Are tricks of custom, but in a man that's just
They're close dilations, working from the heart
140   That passion cannot rule.

IAGO   For Michael Cassio,
I dare be sworn I think that he is honest.

OTHELLO   I think so too.

IAGO   Men should be what they seem,
145   Or those that be not, would they might seem none.

OTHELLO   Certain, men should be what they seem.

IAGO   Why then, I think Cassio's an honest man.

OTHELLO   Nay, yet there's more in this!
I prithee speak to me as to thy thinkings,
150   As thou dost ruminate, and give thy worst of thoughts
The worst of words.

IAGO   Good my lord, pardon me:
Though I am bound to every act of duty,
I am not bound to that all slaves are free.

---

126 of . . . Of in my confidence during   **128 purse** furrow, knit   **130 conceit** imagining/idea
134 for because   **136 stops** hesitations/abrupt pauses   **137 false** treacherous   **138 custom**
habit   **139 close dilations** secret delays/hidden accusations   **140 rule** control, restrain
145 seem none not be men/not seem to be anything at all, not convince in the slightest
154 that . . . free the thing that even slaves are not bound to do (i.e. speak their thoughts)

155 Utter my thoughts? Why, say they are vile and false,
As where's that palace whereinto foul things
Sometimes intrude not? Who has that breast so pure,
Where no uncleanly apprehensions
Keep leets and law-days and in sessions sit
160 With meditations lawful?

OTHELLO   Thou dost conspire against thy friend, Iago,
If thou but think'st him wronged and mak'st his ear
A stranger to thy thoughts.

IAGO   I do beseech you,
165 Though I perchance am vicious in my guess —
As I confess it is my nature's plague
To spy into abuses, and oft my jealousy
Shapes faults that are not — that your wisdom,
From one that so imperfectly conceits,
170 Would take no notice, nor build yourself a trouble
Out of his scattering and unsure observance.
It were not for your quiet nor your good,
Nor for my manhood, honesty and wisdom,
To let you know my thoughts.

175 OTHELLO   What dost thou mean?

IAGO   Good name in man and woman, dear my lord,
Is the immediate jewel of their souls.
Who steals my purse steals trash, 'tis something, nothing;
'Twas mine, 'tis his, and has been slave to thousands:
180 But he that filches from me my good name
Robs me of that which not enriches him
And makes me poor indeed.

OTHELLO   I'll know thy thoughts.

IAGO   You cannot, if my heart were in your hand,
185 Nor shall not, whilst 'tis in my custody.

OTHELLO   Ha?

---

158 uncleanly morally impure   159 leets courts held by some manorial lords   law-days
days on which courts of law meet   sessions sittings of the law court   160 With together
with   161 thy friend i.e. Othello   165 vicious wicked/faulty/blameworthy   167 jealousy
suspicious nature/anxious vigilance   169 conceits conjectures, imagines   171 scattering
wild/random/disordered   observance observations/dutiful care   177 immediate closest
184 if even if

IAGO   O, beware, my lord, of jealousy:
              It is the green-eyed monster which doth mock
              The meat it feeds on. That cuckold lives in bliss
190   Who, certain of his fate, loves not his wronger:
              But, O, what damnèd minutes tells he o'er
              Who dotes, yet doubts, suspects, yet soundly loves!
OTHELLO   O misery!
IAGO   Poor and content is rich and rich enough,
195   But riches fineless is as poor as winter
              To him that ever fears he shall be poor.
              Good heaven, the souls of all my tribe defend
              From jealousy!
OTHELLO   Why? Why is this?
200   Think'st thou I'd make a life of jealousy,
              To follow still the changes of the moon
              With fresh suspicions? No: to be once in doubt
              Is to be resolved. Exchange me for a goat
              When I shall turn the business of my soul
205   To such exsufflicate and blowed surmises
              Matching thy inference. 'Tis not to make me jealous
              To say my wife is fair, feeds well, loves company,
              Is free of speech, sings, plays and dances:
              Where virtue is, these are more virtuous:
210   Nor from mine own weak merits will I draw
              The smallest fear or doubt of her revolt,
              For she had eyes, and chose me. No, Iago,
              I'll see before I doubt; when I doubt, prove;
              And on the proof, there is no more but this:
215   Away at once with love or jealousy.
IAGO   I am glad of this, for now I shall have reason
              To show the love and duty that I bear you

---

188 mock . . . on taunts the victim (the jealous man) that gives it life   **mock** torment/delude/
ridicule   **189 cuckold** man with an unfaithful wife   **190 wronger** i.e. his wife   **191 tells**
counts   **195 fineless** limitless   **201 follow . . . suspicions** imitate the waxing moon by
growing in suspicion/like a madman, respond to each new phase of the moon with new
suspicions   **203 goat** proverbially lecherous animal   **205 exsufflicate** puffed-up   **blowed**
blown-up/whispered/flyblown (i.e. putrid, full of flies' eggs)   **206 inference** conclusion/
implication   **210 merits** qualities/worth   **211 revolt** disobedience, infidelity

With franker spirit: therefore, as I am bound,
Receive it from me. I speak not yet of proof:
220   Look to your wife, observe her well with Cassio,
Wear your eyes thus, not jealous nor secure.
I would not have your free and noble nature,
Out of self-bounty, be abused: look to't.
I know our country disposition well:
225   In Venice they do let heaven see the pranks
They dare not show their husbands: their best conscience
Is not to leave't undone, but kept unknown.

OTHELLO   Dost thou say so?

IAGO   She did deceive her father, marrying you:
230   And when she seemed to shake and fear your looks,
She loved them most.

OTHELLO   And so she did.

IAGO   Why, go to then:
She that so young could give out such a seeming,
235   To seel her father's eyes up close as oak,
He thought 'twas witchcraft. But I am much to blame:
I humbly do beseech you of your pardon
For too much loving you.

OTHELLO   I am bound to thee for ever.

240   IAGO   I see this hath a little dashed your spirits.

OTHELLO   Not a jot, not a jot.

IAGO   Trust me, I fear it has.
I hope you will consider what is spoke
Comes from your love. But I do see you're moved:
245   I am to pray you not to strain my speech
To grosser issues nor to larger reach
Than to suspicion.

---

221 secure free from doubt/overconfident   223 self-bounty inherent generosity/good nature
224 country contains a pun on "cunt" (a similar quibble on "con" may lie within conscience)
225 pranks sexual mischief   227 undone plays on sense of "not copulated with"   233 go to
expression of dismissive contempt   235 seel sew (as a young hawk's eyes are for training
purposes)   oak a closely grained wood   239 bound indebted (plays on sense of "tied,
shackled")   244 your love love for you   246 grosser larger/more lewd   issues conclusions
larger broader/coarser   reach "stretch, aim" (verb) or "scope, range" (noun)   247 suspicion
mere conjecture

OTHELLO   I will not.

IAGO   Should you do so, my lord,
250   My speech should fall into such vile success
Which my thoughts aimed not. Cassio's my worthy friend.
My lord, I see you're moved.

OTHELLO   No, not much moved:
I do not think but Desdemona's honest.

255   IAGO   Long live she so; and long live you to think so!

OTHELLO   And yet, how nature erring from itself—

IAGO   Ay, there's the point: as — to be bold with you —
Not to affect many proposèd matches
Of her own clime, complexion and degree,
260   Whereto we see in all things nature tends—
Foh, one may smell in such a will most rank,
Foul disproportions, thoughts unnatural.
But pardon me: I do not in position
Distinctly speak of her, though I may fear
265   Her will, recoiling to her better judgement,
May fall to match you with her country forms
And happily repent.

OTHELLO   Farewell, farewell.
If more thou dost perceive, let me know more:
270   Set on thy wife to observe. Leave me, Iago.

IAGO   My lord, I take my leave.   *Starts to leave*

OTHELLO   Why did I marry? This honest creature doubtless
Sees and knows more, much more, than he unfolds.

IAGO   My lord, I would I might entreat your   *Returns*
honour
275   To scan this thing no further: leave it to time.
Although 'tis fit that Cassio have his place,

---

250 success outcome   **254 honest** chaste/virtuous   **258 affect** like, prefer   **259 clime . . .
degree** country, race, and rank   **261 will** inclination/willfulness/sexual appetite   **rank**
rebellious/corrupt/rancid, foul-smelling/lascivious   **262 Foul** abhorrent/morally
impure/dirty, blackened/choked with foreign matter   **disproportions** deformities/lack of
symmetry   **263 in position** in this assertion   **264 Distinctly** specifically   **266 fall . . . forms**
come to compare you with men of her own nationality (conceivably **country** puns on "cunt")
267 happily perhaps/with pleasure   **275 scan** examine   **276 place** official position (though
fills it up generates a vaginal sense)

For sure he fills it up with great ability,
Yet, if you please to put him off awhile,
You shall by that perceive him and his means.
280 Note, if your lady strain his entertainment
With any strong or vehement importunity,
Much will be seen in that. In the meantime,
Let me be thought too busy in my fears —
As worthy cause I have to fear I am —
285 And hold her free, I do beseech your honour.

OTHELLO   Fear not my government.

IAGO   I once more take my leave.   *Exit*

OTHELLO   This fellow's of exceeding honesty,
And knows all quantities, with a learnèd spirit,
290 Of human dealings. If I do prove her haggard,
Though that her jesses were my dear heartstrings,
I'd whistle her off and let her down the wind
To prey at fortune. Haply, for I am black
And have not those soft parts of conversation
295 That chamberers have, or for I am declined
Into the vale of years — yet that's not much —
She's gone. I am abused, and my relief
Must be to loathe her. O curse of marriage!
That we can call these delicate creatures ours
300 And not their appetites! I had rather be a toad
And live upon the vapour of a dungeon
Than keep a corner in the thing I love
For others' uses. Yet, 'tis the plague to great ones,
Prerogatived are they less than the base:

279 **means** methods/intentions   280 **strain his entertainment** urge his reinstatement
283 **busy** overzealous/interfering   285 **hold her free** consider her innocent, plays on negative
sense of "sexually available"   286 **government** self-control   289 **quantities** dimensions,
aspects   290 **dealings** behavior/interaction/sexual dealings   **haggard** wild (a haggard is an
untamed female hawk)   291 **jesses** straps fastened around the legs of a hawk to help keep it
attached to the falconer   292 **whistle . . . wind** set her free (a falconer dismissed a hawk with a
whistle; unwanted hawks were released in the same direction as the wind was blowing)
293 **prey at fortune** fend for herself, hunt randomly   **Haply, for** perhaps, because   294 **soft . . .**
conversation pleasing sociable accomplishments   295 **chamberers** fashionable men who
frequent ladies' chambers   297 **abused** wronged/deceived   299 **delicate** charming/pleasure-
seeking   302 **corner** nook/vagina   303 **uses** sexual employment   304 **Prerogatived**
privileged, advantaged

305   'Tis destiny unshunnable, like death:
           Even then this forkèd plague is fated to us
           When we do quicken. Look where she comes:
           Enter Desdemona and Emilia
               If she be false, heaven mocked itself!
               I'll not believe't.
310   DESDEMONA How now, my dear Othello?
               Your dinner, and the generous islanders
               By you invited, do attend your presence.
           OTHELLO   I am to blame.
           DESDEMONA Why do you speak so faintly?
315   Are you not well?
           OTHELLO   I have a pain upon my forehead here.
           DESDEMONA Why, that's with watching. 'Twill away again:
               Let me but bind it hard, within this hour   *Offers her handkerchief*
               It will be well.
320   OTHELLO   Your napkin is too little: *He pushes away*
                                                 the handkerchief and it drops
               Let it alone. Come, I'll go in with you.   *Exit*
           DESDEMONA I am very sorry that you are not well.   *Following him*
           EMILIA   I am glad I have found this napkin: *Picks up the*
               This was her first remembrance from the Moor: *handkerchief*
325   My wayward husband hath a hundred times
               Wooed me to steal it, but she so loves the token —
               For he conjured her she should ever keep it —
               That she reserves it evermore about her
               To kiss and talk to. I'll have the work ta'en out,
330   And give't Iago: what he will do with it
               Heaven knows, not I:
               I nothing but to please his fantasy.
           Enter Iago

---

306 forkèd plague horned affliction (cuckolds were traditionally supposed to grow horns)
307 do quicken are conceived   **308 mocked** deceived/flouted/parodied   **311 generous** noble
312 attend await   **316 pain . . . forehead** suggestive of the cuckold's horns   **317 watching**
not sleeping   **320 napkin** handkerchief   **324 remembrance** love token   **326 Wooed**
entreated, enticed   **327 conjured her** entreated her/made her swear   **328 reserves** keeps
329 work ta'en out embroidery copied   **332 I nothing** I am nothing to him/I know nothing
fantasy whim/desire

	IAGO	How now? What do you here alone?
	EMILIA	Do not you chide: I have a thing for you.
335	IAGO	You have a thing for me? It is a common thing—
	EMILIA	Ha?
	IAGO	To have a foolish wife.
	EMILIA	O, is that all? What will you give me now

For the same handkerchief?

	IAGO	What handkerchief?
340	EMILIA	What handkerchief?

Why, that the Moor first gave to Desdemona,
That which so often you did bid me steal.

	IAGO	Hast stol'n it from her?
345	EMILIA	No, but she let it drop by negligence.

And, to th'advantage, I, being here, took't up.
Look, here 'tis.

	IAGO	A good wench: give it me.
	EMILIA	What will you do with't, that you have been
350		So earnest to have me filch it?
	IAGO	Why, what is that to you? _Snatches it_
	EMILIA	If it be not for some purpose of import,

Give't me again: poor lady, she'll run mad
When she shall lack it.

	IAGO	Be not acknown on't: I have use for it.
355		Go, leave me. _Exit Emilia_

I will in Cassio's lodging loose this napkin
And let him find it. Trifles light as air
Are to the jealous confirmations strong
As proofs of holy writ: this may do something.
The Moor already changes with my poison:
Dangerous conceits are in their natures poisons,
Which at the first are scarce found to distaste,
But with a little act upon the blood,
Burn like the mines of sulphur. I did say so:

---

335 common unremarkable/vulgar/open to use by all   **thing** plays on the sense of "vagina"
346 to th'advantage opportunely, taking the advantage   **354 lack** miss/need   **355 Be . . .
on't** do not admit that you know anything about it   **360 holy writ** scripture   **362 conceits**
ideas/imaginings   **363 distaste** be distasteful   **364 act** action

Enter Othello   *At a distance*

Look, where he comes! Not poppy, nor mandragora,
Nor all the drowsy syrups of the world
Shall ever medicine thee to that sweet sleep
Which thou owed'st yesterday.

370 OTHELLO   Ha, ha, false to me?

IAGO   Why how now, general? No more of that.

OTHELLO   Avaunt, be gone! Thou hast set me on the rack:
I swear 'tis better to be much abused
Than but to know't a little.

375 IAGO   How now, my lord?

OTHELLO   What sense had I in her stol'n hours of lust?
I saw't not, thought it not, it harmed not me:
I slept the next night well, fed well, was free and merry:
I found not Cassio's kisses on her lips.

380 He that is robbed, not wanting what is stol'n,
Let him not know't and he's not robbed at all.

IAGO   I am sorry to hear this.

OTHELLO   I had been happy, if the general camp,
Pioneers and all, had tasted her sweet body,

385 So I had nothing known. O, now, for ever
Farewell the tranquil mind; farewell content;
Farewell the plumèd troops and the big wars
That makes ambition virtue! O, farewell!
Farewell the neighing steed and the shrill trump,

390 The spirit-stirring drum, th'ear-piercing fife,
The royal banner, and all quality,
Pride, pomp and circumstance of glorious war!
And, O, you mortal engines, whose rude throats

---

366 poppy opium   **mandragora** sedative made from the root of the mandragora, or
mandrake, plant   **369 owed'st** owned   **372 Avaunt** get away   **rack** torture device that
stretched the limbs   **378 free** unconstrained, untroubled   **380 wanting** missing
384 Pioneers footsoldiers, the lowest kind of soldier   **385 So** as long as   **387 plumèd**
wearing helmets adorned with feathers   **389 trump** trumpet   **390 fife** flute-like instrument,
often used in military music   **391 quality** essential nature   **392 Pride** glory/proud
magnificence   **pomp and circumstance** splendid display and ceremony   **393 mortal
engines** deadly machines (i.e. cannon)   **rude** rough, raucous

Th'immortal Jove's dread clamours counterfeit,

395 Farewell! Othello's occupation's gone.

IAGO   Is't possible, my lord?

OTHELLO   Villain, be sure thou prove my love a   *Grabs him*
whore;

Be sure of it: give me the ocular proof,

Or by the worth of mine eternal soul,

400 Thou hadst been better have been born a dog

Than answer my waked wrath!

IAGO   Is't come to this?

OTHELLO   Make me to see't, or at the least so prove it

That the probation bear no hinge nor loop

405 To hang a doubt on, or woe upon thy life!

IAGO   My noble lord—

OTHELLO   If thou dost slander her and torture me,

Never pray more: abandon all remorse,

On horror's head horrors accumulate,

410 Do deeds to make heaven weep, all earth amazed,

For nothing canst thou to damnation add

Greater than that.

IAGO   O grace! O heaven forgive me!

Are you a man? Have you a soul? Or sense?

415 God b'wi'you, take mine office. O wretched fool,

That lov'st to make thine honesty a vice!

O monstrous world! Take note, take note, O world,

To be direct and honest is not safe.

I thank you for this profit, and from hence

420 I'll love no friend, sith love breeds such offence.

OTHELLO   Nay, stay: thou shouldst be honest.

IAGO   I should be wise, for honesty's a fool

And loses that it works for.

---

394 **Jove's dread clamours** i.e. thunder, Jove's weapon   404 **probation** proof   408 **remorse** pity/penitence   410 **amazed** full of terror and consternation   415 **God b'wi'you** God be with you, i.e. good-bye   **O wretched fool** Iago addresses himself   419 **profit** profitable lesson   420 **sith** since   **offence** hurt (to me)/antagonism (in my **friend**)   421 **shouldst be** seem to be   422 **should be** ought to be   423 **that** that which

OTHELLO   By the world,

425   I think my wife be honest and think she is not:
I think that thou art just and think thou art not.
I'll have some proof. My name, that was as fresh
As Dian's visage, is now begrimed and black
As mine own face. If there be cords, or knives,

430   Poison, or fire, or suffocating streams,
I'll not endure it. Would I were satisfied!

IAGO   I see you are eaten up with passion:
I do repent me that I put it to you.
You would be satisfied?

435   OTHELLO   Would? Nay, and I will.

IAGO   And may: but, how? How satisfied, my lord?
Would you the supervision grossly gape on?
Behold her topped?

OTHELLO   Death and damnation! O!

440   IAGO   It were a tedious difficulty, I think,
To bring them to that prospect: damn them then,
If ever mortal eyes do see them bolster
More than their own. What then? How then?
What shall I say? Where's satisfaction?

445   It is impossible you should see this,
Were they as prime as goats, as hot as monkeys,
As salt as wolves in pride, and fools as gross
As ignorance made drunk. But yet, I say,
If imputation and strong circumstances

450   Which lead directly to the door of truth
Will give you satisfaction, you might have't.

OTHELLO   Give me a living reason she's disloyal.

---

428 Dian i.e. Diana, Roman goddess of chastity and the moon   **429 cords . . . streams** i.e. means of committing suicide, or perhaps murder   **437 supervision** sight that you are gazing down on   **grossly** blatantly/coarsely   **438 topped** mounted sexually   **441 prospect** point from which they might be viewed   **442 bolster** share a bed/have sex   **443 More** other   **own** i.e. own eyes   **444 satisfaction** proof/freedom from doubt (plays on the sense of "sexual fulfillment")   **446 prime** lecherous   **hot** sexually excited   **447 salt** lustful   **wolves** reputed to be libidinous, especially females   **in pride** in heat   **fools** idiots/lewd people   **gross** great/coarse   **449 imputation . . . circumstances** attribution and convincing circumstantial details

IAGO   I do not like the office,
But sith I am entered in this cause so far —
455   Pricked to't by foolish honesty and love —
I will go on. I lay with Cassio lately,
And being troubled with a raging tooth
I could not sleep. There are a kind of men
So loose of soul that in their sleeps will mutter
460   Their affairs: one of this kind is Cassio.
In sleep I heard him say, 'Sweet Desdemona,
Let us be wary, let us hide our loves':
And then, sir, would he grip and wring my hand,
Cry 'O sweet creature!' then kiss me hard,
465   As if he plucked up kisses by the roots
That grew upon my lips, laid his leg
O'er my thigh, and sigh, and kiss, and then
Cry, 'Cursèd fate that gave thee to the Moor!'

OTHELLO   O monstrous! Monstrous!

470   IAGO   Nay, this was but his dream.

OTHELLO   But this denoted a foregone conclusion:
'Tis a shrewd doubt, though it be but a dream.

IAGO   And this may help to thicken other proofs
That do demonstrate thinly.

475   OTHELLO   I'll tear her all to pieces.

IAGO   Nay, yet be wise: yet we see nothing done,
She may be honest yet. Tell me but this:
Have you not sometimes seen a handkerchief
Spotted with strawberries in your wife's hand?

480   OTHELLO   I gave her such a one: 'twas my first gift.

IAGO   I know not that, but such a handkerchief —
I am sure it was your wife's — did I today
See Cassio wipe his beard with.

OTHELLO   If it be that—

485   IAGO   If it be that, or any it was hers,
It speaks against her with the other proofs.

---

455 Pricked spurred   **456 lay** shared a bed   **467 sigh** Iago moves into the present tense to give his account an air of horrible immediacy   **471 foregone conclusion** event that had already occurred   **472 shrewd doubt** grievous suspicion   **476 yet we** as yet we

OTHELLO   O, that the slave had forty thousand lives:
One is too poor, too weak for my revenge.
Now do I see 'tis true. Look here, Iago,
490   All my fond love thus do I blow to heaven.
'Tis gone.
Arise, black vengeance, from thy hollow hell!
Yield up, O love, thy crown and hearted throne
To tyrannous hate! Swell, bosom, with thy fraught,
495   For 'tis of aspics' tongues!

IAGO   Yet be content.

OTHELLO   O, blood, blood, blood!

IAGO   Patience, I say: your mind may change.

OTHELLO   Never, Iago. Like to the Pontic sea,
500   Whose icy current and compulsive course
Ne'er feels retiring ebb, but keeps due on
To the Propontic and the Hellespont,
Even so my bloody thoughts with violent pace
Shall ne'er look back, ne'er ebb to humble love,
505   Till that a capable and wide revenge
Swallow them up. Now, by yond marble heaven,   *Kneels*
In the due reverence of a sacred vow
I here engage my words.   *Attempts to rise*

IAGO   Do not rise yet.   *Kneels*
510   Witness, you ever-burning lights above,
You elements that clip us round about,
Witness that here Iago doth give up
The execution of his wit, hands, heart,
To wronged Othello's service! Let him command,
515   And to obey shall be in me remorse,
What bloody business ever.   *They rise*

---

487 slave villain   **490 fond** foolish/doting/infatuated   **493 hearted** fixed in the heart
494 fraught burden   **495 aspics** asps (venomous snakes)   **499 Pontic sea** Black Sea
500 compulsive onward-flowing, driven   **502 Propontic** Sea of Marmora (situated between
the Aegean and the Black Sea)   **Hellespont** the Dardanelles (the strait between the Aegean
and the Sea of Marmora)   **505 capable** capacious   **506 marble** i.e. dappled with clouds/hard
and indifferent   **508 engage** pledge, commit   **511 clip** embrace   **513 execution** action,
performance   **wit** mind   **515 remorse** (an act of) compassion (for Othello)   **516 What . . .
ever** whatever the bloodthirsty business

OTHELLO   I greet thy love,
Not with vain thanks, but with acceptance bounteous,
And will upon the instant put thee to't:
520   Within these three days let me hear thee say
That Cassio's not alive.

IAGO   My friend is dead:
'Tis done at your request. But let her live.

OTHELLO   Damn her, lewd minx! O, damn her, damn her!
525   Come, go with me apart: I will withdraw
To furnish me with some swift means of death
For the fair devil. Now art thou my lieutenant.

IAGO   I am your own for ever.   *Exeunt*

Act 3 Scene 4

running scene 8

Enter Desdemona, Emilia and Clown

DESDEMONA   Do you know, sirrah, where Lieutenant Cassio lies?

CLOWN   I dare not say he lies anywhere.

DESDEMONA   Why, man?

CLOWN   He's a soldier, and for me to say a soldier lies, 'tis
5   stabbing.

DESDEMONA   Go to: where lodges he?

CLOWN   To tell you where he lodges is to tell you where I lie.

DESDEMONA   Can anything be made of this?

CLOWN   I know not where he lodges, and for me to devise a
10   lodging and say he lies here or he lies there, were to lie in
mine own throat.

DESDEMONA   Can you inquire him out, and be edified by report?

CLOWN   I will catechize the world for him, that is, make
questions, and by them answer.

---

519 to't to the test   **524 minx** lewd, wanton woman/prostitute   **3.4** *Location: Cyprus
(presumably outside the citadel)*   **1 sirrah** sir (used to a social inferior)   **2 lies** lodges
(the Clown puns on the sense of "to fib")   **5 stabbing** an offense one may be stabbed for
10 lie . . . throat fib outrageously   **12 edified** instructed (the Clown plays on the sense of
"spiritually improved")   **13 catechize** question; the catechism is a form of instruction used by
the Church in which a person answers a set of questions about the Christian faith

15 DESDEMONA Seek him, bid him come hither: tell him I have
moved my lord on his behalf and hope all will be well.

CLOWN   To do this is within the compass of man's wit, and
therefore I will attempt the doing it.   *Exit Clown*

DESDEMONA Where should I lose the handkerchief, Emilia?

20 EMILIA   I know not, madam.

DESDEMONA Believe me, I had rather have lost my purse
Full of crusadoes: and but my noble Moor
Is true of mind and made of no such baseness
As jealous creatures are, it were enough

25 To put him to ill thinking.

EMILIA   Is he not jealous?

DESDEMONA Who, he? I think the sun where he was born
Drew all such humours from him.

EMILIA   Look where he comes.

Enter Othello

30 DESDEMONA I will not leave him now till Cassio
Be called to him.— How is't with you, my lord?

OTHELLO   Well, my good lady.— O, hardness to   *Aside*
dissemble!—
How do you, Desdemona?

DESDEMONA Well, my good lord.

35 OTHELLO   Give me your hand. This hand is moist, my lady.

DESDEMONA It hath felt no age nor known no sorrow.

OTHELLO   This argues fruitfulness and liberal   *Partially aside?*
heart:
Hot, hot, and moist. This hand of yours requires
A sequester from liberty, fasting and prayer,

40 Much castigation, exercise devout,
For here's a young and sweating devil here

---

16 moved petitioned/persuaded   **22 crusadoes** Portuguese gold coins   **but** were it not
that   **27 sun . . . Drew** just as the sun was supposed to draw noxious vapors from the earth
28 humours moods (literally, bodily fluids thought to govern a person's temperament)
32 dissemble deceive/disguise one's feelings   **37 fruitfulness** generosity/fertility/sexual
liberality   **liberal** open/generous/licentious   **39 sequester** seclusion/separation
40 castigation chastisement/corrective discipline   **exercise** religious observances

That commonly rebels. 'Tis a good hand,
A frank one.

DESDEMONA You may, indeed, say so,
45 For 'twas that hand that gave away my heart.

OTHELLO   A liberal hand: the hearts of old gave hands,
But our new heraldry is hands, not hearts.

DESDEMONA I cannot speak of this. Come now, your promise.

OTHELLO   What promise, chuck?

50 DESDEMONA I have sent to bid Cassio come speak with you.

OTHELLO   I have a salt and sorry rheum offends me:
Lend me thy handkerchief.

DESDEMONA Here, my lord.   *Offers him a handkerchief*

OTHELLO   That which I gave you.

55 DESDEMONA I have it not about me.

OTHELLO   Not?

DESDEMONA No, indeed, my lord.

OTHELLO   That's a fault. That handkerchief
Did an Egyptian to my mother give:
60 She was a charmer, and could almost read
The thoughts of people: she told her, while she kept it,
'Twould make her amiable and subdue my father
Entirely to her love, but if she lost it
Or made a gift of it, my father's eye
65 Should hold her loathèd and his spirits should hunt
After new fancies: she, dying, gave it me,
And bid me, when my fate would have me wived,
To give it her: I did so; and take heed on't,
Make it a darling like your precious eye:
70 To lose't or give't away were such perdition
As nothing else could match.

DESDEMONA Is't possible?

---

43 frank free/generous/sexually open   **46 the . . . hearts** i.e. whereas once people gave away
their hands (in marriage) together with their hearts, nowadays people give away their hands
without their hearts   **49 chuck** chick (term of endearment)   **51 salt . . . rheum** miserable
running cold   **62 amiable** lovable   **66 fancies** loves   **68 her** i.e. my wife   **heed** careful
attention

OTHELLO   'Tis true. There's magic in the web of it:
A sibyl, that had numbered in the world
75   The sun to course two hundred compasses,
In her prophetic fury sewed the work:
The worms were hallowed that did breed the silk,
And it was dyed in mummy which the skilful
Conserved of maidens' hearts.

80   DESDEMONA   Indeed? Is't true?

OTHELLO   Most veritable: therefore look to't well.

DESDEMONA   Then would to heaven that I had never seen't!

OTHELLO   Ha? Wherefore?

DESDEMONA   Why do you speak so startingly and rash?

85   OTHELLO   Is't lost? Is't gone? Speak, is't out o'th'way?

DESDEMONA   Bless us!

OTHELLO   Say you?

DESDEMONA   It is not lost, but what an if it were?

OTHELLO   How?

90   DESDEMONA   I say it is not lost.

OTHELLO   Fetch't, let me see't.

DESDEMONA   Why, so I can, but I will not now.
This is a trick to put me from my suit:
Pray you let Cassio be received again.

95   OTHELLO   Fetch me the handkerchief: my mind misgives.

DESDEMONA   Come, come,
You'll never meet a more sufficient man.

OTHELLO   The handkerchief.

DESDEMONA   A man that all his time
100   Hath founded his good fortunes on your love,
Shared dangers with you—

OTHELLO   The handkerchief.

DESDEMONA   In sooth, you are to blame.

---

73 **web** weave   74 **sibyl** prophetess   75 **compasses** annual circuits, i.e. years
76 **prophetic fury** frenzy of prophetic inspiration   77 **hallowed** holy, consecrated
78 **mummy** medicinal substance obtained from mummified bodies   79 **Conserved of**
prepared/preserved from   84 **startingly and rash** abruptly and impetuously   85 **out**
o'th'way misplaced   88 **an if** if   89 **How?** What?   95 **misgives** is filled with suspicion/
foreboding   97 **sufficient** competent, able (with unwitting sexual connotations)   103 **In**
sooth truly

OTHELLO	Away!	*Exit Othello*

105 EMILIA   Is not this man jealous?

DESDEMONA   I ne'er saw this before.

Sure, there's some wonder in this handkerchief:
I am most unhappy in the loss of it.

EMILIA   'Tis not a year or two shows us a man:
110   They are all but stomachs, and we all but food:
They eat us hungerly, and when they are full
They belch us.

Enter Iago and Cassio

Look you, Cassio and my husband.

IAGO   There is no other way: 'tis she must do't.
115   And, lo, the happiness! Go and importune her.

DESDEMONA   How now, good Cassio, what's the news with you?

CASSIO   Madam, my former suit: I do beseech you
That by your virtuous means I may again
Exist, and be a member of his love
120   Whom I with all the office of my heart
Entirely honour. I would not be delayed.
If my offence be of such mortal kind
That nor my service past, nor present sorrows,
Nor purposed merit in futurity,
125   Can ransom me into his love again,
But to know so must be my benefit:
So shall I clothe me in a forced content,
And shut myself up in some other course,
To fortune's alms.

130 DESDEMONA   Alas, thrice-gentle Cassio,
My advocation is not now in tune;
My lord is not my lord; nor should I know him,
Were he in favour as in humour altered.

---

107 **wonder** extraordinary or magical quality   108 **unhappy** unfortunate/miserable
111 **hungerly** hungrily   112 **belch** burp/vomit   115 **happiness** good fortune (at meeting
Desdemona)   118 **virtuous** good/effective   120 **office** duty/functioning   122 **mortal** fatal
123 **nor** neither   124 **purposed . . . futurity** the merit I intend to display in the future
126 **But** merely   **be my benefit** content me/be my gain (as I will know the worst)   128 **shut . . .
in** confine/devote myself to   129 **To fortune's alms** relying on the charity of fortune
131 **advocation** advocacy, pleading (on your behalf)   133 **favour** appearance   **humour** mood

So help me every spirit sanctified
135 As I have spoken for you all my best
And stood within the blank of his displeasure
For my free speech! You must awhile be patient:
What I can do I will, and more I will
Than for myself I dare: let that suffice you.

140 IAGO   Is my lord angry?

EMILIA   He went hence but now,
And certainly in strange unquietness.

IAGO   Can he be angry? I have seen the cannon
When it hath blown his ranks into the air,
145 And like the devil from his very arm
Puffed his own brother: and is he angry?
Something of moment then. I will go meet him:
There's matter in't indeed, if he be angry.   *Exit*

DESDEMONA   I prithee do so. Something, sure, of state,
150 Either from Venice, or some unhatched practice
Made demonstrable here in Cyprus to him,
Hath puddled his clear spirit: and in such cases
Men's natures wrangle with inferior things,
Though great ones are their object. 'Tis even so,
155 For let our finger ache, and it indues
Our other healthful members even to a sense
Of pain. Nay, we must think men are not gods,
Nor of them look for such observancy
As fits the bridal. Beshrew me much, Emilia,
160 I was — unhandsome warrior as I am —
Arraigning his unkindness with my soul,
But now I find I had suborned the witness,
And he's indicted falsely.

EMILIA   Pray heaven it be state matters, as you think,

---

136 within the blank at the center of the target/at point-blank range   139 suffice content
144 his ranks Othello's troops   146 brother brother-in-arms, dearly loved comrade
147 moment momentous importance   149 of state connected with state affairs
150 practice plot, treachery   152 puddled muddied   155 indues brings   156 members
limbs   158 observancy . . . bridal proper attentions as those that befit the wedding
159 Beshrew curse   160 unhandsome inadequate   161 Arraigning indicting, accusing
162 suborned the witness bribed or influenced the witness to give false evidence

165   And no conception nor no jealous toy
     Concerning you.

DESDEMONA Alas the day! I never gave him cause.

EMILIA   But jealous souls will not be answered so;
     They are not ever jealous for the cause,
170   But jealous for they're jealous: it is a monster
     Begot upon itself, born on itself.

DESDEMONA Heaven keep the monster from Othello's mind!

EMILIA   Lady, amen.

DESDEMONA I will go seek him.— Cassio, walk hereabout:
175   If I do find him fit, I'll move your suit
     And seek to effect it to my uttermost.

                     Exeunt [Desdemona and Emilia]

CASSIO   I humbly thank your ladyship.

Enter Bianca

BIANCA   Save you, friend Cassio!

CASSIO   What make you from home?
180   How is't with you, my most fair Bianca?
     Indeed, sweet love, I was coming to your house.

BIANCA   And I was going to your lodging, Cassio.
     What, keep a week away? Seven days and nights?
     Eight score eight hours? And lovers' absent hours
185   More tedious than the dial eight score times?
     O weary reck'ning!

CASSIO   Pardon me, Bianca:
     I have this while with leaden thoughts been pressed:
     But I shall, in a more continuate time,
190   Strike off this score of absence. Sweet   *Gives her*
     Bianca,   *Desdemona's handkerchief*
     Take me this work out.

BIANCA   O Cassio, whence came this?

---

165 toy fancy, nonsensical notion   **171 Begot upon** conceived from   **178 Save** God save (common greeting)   **friend** friend/lover   **179 make you** are you doing   **184 Eight score eight** i.e. 168 (the number of hours in a week)   **score** twenty   **185 dial** (hours on the) clock   **186 reck'ning** counting/total, account   **189 continuate** uninterrupted   **190 Strike . . . score** settle this account/repay my sexual debt with copulation   **191 Take . . . out** copy this embroidery for me

This is some token from a newer friend:
To the felt absence now I feel a cause.
195 Is't come to this? Well, well.

CASSIO   Go to, woman!
Throw your vile guesses in the devil's teeth,
From whence you have them. You are jealous now
That this is from some mistress, some remembrance;
200 No, in good troth, Bianca.

BIANCA   Why, whose is it?

CASSIO   I know not, neither: I found it in my chamber.
I like the work well. Ere it be demanded —
As like enough it will — I would have it copied:
205 Take it, and do't, and leave me for this time.

BIANCA   Leave you? Wherefore?

CASSIO   I do attend here on the general,
And think it no addition, nor my wish,
To have him see me womaned.

210 BIANCA   Why, I pray you?

CASSIO   Not that I love you not.

BIANCA   But that you do not love me.
I pray you bring me on the way a little,
And say if I shall see you soon at night.

215 CASSIO   'Tis but a little way that I can bring you,
For I attend here: but I'll see you soon.

BIANCA   'Tis very good: I must be circumstanced.   *Exeunt*

Act 4 Scene 1   *running scene 8 continues*

Enter Othello and Iago

IAGO   Will you think so?

OTHELLO   Think so, Iago?

IAGO   What, to kiss in private?

---

193 friend lover, mistress   **194 To . . . cause** I now discern a cause for the absence I have
suffered   **203 demanded** asked after   **209 womaned** with a woman or paramour
213 bring accompany   **214 soon at night** soon, tonight/early this evening
217 circumstanced subject to circumstances, i.e. accept the situation

OTHELLO   An unauthorized kiss!

5   IAGO   Or to be naked with her friend in bed
An hour or more, not meaning any harm?

OTHELLO   Naked in bed, Iago, and not mean harm?
It is hypocrisy against the devil:
They that mean virtuously, and yet do so,
10   The devil their virtue tempts, and they tempt heaven.

IAGO   If they do nothing, 'tis a venial slip:
But if I give my wife a handkerchief—

OTHELLO   What then?

IAGO   Why, then, 'tis hers, my lord, and being hers,
15   She may, I think, bestow't on any man.

OTHELLO   She is protectress of her honour too:
May she give that?

IAGO   Her honour is an essence that's not seen:
They have it very oft that have it not.
20   But, for the handkerchief—

OTHELLO   By heaven, I would most gladly have forgot it.
Thou said'st — O, it comes o'er my memory
As doth the raven o'er the infectious house,
Boding to all — he had my handkerchief.

25   IAGO   Ay, what of that?

OTHELLO   That's not so good now.

IAGO   What if I had said I had seen him do you wrong?
Or heard him say — as knaves be such abroad,
Who having by their own importunate suit,
30   Or voluntary dotage of some mistress,
Convincèd or supplied them, cannot choose
But they must blab—

OTHELLO   Hath he said anything?

4.1   **8 hypocrisy . . . devil** i.e. by seeming to do something wicked, but in fact having
virtuous intentions   **11 venial** light, pardonable   **19 They . . . not** those that have lost
it often still appear to possess it   **23 raven** a bird of ill omen, whose cry was thought to
herald death   **infectious** disease-ridden   **24 Boding** predicting ominously (i.e. making
its croaking cry)   **28 abroad** out and about, at large   **29 importunate** persistent
30 voluntary dotage willing infatuation   **31 Convincèd** conquered sexually   **supplied**
filled up, satisfied sexually

IAGO   He hath, my lord, but be you well assured,
35   No more than he'll unswear.

OTHELLO   What hath he said?

IAGO   Why, that he did: I know not what he did.

OTHELLO   What? What?

IAGO   Lie—

40   OTHELLO   With her?

IAGO   With her? On her: what you will.

OTHELLO   Lie with her? Lie on her? We say 'Lie on her' when
they belie her. Lie with her! That's fulsome: handkerchief —
confessions — handkerchief! To confess and be hanged for
45   his labour: first to be hanged and then to confess: I tremble at
it. Nature would not invest herself in such shadowing
passion without some instruction. It is not words that shakes
me thus. Pish! Noses, ears and lips. Is't possible? Confess?
Handkerchief? O devil!   *Falls in a trance*

50   IAGO   Work on,
My medicine works! Thus credulous fools are caught,
And many worthy and chaste dames even thus,
All guiltless, meet reproach.— What, ho? My lord?
My lord, I say! Othello!—

Enter Cassio

How now, Cassio?

55   CASSIO   What's the matter?

IAGO   My lord is fall'n into an epilepsy.
This is his second fit: he had one yesterday.

CASSIO   Rub him about the temples.

IAGO   The lethargy must have his quiet course:
60   If not, he foams at mouth and by and by
Breaks out to savage madness. Look he stirs:
Do you withdraw yourself a little while,
He will recover straight. When he is gone,

---

37 did plays on the sense of "had sex (with)"   **42 Lie on her** tell lies about her   **43 belie**
slander   **fulsome** repulsive/lustful   **46–47 Nature . . . instruction** i.e. I would not be losing
consciousness and suffering a fit (**passion**) without good reason   **invest** clothe, envelop
shadowing darkening/ominous   **instruction** reliable information   **48 Noses** displaced
image of the penis   **lips** also the vaginal labia   **51 medicine** poison   **53 reproach** disgrace
59 lethargy faint, torpor

I would on great occasion speak with you.   [*Exit Cassio*]

65   How is it, general? Have you not hurt your head?

OTHELLO   Dost thou mock me?

IAGO   I mock you not, by heaven.

Would you would bear your fortune like a man!

OTHELLO   A hornèd man's a monster and a beast.

70   IAGO   There's many a beast then in a populous city,

And many a civil monster.

OTHELLO   Did he confess it?

IAGO   Good sir, be a man.

Think every bearded fellow that's but yoked

75   May draw with you: there's millions now alive

That nightly lie in those unproper beds

Which they dare swear peculiar: your case is better.

O, 'tis the spite of hell, the fiend's arch-mock,

To lip a wanton in a secure couch

80   And to suppose her chaste! No, let me know,

And knowing what I am, I know what she shall be.

OTHELLO   O, thou art wise: 'tis certain.

IAGO   Stand you awhile apart,

Confine yourself but in a patient list.

85   Whilst you were here o'erwhelmèd with your grief —

A passion most unsuiting such a man —

Cassio came hither: I shifted him away,

And laid good 'scuses upon your ecstasy,

Bade him anon return and here speak with me,

90   The which he promised. Do but encave yourself

And mark the fleers, the gibes and notable scorns

That dwell in every region of his face,

For I will make him tell the tale anew,

---

64 on great occasion about an important matter   66 Dost . . . me? Othello thinks that Iago is
referring to the growth of a cuckold's horns on the head   69 hornèd cuckolded   71 civil city-
dwelling/civilized   74 bearded i.e. adult   yoked married/constrained and oppressed by
wrongs   75 draw pull the plow like a yoked ox   76 unproper improper/not entirely their own
77 peculiar their own   79 lip kiss   wanton lover/lewd woman   secure couch carefree bed
84 in . . . list within the bounds of patience   87 shifted him away got rid of him/used a ruse to
get him out of the way   88 laid . . . ecstasy gave convincing explanations about your frenzy
89 anon shortly   90 encave conceal   91 fleers sneers

Where, how, how oft, how long ago and when
95   He hath and is again to cope your wife.
I say, but mark his gesture. Marry, patience,
Or I shall say you're all in all in spleen,
And nothing of a man.

OTHELLO   Dost thou hear, Iago?
100   I will be found most cunning in my patience,
But — dost thou hear? — most bloody.

IAGO   That's not amiss,
But yet keep time in all. Will you withdraw?   *Othello withdraws*
Now will I question Cassio of Bianca,
105   A housewife that by selling her desires
Buys herself bread and cloth: it is a creature
That dotes on Cassio — as 'tis the strumpet's plague
To beguile many and be beguiled by one.
He, when he hears of her, cannot restrain
110   From the excess of laughter. Here he comes.

Enter Cassio

As he shall smile, Othello shall go mad,
And his unbookish jealousy must conster
Poor Cassio's smiles, gestures and light behaviours
Quite in the wrong.— How do you, lieutenant?

115   CASSIO   The worser that you give me the addition
Whose want even kills me.

IAGO   Ply Desdemona well, and you are   *Lowers his voice*
sure on't.
Now, if this suit lay in Bianca's power,
How quickly should you speed!

120   CASSIO   Alas, poor caitiff!   *He laughs*

OTHELLO   Look how he laughs already!

IAGO   I never knew woman love man so.

---

95 **cope** have sex with   97 **all . . . spleen** entirely overcome by violent passion   103 **keep**
time remain steady and controlled   105 **housewife** hussy, prostitute   107 **strumpet** whore
108 **beguile** cheat   **beguiled** charmed, ensnared   109 **restrain** refrain   112 **unbookish**
unlearned/ignorant   **conster** construe   113 **light** merry   115 **addition** title (of **lieutenant**)
116 **Whose want** the lack of which   117 **on't** of it   119 **speed** succeed, prosper   120 **caitiff**
wretch

CASSIO	Alas, poor rogue, I think, indeed, she loves me.
OTHELLO	Now he denies it faintly, and laughs it out.
125 IAGO	Do you hear, Cassio?
OTHELLO	Now he importunes him

To tell it o'er: go to, well said, well said.

IAGO	She gives it out that you shall marry her:

Do you intend it?

130 CASSIO	Ha, ha, ha!
OTHELLO	Do ye triumph, Roman? Do you triumph?
CASSIO	I marry? What? A customer? Prithee bear some

charity to my wit: do not think it so unwholesome. Ha, ha, ha!

135 OTHELLO	So, so, so, so: they laugh that wins.
IAGO	Why, the cry goes that you marry her.
CASSIO	Prithee say true.
IAGO	I am a very villain else.
OTHELLO	Have you scored me? Well.
140 CASSIO	This is the monkey's own giving out: she is

persuaded I will marry her, out of her own love and flattery, not out of my promise.

OTHELLO	Iago beckons me: now he begins the story.
CASSIO	She was here even now: she haunts me in every

145 place. I was the other day talking on the sea-bank with certain Venetians, and thither comes the bauble, and falls me thus about my neck—   *Embraces him*

OTHELLO	Crying, 'O dear Cassio!' as it were: his gesture

imports it.

150 CASSIO	So hangs and lolls and weeps upon me, so shakes

and pulls me. Ha, ha, ha!

---

124 faintly without serious intent/unconvincingly   **127 said** done   **131 triumph** exult, gloat (literally "hold a victory procession," an ancient **Roman** celebration during which shackled captives were paraded through the streets)   **132 A customer?** i.e. Marry a whore? I, who pay her for sex?   **bear . . . wit** be more charitable toward my judgment; **wit** plays on the sense of "penis"   **133 unwholesome** unsound/diseased (i.e. with venereal disease)   **136 cry** rumor   **138 else** if it is not so   **139 scored me** wounded me/got one over on me sexually   **141 love and flattery** love for me and self-flattery   **144 haunts** follows, hangs around   **145 sea-bank** seashore   **146 bauble** plaything/worthless trifle   **falls me** falls (**me** is emphatic)   **149 imports** signifies, shows

OTHELLO   Now he tells how she plucked him to my chamber.
            O, I see that nose of yours, but not that dog I shall throw it to.
CASSIO   Well, I must leave her company.
155 IAGO   Before me, look where she comes.

Enter Bianca

CASSIO   'Tis such another fitchew! Marry, a perfumed
            one!— What do you mean by this haunting of me?
BIANCA   Let the devil and his dam haunt you! What did you
            mean by that same handkerchief you gave me even now? I
160   was a fine fool to take it. I must take out the work? A likely
            piece of work, that you should find it in your chamber and
            know not who left it there. This is some minx's token, and I
            must take out the work? There, give it your hobby-horse:
            wheresoever you had it, I'll take out no work   *She gives him*
165   on't.   *the handkerchief*
CASSIO   How now, my sweet Bianca? How now? How now?
OTHELLO   By heaven, that should be my handkerchief!
BIANCA   If you'll come to supper tonight, you may: if you
            will not, come when you are next prepared for.   *Exit*
170 IAGO   After her, after her.
CASSIO   I must: she'll rail in the streets else.
IAGO   Will you sup there?
CASSIO   Yes, I intend so.
IAGO   Well, I may chance to see you, for I would very fain
175   speak with you.
CASSIO   Prithee come. Will you?
IAGO   Go to: say no more.   *[Exit Cassio]*
OTHELLO   How shall I murder him, Iago?   *Comes forward*
IAGO   Did you perceive how he laughed at his vice?
180 OTHELLO O, Iago!
IAGO   And did you see the handkerchief?
OTHELLO   Was that mine?

---

152 plucked drew   **153 nose** probably a surrogate for the penis   **156 such another** just
another, a commonplace   **fitchew** polecat (known for its foul smell and lechery; also a term
for a prostitute)   **158 dam** mother   **161 piece of work** puns on the senses of "prostitute"
and "sexual act"   **162 minx** whore   **163 hobby-horse** prostitute   **167 should** must
168 supper also suggests sex   **171 rail** rant abusively

IAGO   Yours by this hand: and to see how he prizes the
foolish woman your wife! She gave it him, and he hath giv'n
185   it his whore.

OTHELLO   I would have him nine years a-killing. A fine
woman! A fair woman! A sweet woman!

IAGO   Nay, you must forget that.

OTHELLO   Ay, let her rot and perish, and be damned tonight,
190   for she shall not live. No, my heart is turned to stone: I strike
it, and it hurts my hand. O, the world hath not a sweeter
creature: she might lie by an emperor's side and command
him tasks.

IAGO   Nay, that's not your way.

195   OTHELLO   Hang her! I do but say what she is: so delicate with
her needle, an admirable musician. O, she will sing the
savageness out of a bear. Of so high and plenteous wit and
invention!

IAGO   She's the worse for all this.

200   OTHELLO   O, a thousand, a thousand times! And then, of so
gentle a condition!

IAGO   Ay, too gentle.

OTHELLO   Nay, that's certain. But yet the pity of it, Iago! O,
Iago, the pity of it, Iago!

205   IAGO   If you are so fond over her iniquity, give her patent
to offend, for if it touch not you, it comes near nobody.

OTHELLO   I will chop her into messes. Cuckold me?

IAGO   O, 'tis foul in her.

OTHELLO   With mine officer?

210   IAGO   That's fouler.

OTHELLO   Get me some poison, Iago, this night: I'll not
expostulate with her, lest her body and beauty unprovide my
mind again: this night, Iago.

IAGO   Do it not with poison: strangle her in her bed, even
215   the bed she hath contaminated.

---

184 foolish stupid/lewd   **194 your way** the right attitude or course of action   **198 invention**
imagination   **200 so . . . condition** such a well-bred nature/such a sweet and kind disposition
202 gentle yielding   **205 patent** licence   **206 touch** affect/provoke   **207 messes** portions of
meat   **212 expostulate** argue, remonstrate   **unprovide** disarm

OTHELLO   Good, good: the justice of it pleases. Very good.

IAGO   And for Cassio, let me be his undertaker: you shall
hear more by midnight.

Enter Lodovico, Desdemona and Attendants

OTHELLO   Excellent good.   *A trumpet within*

220   What trumpet is that same?

IAGO   I warrant something from Venice.
'Tis Lodovico: this comes from the duke.
See, your wife's with him.

LODOVICO   Save you, worthy general!

225   OTHELLO   With all my heart, sir.

LODOVICO   The duke and the senators of Venice   *Gives a letter*
greet you.

OTHELLO   I kiss the instrument of their pleasures.   *Opens letter*

DESDEMONA   And what's the news, good cousin   *and reads*
Lodovico?

IAGO   I am very glad to see you, signior.

230   Welcome to Cyprus.

LODOVICO   I thank you. How does Lieutenant Cassio?

IAGO   Lives, sir.

DESDEMONA   Cousin, there's fall'n between him and my lord
An unkind breach: but you shall make all well.

235   OTHELLO   Are you sure of that?

DESDEMONA   My lord?

OTHELLO   'This fail you not to do, as you will—'   *Reads*

LODOVICO   He did not call: he's busy in the paper.
Is there division 'twixt my lord and Cassio?

240   DESDEMONA   A most unhappy one: I would do much
T'atone them, for the love I bear to Cassio.

OTHELLO   Fire and brimstone!

DESDEMONA   My lord?

OTHELLO   Are you wise?

---

217 his undertaker the one to undertake the task of dealing with him   **227 instrument . . .
pleasures** i.e. the letter containing their instructions   **228 cousin** general term for any
relative other than parent or sibling   **234 unkind breach** unnatural separation, unfriendly
quarrel   **241 T'atone** to reconcile   **244 wise** in your right mind

245   DESDEMONA   What? Is he angry?

      LODOVICO   Maybe th'letter moved him,
      For, as I think, they do command him home,
      Deputing Cassio in his government.

      DESDEMONA   Trust me, I am glad on't.

250   OTHELLO   Indeed?

      DESDEMONA   My lord?

      OTHELLO   I am glad to see you mad.

      DESDEMONA   Why, sweet Othello?

      OTHELLO   Devil!   *Strikes her*

255   DESDEMONA   I have not deserved this.

      LODOVICO   My lord, this would not be believed in Venice,
      Though I should swear I saw't. 'Tis very much:
      Make her amends, she weeps.

      OTHELLO   O devil, devil!

260   If that the earth could teem with woman's tears,
      Each drop she falls would prove a crocodile.—
      Out of my sight!

      DESDEMONA   I will not stay to offend you.   *Starts to leave*

      LODOVICO   Truly, an obedient lady:

265   I do beseech your lordship, call her back.

      OTHELLO   Mistress!

      DESDEMONA   My lord?   *Returns*

      OTHELLO   What would you with her, sir?

      LODOVICO   Who, I, my lord?

270   OTHELLO   Ay, you did wish that I would make her turn:
      Sir, she can turn, and turn, and yet go on
      And turn again: and she can weep, sir, weep:
      And she's obedient, as you say, obedient:
      Very obedient.— Proceed you in your tears.—

---

249 on't of it   **252 mad** i.e. insane enough to publicly welcome Cassio's promotion
and make your love for him obvious   **257 very much** too much   **260 teem** be fertile,
conceive   **261 crocodile** because crocodiles were supposed to weep insincere tears
271 turn introduces the additional meanings of "have sex"/"change her affections"
go on continue (to have sex/change affections)   **273 obedient** compliant (plays on sexual
sense)

275   Concerning this, sir, — O well-painted passion! —
I am commanded home.— Get you away:
I'll send for you anon.— Sir, I obey the mandate,
And will return to Venice.— Hence, avaunt!

[Exit Desdemona]

Cassio shall have my place. And, sir, tonight
280   I do entreat that we may sup together:
You are welcome, sir, to Cyprus.— Goats and monkeys!   *Exit*

LODOVICO   Is this the noble Moor whom our full senate
Call all in all sufficient? Is this the nature
Whom passion could not shake? Whose solid virtue
285   The shot of accident nor dart of chance
Could neither graze nor pierce?

IAGO   He is much changed.

LODOVICO   Are his wits safe? Is he not light of brain?

IAGO   He's that he is: I may not breathe my censure
290   What he might be: if what he might he is not,
I would to heaven he were!

LODOVICO   What, strike his wife?

IAGO   Faith, that was not so well, yet would I knew
That stroke would prove the worst!

295   **LODOVICO**   Is it his use?
Or did the letters work upon his blood
And new-create his fault?

IAGO   Alas, alas!
It is not honesty in me to speak
300   What I have seen and known. You shall observe him,
And his own courses will denote him so
That I may save my speech: do but go after,
And mark how he continues.

LODOVICO   I am sorry that I am deceived in him.   *Exeunt*

---

275 well-painted passion well-faked sorrow   **279 my place** i.e. as governor of Cyprus/as Desdemona's lover   **281 monkeys** proverbially lustful creatures   **282 full** complete, entire   **283 all . . . sufficient** competent in everything   **289 censure** judgement (quibbling on the sense of "condemnation")   **290 if . . . were** if he is not what he might be (i.e. mad), I heartily wish he was (as only madness would explain and partly excuse his behavior)   **293 well** good **would** I wish   **295 use** habit   **301 courses will denote** actions will signify

Act 4 Scene 2

Enter Othello and Emilia

	OTHELLO	You have seen nothing then?
	EMILIA	Nor ever heard, nor ever did suspect.
	OTHELLO	Yes, you have seen Cassio and she together.
	EMILIA	But then I saw no harm, and then I heard
5		Each syllable that breath made up between them.
	OTHELLO	What, did they never whisper?
	EMILIA	Never, my lord.
	OTHELLO	Nor send you out o'th'way?
	EMILIA	Never.
10	OTHELLO	To fetch her fan, her gloves, her mask, nor nothing?
	EMILIA	Never, my lord.
	OTHELLO	That's strange.
	EMILIA	I durst, my lord, to wager she is honest,

Lay down my soul at stake: if you think other,
15 Remove your thought, it doth abuse your bosom:
If any wretch have put this in your head,
Let heaven requite it with the serpent's curse!
For if she be not honest, chaste and true,
There's no man happy: the purest of their wives
20 Is foul as slander.

OTHELLO   Bid her come hither: go.   *Exit Emilia*
She says enough, yet she's a simple bawd
That cannot say as much. This is a subtle whore,
A closet lock and key of villainous secrets:
25 And yet she'll kneel and pray, I have seen her do't.

Enter Desdemona and Emilia

DESDEMONA My lord, what is your will?
OTHELLO   Pray you, chuck, come hither.
DESDEMONA What is your pleasure?

4.2 *Location: Cyprus (within the citadel)*   **13 durst** dare   **14 at stake** as the stake in
the **wager**   **17 serpent's curse** after the serpent's temptation of Eve in the Garden of Eden,
God cursed him and decreed that he should be the lowest and most reviled of all creatures
22 bawd procuress   **23 This** i.e. Desdemona   **subtle** cunning   **24 closet . . . key** cabinet (or
room) complete with lock and key

OTHELLO	Let me see your eyes: look in my face.	
30 DESDEMONA	What horrible fancy's this?	
OTHELLO	Some of your function, mistress:	*To Emilia*

Leave procreants alone and shut the door:
Cough or cry 'Hem' if anybody come.
Your mystery, your mystery: nay, dispatch.   *Exit Emilia*

35 DESDEMONA Upon my knee, what doth your speech   *Kneels*
       import?
    I understand a fury in your words.

OTHELLO Why, what art thou?

DESDEMONA Your wife, my lord, your true and loyal wife.

OTHELLO Come, swear it, damn thyself
40 Lest, being like one of heaven, the devils themselves
    Should fear to seize thee: therefore be double damned:
    Swear thou art honest.

DESDEMONA Heaven doth truly know it.

OTHELLO Heaven truly knows that thou art false as hell.

45 DESDEMONA To whom, my lord? With whom? How am I false?

OTHELLO Ah Desdemon! Away, away, away!   *Weeps*

DESDEMONA Alas the heavy day! Why do you weep?
    Am I the motive of these tears, my lord?
    If haply you my father do suspect
50 An instrument of this your calling back,
    Lay not your blame on me: if you have lost him,
    I have lost him too.

OTHELLO Had it pleased heaven
    To try me with affliction, had they rained
55 All kind of sores and shames on my bare head,
    Steeped me in poverty to the very lips,
    Given to captivity me and my utmost hopes,
    I should have found in some place of my soul
    A drop of patience: but, alas, to make me
60 The fixèd figure for the time of scorn

---

31 Some . . . function behave as one in your role (as a **bawd**) should   **32 procreants** breeders, fornicators   **34 mystery** trade, occupation   **dispatch** hurry up   **40 being . . . heaven** resembling an angel   **47 heavy** sorrowful   **49 haply** perhaps   **55 sores** afflictions   **56 Steeped** immersed   **60 figure** number (on a clock face)

To point his slow and moving finger at!
Yet could I bear that too, well, very well,
But there where I have garnered up my heart,
Where either I must live, or bear no life,
65   The fountain from the which my current runs
Or else dries up: to be discarded thence!
Or keep it as a cistern for foul toads
To knot and gender in! Turn thy complexion there,
Patience, thou young and rose-lipped cherubin:
70   Ay, here look grim as hell!
DESDEMONA   I hope my noble lord esteems me honest.
OTHELLO   O, ay, as summer flies are in the shambles,
That quicken even with blowing. O, thou weed,
Who art so lovely fair and smell'st so sweet
75   That the sense aches at thee, would thou hadst never been
       born!
DESDEMONA   Alas, what ignorant sin have I committed?
OTHELLO   Was this fair paper, this most goodly book,
Made to write 'whore' upon? What committed?
Committed? O, thou public commoner,
80   I should make very forges of my cheeks,
That would to cinders burn up modesty,
Did I but speak thy deeds. What committed?
Heaven stops the nose at it and the moon winks,
The bawdy wind that kisses all it meets
85   Is hushed within the hollow mine of earth
And will not hear't. What committed?
DESDEMONA   By heaven, you do me wrong.
OTHELLO   Are not you a strumpet?

---

61 finger i.e. hour hand of a clock   **63 garnered** stored   **65 fountain** spring, source
67 cistern pond/water tank   **68 knot and gender** copulate   **Turn . . . there** turn your face
toward it/change your appearance (or nature) when you see it   **69 cherubin** angel (correctly
"cherubim," one of the biblical orders of angels)   **70 grim** cruel, unforgiving/ugly
71 honest truthful, but more specifically "sexually faithful," "chaste"   **72 shambles**
slaughterhouse   **73 quicken . . . blowing** give life even though they deposit their eggs in
rotting meat   **76 ignorant** unwitting   **78 committed** Othello picks up on the senses of
"committed adultery" and "fornicated"   **79 commoner** prostitute   **83 stops** stops up, closes
moon a symbol of chastity   **winks** closes its eyes   **85 mine** cave   **88 strumpet** harlot,
prostitute

DESDEMONA No, as I am a Christian:
90   If to preserve this vessel for my lord
        From any other foul unlawful touch
        Be not to be a strumpet, I am none.
OTHELLO   What, not a whore?
DESDEMONA No, as I shall be saved.
95 OTHELLO   Is't possible?
DESDEMONA O, heaven forgive us!
OTHELLO   I cry you mercy, then:
        I took you for that cunning whore of Venice
        That married with Othello.— You, mistress,   *Calls*
Enter Emilia
100   That have the office opposite to Saint Peter
        And keeps the gate of hell! You, you, ay, you!
        We have done our course: there's money for your pains.
        I pray you turn the key and keep our counsel.   *Exit*

                                                        Gives money

EMILIA   Alas, what does this gentleman conceive?
105   How do you, madam? How do you, my good lady?
DESDEMONA Faith, half asleep.
EMILIA   Good madam, what's the matter with my lord?
DESDEMONA With who?
EMILIA   Why, with my lord, madam.
110 DESDEMONA Who is thy lord?
EMILIA   He that is yours, sweet lady.
DESDEMONA I have none. Do not talk to me, Emilia:
        I cannot weep, nor answers have I none
        But what should go by water. Prithee, tonight
115   Lay on my bed my wedding sheets: remember,
        And call thy husband hither.
EMILIA   Here's a change indeed!   *Exit*
DESDEMONA 'Tis meet I should be used so, very meet.

---

90 vessel body   **97 cry you mercy** beg your pardon   **100 office opposite** opposing job
Saint Peter heaven's gatekeeper   **101 gate of hell** vaginal connotations (**hell** was a slang
term for the vagina)   **102 done our course** finished our business/had our bout of sex
103 counsel secret   **104 conceive** think, imagine   **106 asleep** stunned   **114 go by water**
be expressed through tears   **118 meet** fitting   **used** treated

How have I been behaved, that he might stick
120 The small'st opinion on my least misuse?

Enter Iago and Emilia

IAGO   What is your pleasure, madam?
How is't with you?

DESDEMONA   I cannot tell. Those that do teach young babes
Do it with gentle means and easy tasks:
125 He might have chid me so, for, in good faith,
I am a child to chiding.

IAGO   What's the matter, lady?

EMILIA   Alas, Iago, my lord hath so bewhored her,
Thrown such despite and heavy terms upon her,
130 That true hearts cannot bear it.

DESDEMONA   Am I that name, Iago?

IAGO   What name, fair lady?

DESDEMONA   Such as she said my lord did say I was.

EMILIA   He called her whore: a beggar in his drink
135 Could not have laid such terms upon his callet.

IAGO   Why did he so?

DESDEMONA   I do not know: I am sure I am none such.   *Weeps*

IAGO   Do not weep, do not weep. Alas the day!

EMILIA   Hath she forsook so many noble matches?
140 Her father? And her country? And her friends?
To be called whore? Would it not make one weep?

DESDEMONA   It is my wretched fortune.

IAGO   Beshrew him for't!
How comes this trick upon him?

145 DESDEMONA   Nay, heaven doth know.

EMILIA   I will be hanged if some eternal villain,
Some busy and insinuating rogue,
Some cogging, cozening slave, to get some office,
Have not devised this slander: I will be hanged else.

---

119 How . . . misuse? What must I have done to cause him to attach even the slightest condemnation to my most minor misconduct?   **126 a . . . chiding** i.e. know little of being rebuked   **128 bewhored her** called her a whore   **129 despite** contempt/malice/abuse **heavy** serious/angry/violent/distressing   **135 callet** drab, trull, whore   **139 forsook** declined/given up   **143 Beshrew** curse   **144 trick** delusion   **148 cogging** cheating **cozening** deceiving

150	IAGO	Fie, there is no such man: it is impossible.
	DESDEMONA	If any such there be, heaven pardon him!
	EMILIA	A halter pardon him! And hell gnaw his bones!

Why should he call her whore? Who keeps her company?
What place? What time? What form? What likelihood?
155   The Moor's abused by some most villainous knave,
Some base notorious knave, some scurvy fellow.
O heavens, that such companions thou'dst unfold,
And put in every honest hand a whip
To lash the rascals naked through the world
160   Even from the east to th'west!

	IAGO	Speak within door.
	EMILIA	O, fie upon them! Some such squire he was

That turned your wit the seamy side without
And made you to suspect me with the Moor.

165	IAGO	You are a fool: go to.
	DESDEMONA	Alas, Iago,

What shall I do to win my lord again?
Good friend, go to him, for, by this light of heaven,
I know not how I lost him. Here I kneel: *Kneels*
170   If e'er my will did trespass gainst his love,
Either in discourse of thought or actual deed,
Or that mine eyes, mine ears, or any sense
Delighted them, or any other form,
Or that I do not yet, and ever did,
175   And ever will — though he do shake me off
To beggarly divorcement — love him dearly,
Comfort forswear me! Unkindness may do much,
And his unkindness may defeat my life,
But never taint my love. I cannot say 'whore':
180   It does abhor me now I speak the word:

---

152 halter hangman's noose   **154 form** manner, way   **156 scurvy** contemptible
157 companions rogues   **unfold** reveal, expose   **161 within door** i.e. more quietly
162 squire fellow (contemptuous)   **163 the . . . without** inside out (with the seams on the outside)   **171 discourse** course, process   **172 that** if   **174 yet** still   **177 forswear** abandon
180 abhor revolt (puns on *whore*)

To do the act that might the addition earn
Not the world's mass of vanity could make me.

IAGO   I pray you be content: 'tis but his humour.
The business of the state does him offence.

185 DESDEMONA If 'twere no other—

IAGO   It is but so, I warrant.   *Trumpets within*
Hark, how these instruments summon to supper!
The messengers of Venice stays the meat:
Go in, and weep not: all things shall be well.

Exeunt Desdemona and Emilia

Enter Rodorigo

190 How now, Rodorigo?

RODORIGO   I do not find that thou deal'st justly with me.

IAGO   What in the contrary?

RODORIGO   Every day thou daff'st me with some device, Iago,
and rather, as it seems to me now, keep'st from me all
195 conveniency than suppliest me with the least advantage of
hope. I will indeed no longer endure it, nor am I yet
persuaded to put up in peace what already I have foolishly
suffered.

IAGO   Will you hear me, Rodorigo?

200 RODORIGO   I have heard too much, and your words and
performances are no kin together.

IAGO   You charge me most unjustly.

RODORIGO   With naught but truth: I have wasted myself out
of my means. The jewels you have had from me to
205 deliver Desdemona would half have corrupted a votarist:
you have told me she hath received them and returned
me expectations and comforts of sudden respect and
acquaintance, but I find none.

IAGO   Well, go to, very well.

---

181 addition title, name   182 vanity worthless finery   183 humour mood   188 stays await
meat food   193 daff'st me put me off, deflect me   device trick/stratagem   195 conveniency
opportunity   197 put up endure, tolerate   205 votarist nun   207 comforts encouraging
hopes   sudden respect imminent esteem and favor   208 acquaintance familiarity/sexual
intimacy (possibly with pun on "quaint," i.e. vagina)

210   RODORIGO   'Very well'! 'Go to'! I cannot go to, man, nor 'tis not
very well: nay, I think it is scurvy, and begin to find myself
fopped in it.

IAGO   Very well.

RODORIGO   I tell you 'tis not very well. I will make myself
215   known to Desdemona: if she will return me my jewels, I will
give over my suit and repent my unlawful solicitation: if not,
assure yourself I will seek satisfaction of you.

IAGO   You have said now.

RODORIGO   Ay, and said nothing but what I protest intendment
220   of doing.

IAGO   Why, now I see there's mettle in thee, and even from
this instant do build on thee a better opinion than ever
before. Give me thy hand, Rodorigo: thou hast taken against
me a most just exception, but yet I protest I have dealt most
225   directly in thy affair.

RODORIGO   It hath not appeared.

IAGO   I grant indeed it hath not appeared, and your
suspicion is not without wit and judgement. But, Rodorigo, if
thou hast that in thee indeed which I have greater reason to
230   believe now than ever — I mean purpose, courage and
valour — this night show it: if thou the next night following
enjoy not Desdemona, take me from this world with
treachery and devise engines for my life.

RODORIGO   Well, what is it? Is it within reason and compass?

235   IAGO   Sir, there is especial commission come from Venice
to depute Cassio in Othello's place.

RODORIGO   Is that true? Why then Othello and Desdemona
return again to Venice.

IAGO   O, no. He goes into Mauritania and taketh away
240   with him the fair Desdemona, unless his abode be lingered

---

210 **go to** Rodorigo shifts the sense to "have sex"   212 **fopped** deceived, cheated
217 **satisfaction** recompense   218 **said** had your say   219 **protest intendment** declare
I have the intention   221 **mettle** spirit, vigor   224 **exception** objection   225 **directly**
straightforwardly/fairly   233 **engines** plots against   234 **compass** range   239 **Mauritania**
region in north Africa consisting of parts of Morocco and Algeria   240 **abode be lingered**
stay be prolonged

here by some accident, wherein none can be so determinate
as the removing of Cassio.

RODORIGO   How do you mean, removing him?

IAGO   Why, by making him uncapable of Othello's place:
245   knocking out his brains.

RODORIGO   And that you would have me to do?

IAGO   Ay, if you dare do yourself a profit and a right. He
sups tonight with a harlotry, and thither will I go to him. He
knows not yet of his honourable fortune: if you will watch
250   his going thence — which I will fashion to fall out between
twelve and one — you may take him at your pleasure. I will
be near to second your attempt, and he shall fall between us.
Come, stand not amazed at it, but go along with me: I will
show you such a necessity in his death that you shall think
255   yourself bound to put it on him. It is now high suppertime,
and the night grows to waste: about it.

RODORIGO   I will hear further reason for this.

IAGO   And you shall be satisfied.   *Exeunt*

Act 4 Scene 3   *running scene 9 continues*

Enter Othello, Lodovico, Desdemona, Emilia and Attendants

LODOVICO   I do beseech you, sir, trouble yourself no further.

OTHELLO   O, pardon me: 'twill do me good to walk.

LODOVICO   Madam, goodnight. I humbly thank your ladyship.

DESDEMONA   Your honour is most welcome.

5   OTHELLO   Will you walk, sir?— O, Desdemona!

DESDEMONA   My lord?

OTHELLO   Get you to bed on th'instant, I will be returned
forthwith. Dismiss your attendant there: look't be done.

Exeunt [Othello, Lodovico and Attendants]

DESDEMONA   I will, my lord.

10   EMILIA   How goes it now? He looks gentler than he did.

---

241 **determinate** decisive   248 **harlotry** harlot   250 **fashion . . . out** arrange to occur
252 **second** support, back   253 **amazed** dumbstruck, stunned   255 **high** fully   256 **grows
to waste** is passing/being wasted

DESDEMONA   He says he will return incontinent,
And hath commanded me to go to bed,
And bid me to dismiss you.

EMILIA   Dismiss me?

15   DESDEMONA   It was his bidding: therefore, good Emilia,
Give me my nightly wearing, and adieu.
We must not now displease him.

EMILIA   I would you had never seen him.

DESDEMONA   So would not I: my love doth so approve him

20   That even his stubbornness, his checks, his frowns —
Prithee unpin me — have grace and favour.

EMILIA   I have laid those sheets you bade me on the bed.

DESDEMONA   All's one.— Good father, how foolish are our
minds!—
If I do die before, prithee shroud me

25   In one of these same sheets.

EMILIA   Come, come, you talk.

DESDEMONA   My mother had a maid called Barbary:
She was in love, and he she loved proved mad
And did forsake her. She had a song of 'willow',

30   An old thing 'twas, but it expressed her fortune,
And she died singing it: that song tonight
Will not go from my mind: I have much to do
But to go hang my head all at one side
And sing it like poor Barbary. Prithee dispatch.

35   EMILIA   Shall I go fetch your nightgown?

DESDEMONA   No, unpin me here.
This Lodovico is a proper man.

EMILIA   A very handsome man.

4.3   11   incontinent immediately, plays on sense of "loosely, unchastely"   **16 nightly
wearing** nightclothes   **19 approve** commend   **20 stubbornness** inflexibility, obstinacy/
ruthlessness, ferocity   **21 unpin me** i.e. loosen or detach parts of my clothing (sleeves etc.
were secured on with pins)/unpin my hair or remove my hair accessory   **23 All's one** it makes
no difference/all right   **Good father** i.e. God in heaven   **24 before** i.e. before you   **shroud**
lay, wrap (ready for burial)   **26 talk** talk nonsense, talk on idly   **27 Barbary** a form of
Barbara, but the name has obvious north African associations   **28 mad** insane/wild/faithless
29 willow the tree symbolized lost or unrequited love   **32 I . . . to** it is all I can do not to
37 proper handsome/accomplished

DESDEMONA He speaks well.

40   EMILIA   I know a lady in Venice would have walked barefoot
to Palestine for a touch of his nether lip.

DESDEMONA The poor soul sat singing by a sycamore tree,   *Sings*
Sing all a green willow:
Her hand on her bosom, her head on her knee,
45   Sing willow, willow, willow.
The fresh streams ran by her, and murmured her
moans,
Sing willow, willow, willow:
Her salt tears fell from her, and softened the
stones,
Sing willow—
50   Lay by these—   *To Emilia*
Willow, willow—   *Sings*
Prithee, hie thee: he'll come anon—
Sing all a green willow must be my garland.   *Sings*
Let nobody blame him, his scorn I approve—
55   Nay, that's not next.— Hark, who is't that knocks?

EMILIA   It's the wind.

DESDEMONA I called my love false love, but what said he   *Sings*
then?
Sing willow, willow, willow:
If I court more women, you'll couch with more
men!—
60   So, get thee gone, goodnight. Mine eyes do itch:
Doth that bode weeping?

EMILIA   'Tis neither here nor there.

DESDEMONA I have heard it said so. O, these men, these men!
Dost thou in conscience think — tell me, Emilia —
65   That there be women do abuse their husbands
In such gross kind?

---

41 nether lower (possibly with bawdy implication)   **42 sycamore** type of fig-tree or, as now, a species of maple; puns on "sick amour"   **50 Lay by these** put these aside (presumably parts of her clothing or accessories)   **52 hie thee** hurry yourself   **59 couch** lie, sleep   **61 bode** foretell   **65 abuse** deceive, wrong   **66 gross kind** a great way/a coarse manner

EMILIA	There be some such, no question.
DESDEMONA	Wouldst thou do such a deed for all the world?
EMILIA	Why, would not you?

70 DESDEMONA   No, by this heavenly light!

EMILIA   Nor I neither by this heavenly light:
I might do't as well i'th'dark.

DESDEMONA   Wouldst thou do such a deed for all the world?

EMILIA   The world's a huge thing: it is a great price
75   For a small vice.

DESDEMONA   In troth, I think thou wouldst not.

EMILIA   In troth, I think I should, and undo't when I had
done. Marry, I would not do such a thing for a joint-ring, nor
for measures of lawn, nor for gowns, petticoats, nor caps,
80   nor any petty exhibition: but for all the whole world, why,
who would not make her husband a cuckold to make him a
monarch? I should venture purgatory for't.

DESDEMONA   Beshrew me, if I would do such a wrong
For the whole world.

85   EMILIA   Why, the wrong is but a wrong i'th'world, and
having the world for your labour, 'tis a wrong in your own
world, and you might quickly make it right.

DESDEMONA   I do not think there is any such woman.

EMILIA   Yes, a dozen, and as many to th'vantage as
90   Would store the world they played for.
But I do think it is their husbands' faults
If wives do fall. Say that they slack their duties
And pour our treasures into foreign laps,
Or else break out in peevish jealousies,
95   Throwing restraint upon us, or say they strike us,
Or scant our former having in despite:
Why, we have galls, and though we have some grace,

---

74 **price** prize   78 **joint-ring** ring consisting of two joined halves   79 **lawn** fine linen
80 **exhibition** gift   82 **venture** risk (going to)   89 **to th'vantage** in addition, besides
90 **store** populate   **played** gambled/had sex   92 **fall** succumb sexually   **duties** marital
and sexual duties   93 **our . . . laps** the semen that is due to us into other women's vaginas
94 **peevish** senseless/perverse/willful   96 **scant** reduce/withhold   **our former having** what
we had before/our former financial means   **despite** spite, malice   97 **have galls** are capable
of feeling bitterness and resentment   **grace** charm/virtue/mercy

Yet have we some revenge. Let husbands know
Their wives have sense like them: they see and smell
100   And have their palates both for sweet and sour,
As husbands have. What is it that they do
When they change us for others? Is it sport?
I think it is. And doth affection breed it?
I think it doth. Is't frailty that thus errs?
105   It is so too. And have not we affections?
Desires for sport? And frailty, as men have?
Then let them use us well: else let them know,
The ills we do, their ills instruct us so.

DESDEMONA   Goodnight, goodnight: heaven me such uses send
110   Not to pick bad from bad, but by bad mend!   *Exeunt*

Act 5 Scene 1   *running scene 10*

Enter Iago and Rodorigo

IAGO   Here, stand behind this bulk: straight will he come.
Wear thy good rapier bare, and put it home.
Quick, quick, fear nothing; I'll be at thy elbow.
It makes us or it mars us: think on that,
5   And fix most firm thy resolution.

RODORIGO   Be near at hand: I may miscarry in't.

IAGO   Here, at thy hand: be bold, and take   *Conceals himself*
thy stand.

RODORIGO   I have no great devotion to the deed,
And yet he hath given me satisfying reasons.
10   'Tis but a man gone. Forth, my sword: he dies.   *Draws*

IAGO   I have rubbed this young quat almost to the   *Aside*
sense,

---

98 revenge desire for revenge   **102 change** exchange   **sport** entertainment/sex
103 affection desire, lust   **107 use** treat/employ sexually   **109 uses** habits (of thought)
110 Not . . . mend not to learn bad habits from the bad behavior of others, but to learn from
such examples to improve myself   **5.1   *Location: Cyprus (a street)***   **1 bulk** framework
projecting from the front of a shop, a stall   **2 bare** unsheathed   **put it home** drive it firmly to
the target   **4 mars** destroys   **6 miscarry** go wrong, fail   **11 quat** pimple   **to the sense** raw,
to the tenderest part

And he grows angry. Now, whether he kill Cassio
Or Cassio him, or each do kill the other,
Every way makes my gain. Live Rodorigo,
15 He calls me to a restitution large
Of gold and jewels that I bobbed from him
As gifts to Desdemona:
It must not be. If Cassio do remain,
He hath a daily beauty in his life
20 That makes me ugly: and besides, the Moor
May unfold me to him: there stand I in much peril.
No, he must die. But so: I heard him coming.

Enter Cassio

RODORIGO I know his gait, 'tis he.— Villain, thou diest! *Makes a*
CASSIO That thrust had been mine enemy indeed, *sword thrust*
25 But that my coat is better than thou know'st:
I will make proof of thine. *Draws and wounds Rodorigo*
RODORIGO O, I am slain! *He falls; Iago comes forward and stabs Cassio*

[*Exit Iago*] *on the leg*

CASSIO I am maimed for ever. Help, ho! Murder, *He falls*
murder!

Enter Othello

OTHELLO The voice of Cassio: Iago keeps his word.
30 RODORIGO O, villain that I am!
OTHELLO It is even so.
CASSIO O, help, ho! Light! A surgeon!
OTHELLO 'Tis he. O brave Iago, honest and just,
That hast such noble sense of thy friend's wrong!
35 Thou teachest me.— Minion, your dear lies dead,
And your unblest fate hies. Strumpet, I come:
For of my heart those charms, thine eyes, are blotted,
Thy bed, lust-stained, shall with lust's blood be
spotted.
Exit Othello

---

12 angry inflamed/enraged   14 Live Rodorigo should Rodorigo live   16 bobbed
cheated   17 gifts i.e. supposed gifts   21 unfold reveal   25 coat (thick) overcoat/metal-
plated garment worn under outer clothing   26 proof trial   33 brave excellent/noble
35 Minion whore (addressing Desdemona)   36 unblest unholy, damned   hies hastens
37 of out of, from

Enter Lodovico and Gratiano

CASSIO	What, ho! No watch? No passage? Murder, murder!
40 GRATIANO	'Tis some mischance: the voice is very direful.
CASSIO	O, help!
LODOVICO	Hark!
RODORIGO	O wretched villain!
LODOVICO	Two or three groan. 'Tis heavy night;

45 These may be counterfeits: let's think't unsafe
To come in to the cry without more help.

RODORIGO	Nobody come: then shall I bleed to death.

Enter Iago   *With a light and weapons*

LODOVICO	Hark!
GRATIANO	Here's one comes in his shirt, with light and weapons.
50 IAGO	Who's there? Whose noise is this that cries on murder?
LODOVICO	We do not know.
IAGO	Do not you hear a cry?
CASSIO	Here, here! For heaven sake, help me!
IAGO	What's the matter?
55 GRATIANO	This is Othello's ancient, as I take it. *To Lodovico*
LODOVICO	The same indeed: a very valiant fellow. *To Gratiano*
IAGO	What are you here that cry so grievously?
CASSIO	Iago? O, I am spoiled, undone by villains!

Give me some help.

60 IAGO	O me, lieutenant! What villains have done this?
CASSIO	I think that one of them is hereabout,

And cannot make away.

IAGO	O treacherous villains!— *To Lodovico and Gratiano*

What are you there? Come in, and give some help.

65 RODORIGO	O, help me there!
CASSIO	That's one of them.
IAGO	O murd'rous slave! O villain! *Stabs Rodorigo*

---

39 passage passersby   **40 direful** dreadful, dismal, horrible   **44 heavy** overcast, gloomy
46 come in to approach   **49 in his shirt** in his nightshirt/without a jacket   **58 spoiled** badly
damaged, injured   **undone** ruined

RODORIGO	O damned Iago! O inhuman dog!
IAGO	Kill men i'th'dark!— Where be these bloody thieves?—

70   How silent is this town!— Ho! Murder, murder!—
      What may you be? Are you of good or evil? *To Lodovico and Gratiano*

LODOVICO	As you shall prove us, praise us.
IAGO	Signior Lodovico?
LODOVICO	He, sir.

75   IAGO   I cry you mercy. Here's Cassio hurt by villains.

GRATIANO	Cassio?	
IAGO	How is't, brother?	*To Cassio*
CASSIO	My leg is cut in two.	
IAGO	Marry, heaven forbid!—	

80   Light, gentlemen. I'll bind it with my shirt.
      Enter Bianca

BIANCA	What is the matter, ho? Who is't that cried?
IAGO	Who is't that cried?
BIANCA	O my dear Cassio! My sweet Cassio! O Cassio, Cassio, Cassio!

85   IAGO   O notable strumpet! Cassio, may you suspect
      Who they should be that have thus mangled you?

CASSIO	No.
GRATIANO	I am sorry to find you thus: I have been to seek you.
IAGO	Lend me a garter. So.— O, for a chair

90   To bear him easily hence!

BIANCA	Alas, he faints! O Cassio, Cassio, Cassio!
IAGO	Gentlemen all, I do suspect this trash

      To be a party in this injury.—
      Patience awhile, good Cassio.— Come, come;
95   Lend me a light.   *Shines light on Rodorigo*
                    Know we this face or no?
      Alas, my friend and my dear countryman
      Rodorigo? No. Yes, sure: yes, 'tis Rodorigo.

---

72 prove discover by testing, find   **praise** appraise   **85 may you suspect** do you have any suspicions about   **89 garter** band worn to hold up the stocking or as a belt or sash (Iago requires it for use as a tourniquet)   **92 trash** worthless stuff, whore (i.e. Bianca)

GRATIANO	What, of Venice?
IAGO	Even he, sir: did you know him?
100 GRATIANO	Know him? Ay.
IAGO	Signior Gratiano? I cry your gentle pardon:

These bloody accidents must excuse my manners
That so neglected you.

GRATIANO	I am glad to see you.
105 IAGO	How do you, Cassio?— O, a chair, a chair!
GRATIANO	Rodorigo?
IAGO	He, he 'tis he.—

O, that's well said: the chair!   *Attendants bring in a chair*
Some good man bear him carefully from hence:
110   I'll fetch the general's surgeon.—
For you, mistress,   *To Bianca*
Save you your labour.— He that lies slain here, Cassio,
Was my dear friend: what malice was between you?

CASSIO	None in the world, nor do I know the man!
115 IAGO	What, look you pale?— O, bear him out *To Bianca*

o'th'air.
Stay you, good gentlemen.— Look you pale,
    mistress?—   *Attendants bear off*
Do you perceive the gastness of her eye?—   *Cassio and Rodorigo*
Nay, if you stare, we shall hear more anon.—
Behold her well: I pray you look upon her:
120   Do you see, gentlemen? Nay, guiltiness will speak,
Though tongues were out of use.

[Enter Emilia]

EMILIA	Alas, what is the matter? What is the matter, husband?
IAGO	Cassio hath here been set on in the dark

By Rodorigo and fellows that are scaped:
125   He's almost slain, and Rodorigo quite dead.

EMILIA	Alas, good gentleman! Alas, good Cassio!

---

102 accidents events/mishaps   **108 said** done   **111 For** as for   **112 Save . . . labour** don't
bother to try and help Cassio, leave him alone   **117 the . . . eye** her terrified look   **gastness**
terror, dread   **118 stare** i.e. gaze fixedly in horror (suggestive of guilt and an imminent
confession)

| IAGO | This is the fruits of whoring. Prithee, Emilia, |

IAGO   This is the fruits of whoring. Prithee, Emilia,
Go know of Cassio where he supped tonight.—   *To Bianca*
What, do you shake at that?

130 BIANCA   He supped at my house, but I therefore shake not.

IAGO   O, did he so? I charge you go with me.

EMILIA   O, fie upon thee, strumpet!

BIANCA   I am no strumpet, but of life as honest
As you that thus abuse me.

135 EMILIA   As I? Fie upon thee!

IAGO   Kind gentlemen, let's go see poor Cassio dressed.—
Come, mistress, you must tell's another tale.
Emilia, run you to the citadel
And tell my lord and lady what hath happed.—

140 Will you go on afore?— This is the night   *Aside*
That either makes me or fordoes me quite.   *Exeunt*

Act 5 Scene 2   *running scene 11*

Enter Othello and Desdemona in her bed   *Othello with a light*

OTHELLO   It is the cause, it is the cause, my soul:
Let me not name it to you, you chaste stars:
It is the cause. Yet I'll not shed her blood,
Nor scar that whiter skin of hers than snow,

5 And smooth as monumental alabaster:
Yet she must die, else she'll betray more men.
Put out the light, and then put out the light.
If I quench thee, thou flaming minister,
I can again thy former light restore,

10 Should I repent me: but once put out thy light,
Thou cunning'st pattern of excelling nature,

---

133 honest chaste   **136 Cassio dressed** i.e. Cassio's wound bandaged   **141 fordoes me quite** ruins me completely   **5.2** *Location: Cyprus (citadel/governor's bedroom)*
1 cause offense/reason for action   **5 alabaster** used for the construction of funeral monuments   **7 Put . . . light** quench the torch or candle and then extinguish Desdemona's life   **8 flaming minister** i.e. the torch or candle   **minister** servant   **11 cunning'st pattern** most skillfully made model (**cunning** reverberates with its sense of "deception")

I know not where is that Promethean heat
That can thy light relume. When I have plucked thy rose,
I cannot give it vital growth again:

15   It needs must wither. I'll smell thee on the tree.   *Kisses her*
O balmy breath, that dost almost persuade
Justice to break her sword! One more, one more.
Be thus when thou art dead, and I will kill thee
And love thee after. One more, and that's the last.   *Kisses her*

20   So sweet was ne'er so fatal. I must weep,
But they are cruel tears: this sorrow's heavenly,
It strikes where it doth love. She wakes.

DESDEMONA   Who's there? Othello?

OTHELLO   Ay, Desdemona.

25 DESDEMONA   Will you come to bed, my lord?

OTHELLO   Have you prayed tonight, Desdemon?

DESDEMONA   Ay, my lord.

OTHELLO   If you bethink yourself of any crime
Unreconciled as yet to heaven and grace,

30   Solicit for it straight.

DESDEMONA   Alack, my lord, what may you mean by that?

OTHELLO   Well, do it, and be brief: I will walk by.
I would not kill thy unprepar̀ed spirit,
No, heavens forfend! I would not kill thy soul.

35 DESDEMONA   Talk you of killing?

OTHELLO   Ay, I do.

DESDEMONA   Then heaven have mercy on me!

OTHELLO   Amen, with all my heart!

DESDEMONA   If you say, I hope you will not kill me.

40 OTHELLO   Hum!

DESDEMONA   And yet I fear you, for you're fatal then

---

12 **Promethean** in Greek mythology the Titan Prometheus created humankind, for whom he also stole fire from heaven   13 **relume** relight   14 **vital** living   17 **Justice** traditionally depicted as a blindfolded woman carrying scales and a sword   20 **fatal** deadly, destructive/ doomed   22 **strikes** delivers a blow/withers (used of frost)/destroys (used of God or of malign planetary influence)   27 **Ay** yes; Folio's "I" could mean both "I" and "ay" (yes) and sound identical   30 **Solicit** beg forgiveness   34 **forfend** forbid   39 **say** say so, say that

When your eyes roll so: why I should fear I know not,
Since guiltiness I know not, but yet I feel I fear.

OTHELLO   Think on thy sins.

45   DESDEMONA   They are loves I bear to you.

OTHELLO   Ay, and for that thou diest.

DESDEMONA   That death's unnatural that kills for loving.
Alas, why gnaw you so your nether lip?
Some bloody passion shakes your very frame:

50   These are portents, but yet I hope, I hope,
They do not point on me.

OTHELLO   Peace, and be still!

DESDEMONA   I will so. What's the matter?

OTHELLO   That handkerchief which I so loved and gave thee

55   Thou gav'st to Cassio.

DESDEMONA   No, by my life and soul!
Send for the man and ask him.

OTHELLO   Sweet soul, take heed, take heed of perjury:
Thou art on thy death-bed.

60   DESDEMONA   Ay, but not yet to die.

OTHELLO   Presently:
Therefore confess thee freely of thy sin,
For to deny each article with oath
Cannot remove nor choke the strong conception

65   That I do groan withal. Thou art to die.

DESDEMONA   O, heaven have mercy on me!

OTHELLO   I say, amen.

DESDEMONA   And have you mercy too! I never did
Offend you in my life, never loved Cassio

70   But with such general warranty of heaven
As I might love: I never gave him token.

OTHELLO   By heaven, I saw my handkerchief in's hand.
O perjured woman, thou dost stone my heart,

---

45 They . . . you apparently alludes to the sin of loving a human more than God
61 Presently imminently   **63 article** item forming part of an accusation   **64 conception**
belief/plan   **65 do groan withal** suffer with/am in labor with (playing on sense of pregnancy:
conception)   **69 Offend** sin against, commit a crime against   **70 warranty** authorization
73 stone harden, turn to stone

And makes me call what I intend to do

75 A murder, which I thought a sacrifice:

I saw the handkerchief.

DESDEMONA He found it then:

I never gave it him. Send for him hither,

Let him confess a truth.

80 OTHELLO   He hath confessed.

DESDEMONA What, my lord?

OTHELLO   That he hath used thee.

DESDEMONA How? Unlawfully?

OTHELLO   Ay.

85 DESDEMONA He will not say so.

OTHELLO   No, his mouth is stopped:

Honest Iago hath ta'en order for't.

DESDEMONA O, my fear interprets! What, is he dead?

OTHELLO   Had all his hairs been lives, my great revenge

90 Had stomach for them all.

DESDEMONA Alas, he is betrayed and I undone!

OTHELLO   Out, strumpet! Weep'st thou for him to my face?

DESDEMONA O, banish me, my lord, but kill me not!

OTHELLO   Down, strumpet!

95 DESDEMONA Kill me tomorrow, let me live tonight!

OTHELLO   Nay, if you strive—

DESDEMONA But half an hour!

OTHELLO   Being done, there is no pause.

DESDEMONA But while I say one prayer!

100 OTHELLO   It is too late.   *Smothers her*

Emilia at the door

EMILIA   My lord, my lord! What, ho! My lord, my lord! *Within*

OTHELLO   What noise is this? Not dead? Not yet quite dead?

I that am cruel am yet merciful:

I would not have thee linger in thy pain: so, so.

105 EMILIA   What, ho? My lord, my lord!   *Within*

---

82 used had sex with (Desdemona responds to a more general sense of "employed")   **87 ta'en order** made arrangements   **90 stomach** appetite   **96 strive** struggle   **98 Being done** i.e. as I am resolved to do the deed/while it is being done   **is no pause** must be no hesitation

OTHELLO   Who's there?

EMILIA   O, good my lord, I would speak a word with   *Within*
        you!

OTHELLO   Yes.— 'Tis Emilia.— By and by.— She's dead.
        'Tis like she comes to speak of Cassio's death.—
110   The noise was high. Ha, no more moving?
        Still as the grave. Shall she come in? Were't good?—
        I think she stirs again. No. What's best to do?
        If she come in, she'll sure speak to my wife:
        My wife, my wife! What wife? I have no wife.
115   O insupportable! O heavy hour!
        Methinks it should be now a huge eclipse
        Of sun and moon, and that th'affrighted globe
        Did yawn at alteration.

EMILIA   I do beseech you   *Within*
120   That I may speak with you, O, good my lord!

OTHELLO   I had forgot thee.— O, come in, Emilia.—
        Soft, by and by: let me the curtains draw.—   *Draws the bed curtains*
        Where art thou? What's the matter with thee now?   *and unlocks*
Enter Emilia   *the door*

EMILIA   O, my good lord, yonder's foul murders done!
125   OTHELLO   What? Now?

EMILIA   But now, my lord.

OTHELLO   It is the very error of the moon:
        She comes more nearer earth than she was wont,
        And makes men mad.
130   EMILIA   Cassio, my lord, hath killed a young Venetian
        Called Rodorigo.

OTHELLO   Rodorigo killed? And Cassio killed?

EMILIA   No, Cassio is not killed.

OTHELLO   Not Cassio killed? Then murder's out of tune,
135   And sweet revenge grows harsh.

---

108 By and by in a moment (addressed to Emilia)   **109 like** likely   **110 noise** i.e. following
the attack on Cassio   **high** loud   **118 yawn at alteration** gape open at this great change in
nature   **122 Soft** wait a moment   **curtains** bed curtains   **127 error** roaming, wandering off
course/mistake   **128 wont** accustomed   **135 harsh** jarring, discordant

DESDEMONA O, falsely, falsely murdered!

EMILIA Alas! What cry is that?

OTHELLO That? What?

EMILIA Out, and alas! That was my lady's voice.

140 Help, help, ho, help! O lady, speak again! *Opens the bed curtains*
Sweet Desdemona! O sweet mistress, speak!

DESDEMONA A guiltless death I die.

EMILIA O, who hath done this deed?

DESDEMONA Nobody: I myself. Farewell.

145 Commend me to my kind lord. O, farewell! *Dies*

OTHELLO Why, how should she be murdered?

EMILIA Alas, who knows?

OTHELLO You hear her say herself it was not I.

EMILIA She said so: I must needs report the truth.

150 OTHELLO She's like a liar gone to burning hell:
'Twas I that killed her.

EMILIA O, the more angel she, and you the blacker devil!

OTHELLO She turned to folly, and she was a whore.

EMILIA Thou dost belie her, and thou art a devil.

155 OTHELLO She was false as water.

EMILIA Thou art rash as fire, to say
That she was false: O, she was heavenly true!

OTHELLO Cassio did top her: ask thy husband else.
O, I were damned beneath all depth in hell,
160 But that I did proceed upon just grounds
To this extremity. Thy husband knew it all.

EMILIA My husband?

OTHELLO Thy husband.

EMILIA That she was false to wedlock?

165 OTHELLO Ay, with Cassio. Had she been true,
If heaven would make me such another world
Of one entire and perfect chrysolite,
I'd not have sold her for it.

---

136 falsely wrongfully, unjustly   **139 Out, and alas!** i.e. alas (out is an intensifier)   **153 folly**
lewdness   **154 belie** slander   **158 top** mount sexually   **else** otherwise — i.e. if you do not
believe me   **160 But** were it not   **167 chrysolite** precious stone, a name given to various
gems including the topaz

	EMILIA	My husband?
170	OTHELLO	Ay, 'twas he that told me on her first:

An honest man he is, and hates the slime
That sticks on filthy deeds.

EMILIA   My husband?

OTHELLO   What needs this iterance, woman? I say thy husband.

175   EMILIA   O mistress, villainy hath made mocks with love.
My husband say she was false?

OTHELLO   He, woman;
I say thy husband: dost understand the word?
My friend, thy husband: honest, honest Iago.

180   EMILIA   If he say so, may his pernicious soul
Rot half a grain a day! He lies to th'heart:
She was too fond of her most filthy bargain.

OTHELLO   Ha?

EMILIA   Do thy worst:

185   This deed of thine is no more worthy heaven
Than thou wast worthy her.

OTHELLO   Peace, you were best—

EMILIA   Thou hast not half that power to do me harm
As I have to be hurt. O gull, O dolt,

190   As ignorant as dirt! Thou hast done a deed —
I care not for thy sword — I'll make thee known,
Though I lost twenty lives.— Help, help, ho, help!
The Moor hath killed my mistress! Murder, murder!

Enter Montano, Gratiano and Iago

MONTANO   What is the matter? How now, general?

195   EMILIA   O, are you come, Iago? You have done well,
That men must lay their murders on your neck.

GRATIANO   What is the matter?

EMILIA   Disprove this villain, if thou be'st a man: *To Iago*

---

170 **on** of   171 **slime** viscous substance/semen   172 **filthy deeds** whorish or impure sexual acts   174 **iterance** iteration, repetition   175 **made mocks with** made sport of/made a mockery of   180 **pernicious** destructive/villainous   182 **filthy bargain** i.e. Othello   **filthy** dirty, black   187 **Peace . . . best** you'd be better off remaining silent   189 **be hurt** endure pain inflicted by you   **gull** dupe   191 **make thee known** expose you

He says thou told'st him that his wife was false:
200 I know thou didst not, thou'rt not such a villain.
Speak, for my heart is full.

IAGO   I told him what I thought, and told no more
Than what he found himself was apt and true.

EMILIA   But did you ever tell him she was false?

205 IAGO   I did.

EMILIA   You told a lie, an odious, damnèd lie:
Upon my soul, a lie, a wicked lie.
She false with Cassio? Did you say with Cassio?

IAGO   With Cassio, mistress! Go to, charm your tongue.

210 EMILIA   I will not charm my tongue; I am bound to speak:
My mistress here lies murdered in her bed—

ALL   O, heavens forfend!

EMILIA   And your reports have set the murder on.

OTHELLO   Nay, stare not, masters: it is true indeed.

215 GRATIANO   'Tis a strange truth.

MONTANO   O, monstrous act!

EMILIA   Villainy, villainy, villainy!
I think upon't, I think: I smell't: O villainy!
I thought so then. I'll kill myself for grief.

220 O villainy! Villainy!

IAGO   What, are you mad? I charge you get you home.

EMILIA   Good gentlemen, let me have leave to speak:
'Tis proper I obey him, but not now.
Perchance, Iago, I will ne'er go home.

225 OTHELLO   O, O, O!   *He falls on the bed*

EMILIA   Nay, lay thee down and roar,
For thou hast killed the sweetest innocent
That e'er did lift up eye.

OTHELLO   O, she was foul!   *Rises*

230 I scarce did know you, uncle: there lies your niece,

---

203 apt likely   **209 charm** put a spell on, i.e. silence   **228 lift up eye** i.e. look up to heaven
229 foul corrupt/wicked/guilty of an accusation   **230 uncle** i.e. Gratiano, presumably
Brabantio's brother

Whose breath, indeed, these hands have newly stopped:
I know this act shows horrible and grim.

GRATIANO   Poor Desdemon! I am glad thy father's dead:
Thy match was mortal to him, and pure grief
235   Shore his old thread in twain. Did he live now,
This sight would make him do a desperate turn,
Yea, curse his better angel from his side,
And fall to reprobance.

OTHELLO   'Tis pitiful, but yet Iago knows
240   That she with Cassio hath the act of shame
A thousand times committed: Cassio confessed it,
And she did gratify his amorous works
With that recognizance and pledge of love
Which I first gave her: I saw it in his hand:
245   It was a handkerchief, an antique token
My father gave my mother.

EMILIA   O heaven! O heavenly powers!

IAGO   Come, hold your peace.

EMILIA   'Twill out, 'twill out. I peace?
250   No, I will speak as liberal as the north:
Let heaven and men and devils, let them all,
All, all, cry shame against me, yet I'll speak.

IAGO   Be wise, and get you home.

EMILIA   I will not.   *Iago threatens to stab Emilia*

255   GRATIANO   Fie, your sword upon a woman?

EMILIA   O thou dull Moor! That handkerchief thou
speak'st of
I found by fortune and did give my husband,
For often, with a solemn earnestness —
More than indeed belonged to such a trifle —
260   He begged of me to steal't.

---

232 **grim** cruel, merciless   234 **mortal** fatal   235 **Shore . . . thread** an allusion to the
three Fates: one spun the thread of a man's life, another measured it, and the third cut it
236 **do . . . turn** i.e. kill himself; "despair" or "desperation" are terms for the state of spiritual
hopelessness thought to precede suicide   **turn** act   238 **reprobance** rejection by God
(suicide is a sin)   242 **works** sexual acts   243 **recognizance** token   245 **antique** ancient
249 **peace** be silent   250 **liberal . . . north** freely as the north wind   256 **dull** stupid (plays on
the sense of "dark")   259 **belonged** was appropriate

IAGO	Villainous whore!	
EMILIA	She give it Cassio? No, alas! I found it,	
	And I did give't my husband.	
IAGO	Filth, thou liest!	
265 | EMILIA | By heaven, I do not, I do not, gentlemen. | |

O murd'rous coxcomb! What should such a fool
Do with so good a wife?

OTHELLO   Are there no stones in heaven
But what serves for the thunder?— Precious
villain!   *He runs at Iago but is disarmed; Iago stabs Emilia*

270   GRATIANO   The woman falls: sure, he hath killed his wife.

[Exit Iago]

EMILIA   Ay, ay! O, lay me by my mistress' side.

GRATIANO   He's gone, but his wife's killed.

MONTANO   'Tis a notorious villain. Take you this weapon
Which I have recovered from the Moor:

275   Come, guard the door without: let him not pass,
But kill him rather. I'll after that same villain,
For 'tis a damnèd slave.   *[Exeunt Montano and Gratiano]*

OTHELLO   I am not valiant neither,
But every puny whipster gets my sword:

280   But why should honour outlive honesty?
Let it go all.

EMILIA   What did thy song bode, lady?
Hark, canst thou hear me? I will play the swan,
And die in music:— Willow, willow, willow—   *Sings*

285   Moor, she was chaste: she loved thee, cruel Moor.
So come my soul to bliss, as I speak true,
So speaking as I think, alas, I die.   *Dies*

OTHELLO   I have another weapon in this chamber:
It was a sword of Spain, the ice-brook's temper:

290   O, here it is. Uncle, I must come forth.   *Finds sword*

---

264 Filth foul thing/whore   **266 coxcomb** fool (from the headgear of a professional fool, which resembled a cock's comb)   **268 stones** thunderbolts   **269 Precious** utter, out-and-out **273 notorious** obvious, evident   **274 recovered** taken   **275 without** from the outside **279 whipster** worthless wretch   **280 honour** good reputation   **honesty** integrity (for which honour is gained)   **283 swan . . . music** proverbially, swans sang just before they died   **289 the ice-brook's temper** tempered (i.e. made hard) by immersing it in the water of an ice-cold brook

GRATIANO   If thou attempt it, it will cost thee dear: *Within*
Thou hast no weapon, and perforce must suffer.

OTHELLO   Look in upon me then and speak with me,
Or, naked as I am, I will assault thee.

[Enter Gratiano]

295   GRATIANO   What is the matter?

OTHELLO   Behold, I have a weapon:
A better never did itself sustain
Upon a soldier's thigh. I have seen the day
That, with this little arm and this good sword,
300   I have made my way through more impediments
Than twenty times your stop: but — O vain boast! —
Who can control his fate? 'Tis not so now.
Be not afraid, though you do see me weaponed:
Here is my journey's end, here is my butt
305   And very sea-mark of my utmost sail.
Do you go back dismayed? 'Tis a lost fear:
Man but a rush against Othello's breast
And he retires. Where should Othello go?
Now, how dost thou look now? O ill-starred wench,
310   Pale as thy smock, when we shall meet at compt,
This look of thine will hurl my soul from heaven,
And fiends will snatch at it! Cold, cold, my girl?
Even like thy chastity. O cursèd, cursèd slave!
Whip me, ye devils,
315   From the possession of this heavenly sight,
Blow me about in winds, roast me in sulphur,
Wash me in steep-down gulfs of liquid fire!
O Desdemon! Dead, Desdemon! Dead! O, O!

---

292 perforce of necessity   **294 naked** unarmed   **297 A . . . sustain** i.e. a soldier never wore a
better one   **sustain** maintain a fixed position   **301 your stop** the obstruction presented by
you   **304 Here** various possibilities: "in this place"/"this sword" (i.e. don't be **afraid**, this will
be **my** rather than your death)/Othello uses the sword to indicate the part of himself he is
going to stab/Othello gestures to Desdemona or indicates the sword (with emphasis on **my**)
butt goal, target (archery term)   **305 sea-mark** boundary of the flow of the sea/landmark
used in navigation   **306 lost** wasted   **307 Man . . . rush** use a mere reed   **309 ill-starred** ill-
fated   **310 smock** woman's undergarment   **compt** the day of reckoning, Judgment Day
313 slave i.e. himself/Iago   **317 steep-down** extremely steep

Enter Lodovico, Cassio [carried in a chair], Montano and Iago
[prisoner] with Officers

LODOVICO   Where is this rash and most unfortunate man?

320 OTHELLO   That's he that was Othello: here I am.

LODOVICO   Where is that viper? Bring the villain forth.

OTHELLO   I look down towards his feet, but that's a fable:
If that thou be'st a devil, I cannot kill thee.   *Wounds Iago*

LODOVICO   Wrench his sword from him.

325 IAGO   I bleed, sir, but not killed.

OTHELLO   I am not sorry neither: I'd have thee live,
For in my sense 'tis happiness to die.

LODOVICO   O thou Othello, thou was once so good,
Fall'n in the practice of a cursèd slave,

330 What shall be said to thee?

OTHELLO   Why, anything:
An honourable murderer, if you will,
For nought I did in hate, but all in honour.

LODOVICO   This wretch hath part confessed his villainy.

335 Did you and he consent in Cassio's death?

OTHELLO   Ay.

CASSIO   Dear general, I never gave you cause.

OTHELLO   I do believe it, and I ask your pardon.
Will you, I pray, demand that demi-devil

340 Why he hath thus ensnared my soul and body?

IAGO   Demand me nothing: what you know, you know:
From this time forth I never will speak word.

LODOVICO   What? Not to pray?

GRATIANO   Torments will ope your lips.

345 OTHELLO   Well, thou dost best.

LODOVICO   Sir, you shall understand what hath befall'n —
Which, as I think, you know not. Here is a letter
Found in the pocket of the slain Rodorigo,
And here another: the one of them imports

---

322 I . . . feet i.e. to see if Iago, like the devil, has cloven feet   **327 in my sense** according to
the way I feel   **329 practice** scheming, treachery   **344 Torments** torture   **349 imports**
concerns/indicates

350   The death of Cassio to be undertook
        By Rodorigo.

OTHELLO   O villain!

CASSIO   Most heathenish and most gross!

LODOVICO   Now here's another discontented paper
355   Found in his pocket too: and this, it seems,
        Rodorigo meant t'have sent this damnèd villain,
        But that belike Iago in the interim
        Came in and satisfied him.

OTHELLO   O thou pernicious caitiff!—
360   How came you, Cassio, by that handkerchief
        That was my wife's?

CASSIO   I found it in my chamber,
        And he himself confessed it but even now
        That there he dropped it for a special purpose
365   Which wrought to his desire.

OTHELLO   O fool, fool, fool!

CASSIO   There is besides in Rodorigo's letter
        How he upbraids Iago, that he made him
        Brave me upon the watch, whereon it came
370   That I was cast: and even but now he spake —
        After long seeming dead — Iago hurt him,
        Iago set him on.

LODOVICO   You must forsake this room and go with us: *To Othello*
        Your power and your command is taken off,
375   And Cassio rules in Cyprus. For this slave,
        If there be any cunning cruelty
        That can torment him much and hold him long,
        It shall be his. You shall close prisoner rest
        Till that the nature of your fault be known
380   To the Venetian state.— Come, bring away.

---

353 gross vile/monstrously evident   **354 discontented** filled with discontent   **357 belike** probably/perhaps   **358 satisfied him** provided him with answers and explanations (relating to the issues raised in the letter)   **359 caitiff** wretch   **365 wrought . . . desire** worked in accordance with his wishes   **369 Brave** challenge, confront   **whereon** as a result of which   **370 cast** dismissed   **377 hold him long** keep him alive under torture for a long time   **378 close** securely confined

OTHELLO   Soft you; a word or two before you go.
I have done the state some service, and they know't —
No more of that. I pray you, in your letters,
When you shall these unlucky deeds relate,
385   Speak of me as I am: nothing extenuate,
Nor set down aught in malice. Then must you speak
Of one that loved not wisely but too well:
Of one not easily jealous, but being wrought,
Perplexed in the extreme: of one whose hand,
390   Like the base Judean, threw a pearl away
Richer than all his tribe: of one whose subdued eyes,
Albeit unusèd to the melting mood,
Drops tears as fast as the Arabian trees
Their medicinable gum. Set you down this,
395   And say besides, that in Aleppo once,
Where a malignant and a turbaned Turk
Beat a Venetian and traduced the state,
I took by th'throat the circumcisèd dog
And smote him, thus.   *Stabs himself*
400 LODOVICO   O bloody period!
GRATIANO   All that is spoke is marred.
OTHELLO   I kissed thee ere I killed thee: no way but this,
Killing myself, to die upon a kiss.   *Kisses Desdemona*
                                                                          Dies

CASSIO   This did I fear, but thought he had no weapon,
405   For he was great of heart.
LODOVICO   O Spartan dog,   *To Iago*
More fell than anguish, hunger, or the sea!
Look on the tragic loading of this bed:

---

385 extenuate diminish, disparage   **388 wrought** worked on/worked up   **389 Perplexed** distressed, tormented, agitated   **390 base** unworthy   **Judean** may allude to Judas Iscariot, the Judean disciple who betrayed Christ, or to Herod, the jealous Judean king who accused his wife Mariamne of adultery and had her executed   **391 subdued** overcome (by emotion)   **393 Arabian trees** i.e. myrrh trees, which drip with the gum resin   **394 medicinable** myrrh was used in astringent and expectorant tinctures   **395 Aleppo** city in Turkey   **397 traduced** slandered   **400 period** conclusion   **402 kissed . . . thee** perhaps another reference to Judas, who famously identified Christ to his enemies by kissing him; he later killed himself   **403 die** with shading into sense of "orgasm"   **406 Spartan dog** a particularly fierce breed of hunting dog   **407 fell** fierce/cruel

This is thy work.— The object poisons sight,
410   Let it be hid. Gratiano, keep the house,
And seize upon the fortunes of the Moor,
For they succeed on you.— To you, lord governor,   *To Cassio*
Remains the censure of this hellish villain:
The time, the place, the torture: O, enforce it!
415   Myself will straight aboard, and to the state
This heavy act with heavy heart relate.   *Exeunt*

410 keep guard, secure/remain in/seize   **411 seize upon** take legal possession of
412 succeed on descend to, pass to   **413 censure** judgment/sentencing   **416 heavy**
sorrowful

TEXTUAL NOTES

Q = First Quarto text of 1622
Q2 = a correction introduced in the Second Quarto text of 1630
F = First Folio text of 1623
F2 = a correction introduced in the Second Folio text of 1632
F3 = a correction introduced in the Third Folio text of 1663–64
F4 = a correction introduced in the Fourth Folio text of 1685
Ed = a correction introduced by a later editor
SH = speech heading (i.e. speaker's name)

List of parts based on "The Names of the Actors" at end of F text, with
additional information provided in parenthesis

RODORIGO *spelled thus in* F *(throughout)*. Q = Roderigo *throughout* **EMILIA**
spelled Aemilia *in* F *(throughout)*
1.1.1 Never = F. Q = TVsh, neuer **4 But** = F. Q = S'blood, but **25 toga'd** =
Q *(toged)*. F = Tongued **29 Cyprus** *spelled* Ciprus *in* F *(and elsewhere)*
33 bless = F. Q = God blesse **68 full** = Q. F = fall **thick-lips** = Ed. F =
Thicks-lips. Q = thicklips. **75 chances** = F. Q = changes **90 Sir** = F. Q =
Zounds sir **91 soul:** = Ed. F = soule **117 Sir** = F. Q = Zouns Sir **121 jennets for germans** *spelled* Gennets for Germaines *in* F **125 making** = F. Q
= now making **165 hell-pains** = Ed. F = hell apines. Q = hells paines
168 sign. That = Ed. F = signe) that
1.2.41 haste-post-haste = Ed. F = haste,Post-haste **70 You, Rodorigo?
Come** = F *(corrected)*. F *(uncorrected)* = You *Rodorigo*, Come **98 Whither**
= F2. F = Whether **103 I do** = Q. F = do
1.3.24 gaze. When = Ed. F = gaze, when **58 nor** = Q. F = hor **62 and** =
Q. F = snd **66 SH SENATORS** *ambiguously spelled* Sen. *in* F **84 your** =
Q. F = yonr **100 tale** = Q. F = u Tale **110 maimed** *spelled* main'd *in* F
imperfect = Ed. F = imperfect. **117 wrought upon** = Q. F = wtought vp
on **118 SH DUKE** = Q. *Not in* F **119 overt** = Q. F = ouer **122 SH FIRST
SENATOR** = Q. F = *Sen.* **136 till** = Q. F = tell **152 slavery, of** = Q. F =
slauery. Of **154 antres** *spelled* Antars *in* F **155 rocks, hills** = F. Q =
rocks and hils **157 other** = Q. F = others **158 Anthropophagi** *spelled*
Antropophague *in* F **161 thence** = Q. F = hence **169 intentively** = Q. F =
instinctiuely **173 kisses** = F. Q = sighes **190 speak:** = Ed. F = speake?
217 lovers. = F. Q = louers / Into your fauour **222 preserved** = Q. F =
presern'd **245 couch** = Q. F = Coach **247 alacrity** = Q. F = Alacartie
258 there reside = Q. F = therorecide **265 I love** = F. Q = I did loue

291 against = Q. F = againsf **320 the** = Q. F = the the **334 guinea-hen** *spelled* Gynney Hen *in* F **341 thyme** *spelled* Time *in* F **344 beam** = Ed. F = braine. Q = Ballence **350 scion** *spelled* Seyen *in* F **371 supersubtle** = F. Q = a super subtle **393 a snipe** = Q. F = Snpe **396 He** = Q. F = She
2.1.2 SH FIRST GENTLEMAN = 1. Gent *in* F **9 mortise** = Q. F = Morties. **10 SH SECOND GENTLEMAN** = Q. F = 2 **13 wind-shaked surge** = F3. F = winde-shak'd-Surge **mane** *spelled* Maine *in* F **18 SH MONTANO** = Ed. F = *Men.* **21 SH THIRD GENTLEMAN** = Q. F = 3 **27–8 in . . . Cassio** = Ed. F = in: *A Verennessa, Michael Cassio* **42 th'aerial** = Ed. F = th'Eriall **44 SH THIRD GENTLEMAN** = Q. F = *Gent.* **47 Thanks, you** = Ed. F = Thankes you, **54 hopes** = Ed. F = hope's **56,103 SH [VOICES]** = Ed. F = *Within* **71 engineer** *spelled* Ingeniuer *in* F **97 tell of** = F. Q = tell me of **101 of sea** = F. Q = of the sea **158 indeed, one** = Ed. F = indeed? One **authority** *spelled* authorithy *in* F **180 gyve** = F2. F = giue **185 courtesy** *spelled* Curtsie *in* F **186 clyster-pipes** = Q *(Clisterpipes).* F = Cluster-pipes **228 hither** = Q. F = thither **237 prating?** = Q. F = prating, **248 fortune** = Q. F = Forune **249 does?** = Q. F = do's: **253 has** = Q. F = he's **269 mutabilities** = F. Q = mutualities **279 haply** *spelled* happely *in* F **298 accountant** *spelled* accomptant *in* F **304 evened** *spelled* eeuen'd *in* F **for wife** = Q. F = for wift **311 right** = F. Q = ranke **312 night-cap** = Q. F = Night-Cape
2.2.9 present = Q. F = presenr **Bless** = F. Q = Heauen blesse
[Act 2 Scene 3] = Ed. *Scene is continuous in* F
2.3.26 stoup = Ed. F = stope **53 to put** = Q. F = put to **71 Englishman** = Q. F = Englishmen **85 Then** = Q. F = *And* **auld** = Ed. F = *awl'd.* Q = owd **98 Forgive** = F. Q = God forgiue **100 left** = F. Q = left hand **103 SH GENTLEMEN** = Q. F = *Gent.* **134 You** = F. Q = Zouns, you **148 Sir Montano— Sir** = Ed. F = Sir *Montano:* **151 lieutenant!** = F. Q = Leiutenant, hold, **154 I bleed** = F. Q = Zouns, I bleed **157 sense of place** = Ed. F = place of sense **189 me —** = Ed. F = me. **209 leagued** = Ed. F = league **246 well,** = F. Q = well now, **280 O,** = F. Q = O God, **298 familiar** = Q. F = famillar **306 denotement** = Q. F = deuotement **313 stronger** = Q. F = stonger **319 check me** = F. Q = check me here **330 were't to** = Q. F = were to **360 Does't** = Ed. F = Dos't **371 on:** = Ed. F = on. Q = on, **372 the while** = Ed. F = a while
3.1.8 tail *spelled* tale *in* F **29 SH CASSIO** = Q. *Not in* F
3.2.6 We'll = F3. F = Well
3.3.5 fellow. Do = Ed. F = Fellow, Do **71 In faith** = F4. F = Infaith **73 example** = Ed. F = example) **79 with** = Q. F = wirh **82 much—** = Ed. F = much. **105 you** = Q. F = he **154 that all** = Q. F = that: All **free** = F. Q = free to **158 Where no** = Ed. F = Wherein. Q = But some **167 oft** = Q. F = of **168 wisdom** = F. Q = I intreate then **175 What** = F. Q = Zouns. **183 I'll** = F. Q = By heauen, I'le **203 Is** = F. Q = Is once **205 exsufflicate** *spelled* exufflicate *in* F **208 dances** = F. Q = dances well **278 put** = F2.

Not in F **289 learnèd** = Ed. F = learn'd **290 human** *spelled* humane *in* F
(and elsewhere) **329 talk to** = Q. F = talke too **384 Pioneers** *spelled*
Pyoners *in* F **406 lord—** = Ed. F = Lord. **409 horror's** = Ed. F = Horrors
432 I see you = F. Q = I see sir, you **466 laid** = F. Q = then layed **492 thy**
= Q. F = the **498 mind may** = F. Q = mind perhaps may **501 Ne'er feels**
= Q2. F = Neu'r keepes

3.4.36 It hath felt = F. Q = It has yet felt **70 lose't** *spelled* loose't *in* F
86 Bless = F. Q = Heauen blesse **92 I can, but** = F. Q = I can sir, but
101 you— = Ed. F = you. **121 honour. I** = Ed. F = honour, I **171 born**
spelled borne *in* F **174 hereabout** = F3. F = heere about **184 lovers'** =
Ed. F = Louers **193 friend:** = Ed. F = Friend,

4.1.43 Lie . . . That's = F. Q = lye with her, Zouns, that's **84 list.** = Q. F =
List, **86 unsuiting** = Q *(corrected).* F = resulting **112 conster** = Q. F =
conserue **114 you, lieutenant** = F. Q = you now Leiutenant **118 power**
= Q. F = dowre **132 I marry** = F. Q = I marry her **143 beckons** = Q. F =
becomes **146 and falls me** = Q. F = by this hand she fals **170 I** = F. Q =
Faith I **220 I . . . Venice** = F. Q = Something from *Venice* sure,
221 Lodovico: this comes = Ed. F = *Lodouico*, this, comes **223 Save**
you = F. Q = God saue the **263 an obedient** = Q. F = obedient
300 denote = Q. F *(corrected)* = deonte. F *(uncorrected)* = deuote

4.2.34 nay = Ed. F = May **49 haply** *spelled* happely *in* F *(and elsewhere)*
52 I = F. Q = Why I **70 Ay** *spelled* I *in* F **173 form,** = Ed. F = Forme.
193 daff'st *spelled* dafts *in* F **200 I** = F. Q = Faith I **231 the** = Q. F = rhe
234 within = Q. F = within,

4.3.19 I = Q. F = I, **21 favour** = F. Q = fauour in them **24 before,** = F. Q =
before thee, **34 Barbary** *spelled* Brabarie *in* F **42 singing** = F *(corrected).*
F *(uncorrected)* = sining **45 Sing . . . willow** = Ed. F = *Sing Willough, &c.*
(and elsewhere)

5.1.1 bulk = Q. F = Barke **46 in to** = Ed. F = into **115 him out** = Q. F = him
5.2.39 say = F. Q = say so **61 Presently** = F. Q = Yes, presently **184 worst** =
Q. F = wotst **274 have** = F. Q = haue here **347 not. Here** = Ed. F = not)
heere **361 wife's** = Q. F = wiues **390 Judean** = F. Q, F2 = Indian

QUARTO PASSAGES THAT DO NOT APPEAR IN THE FOLIO

Following 1.3.367 (after "errors of her choice"):
she must have change, she must.

Following 1.3.388:

RODORIGO   What say you?

IAGO   No more of drowning, do you hear?

RODORIGO   I am changed:

Following 2.1.89:
And bring all Cyprus comfort!

Following 3.1.25:

CASSIO   Do, good my friend.

Following 3.1.48:
To take the safest occasion by the front

Following 3.4.98:

DESDEMONA   I pray, talk me of Cassio.

OTHELLO   The handkerchief!

Following 4.2.185:
And he does chide with you.

Following 5.2.100:

DESDEMONA   O, lord, lord, lord!

SCENE-BY-SCENE ANALYSIS

ACT 1 SCENE 1

Lines 1–84: The action begins *in medias res*, establishing the pace of the play. As Iago and Rodorigo hurry along, they reveal events prior to this point. The audience is initially excluded from some key information, however, establishing the themes of secrecy and misunderstanding: Rodorigo complains that, although he has been giving Iago money, Iago has not told him "of this," although we are not told what "this" is. He claims that Iago said that he hated someone, referred to by both of them as "him," and, later, "the Moor"; no one refers to Othello by name in the first scene: he is identified chiefly by his racial "otherness," and "labeled" by pronouns or epithets, creating a negative sense of his identity (another theme) and establishing the power of language. The latter is particularly significant to Iago, who manipulates others through his linguistic skills, evident in his placation of the gullible Rodorigo and description of his hatred for Othello. Iago claims that he is bitter because Othello promoted Cassio to be his lieutenant and made Iago his ensign. Iago complains that he is an experienced soldier, while Cassio's "soldiership" is "Mere prattle without practice," creating tension between words and action. Rodorigo comments that if he were Iago he would not continue to follow Othello, but Iago explains that he is doing it so that he can get his revenge. He explains that he is only "trimmed in forms and visages of duty," establishing the themes of deception and appearance versus reality. Iago declares his false nature: "I am not what I am," a paradoxical statement that emphasizes the ambiguity of his identity. Despite this, Rodorigo continues to trust him, showing his lack of perception.

They arrive at Brabantio's house and Iago instructs Rodorigo to rouse the sleeping household, establishing that it is nighttime. This reinforces the sense of secrecy and introduces the recurring image of darkness, part of the structure of oppositions that run through the play, including dark/light, black/white, words/actions, good/evil, and male/female. Both men shout to wake Brabantio, but Iago's language is more dramatic, alarmist, and effective.

Lines 85–195: Brabantio appears above, demanding to know "the reason of this terrible summons." Rodorigo politely inquires whether all Brabantio's family "is within," but Iago takes over, warning Brabantio that "an old black ram / Is tupping [his] white ewe." His sustained use of base sexual imagery further dehumanizes Othello and enrages Brabantio. Rodorigo identifies himself, but Iago remains anonymous, secretly manipulating events as both "actor" and "director." Rodorigo has previously tried to court Brabantio's daughter, Desdemona, and Brabantio accuses him of coming full of "distempering draughts" to see her. With inflammatory interjections from Iago, Rodorigo explains to Brabantio that they have come to warn him that Desdemona has eloped with "a lascivious Moor." Brabantio rouses his household and Iago leaves, explaining that he cannot appear to be against Othello. Brabantio confirms that Desdemona is missing. His disjointed speech reflects his distress and anger as he suggests that magic has been used on her. Rodorigo offers to take him to Othello and Desdemona.

ACT 1 SCENE 2

Lines 1–64: Iago, feigning loyalty to Othello, expresses concern that Brabantio will try to force a divorce, but Othello assures him that he will "out-tongue" Brabantio's complaints, emphasizing the theme of language. He assures Iago that he genuinely loves "the gentle Desdemona." They see torches approaching and assume that Brabantio has come. Iago urges Othello to go indoors, but Othello is not afraid, reminding Iago of his "parts," "title," and "perfect soul," introducing another opposition in the play, that of the physical versus the spiritual. It is not Brabantio, however, but Cassio and his officers, who have come to tell Othello that the Duke wishes to see him "haste-post-haste" on military business. Othello leaves briefly to "spend a word" in the house and Iago informs Cassio that Othello is married,

again describing the event through coarse sexual innuendo. Brabantio and Rodorigo arrive.

Lines 65–117: Brabantio accuses Othello of being a "foul thief"
who has "enchanted" Desdemona. He dehumanizes Othello, referring to him as "a thing," and tries to arrest him as a "practiser" of
illegal magic. Othello explains that the Duke has summoned him,
and Brabantio decides that he will go as well, certain that the Duke
will sympathize with his complaint against Othello.

ACT 1 SCENE 3

Lines 1–134: The Duke and his senators discuss reports that the
Turkish fleet is heading for Cyprus. A sailor brings news that they
now appear to be traveling toward Rhodes, although a Senator suggests that "'tis a pageant, / To keep us in false gaze," emphasizing the
theme of deception. A Messenger reports that the Turkish fleet has
united with reinforcements and that they are once again heading for
Cyprus. Brabantio and Othello arrive, accompanied by Iago, Cassio,
and Rodorigo. The Duke assumes that Brabantio is there to discuss
the urgent military business, but Brabantio is concerned with his
own worries, creating tension between political and personal concerns. He tells the Duke that his daughter has been "stolen" and
"corrupted / By spells and medicines." The Duke promises that who-
ever is involved in "this foul proceeding" will be punished.

Brabantio names Othello. Othello admits that he has "ta'en
away" Desdemona and married her, but insists that this is his only
offense. He offers to explain, warning that he is "Rude" in his speech,
being only a soldier, and can only tell "a round unvarnished tale,"
but his claims that he is "little blessed with the soft phrase of peace"
are belied by his careful and persuasive arguments. Brabantio maintains that Desdemona was "never bold" and of a "still" spirit, reinforcing the passivity evoked by Othello's description of her as "gentle
Desdemona" in the previous scene and emphasizing the play's concern with the way identity can be created by others, through
repeated use of words and phrases in association with a character.
Othello sends for Desdemona so that she may speak for herself.

Lines 135–320: Othello describes how Brabantio used to invite him to his house and how he would tell Brabantio tales of "moving accidents by flood and field" and "hair-breadth scapes i'th'imminent deadly breach." He tells them that Desdemona loved him "for the dangers" he had undergone and that, in turn, he loved her because "she did pity them." He claims that his words are the only "witchcraft" that he has used, again emphasizing the power of language. The Duke urges Brabantio to make the best of the situation. Desdemona arrives, and Brabantio asks her, of all the assembled "noble company," whom she owes the most obedience to. Desdemona answers that she has a "divided duty" between her father and husband, but points out that, like her mother before her, she must put her husband first. While this speech emphasizes that Desdemona is subject to male authority, it also shows that she is confident and articulate. Brabantio unhappily resigns himself and the Duke tries to encourage him, saying that "To mourn a mischief that is past and gone / Is the next way to draw new mischief on," reminding us of Iago's desire for revenge.

The discussion turns to the military situation and the Duke tells Othello that he must go to Cyprus, suggesting that Desdemona return to Brabantio's home. In a moving speech, Desdemona requests to be allowed to go with Othello. The Duke agrees and leaves with the senators and Brabantio. Othello assigns Iago to escort Desdemona to Cyprus, believing him to be a man "of honesty and trust," a comment that shows Othello's lack of perception and introduces the motif of honesty. Othello and Desdemona leave to prepare for his departure.

Lines 321–390: Rodorigo melodramatically claims that his life is "torment" now that he has lost Desdemona. Iago argues that it "cannot be long that Desdemona should continue her love to the Moor" and claims that Othello will soon tire of Desdemona because "These Moors are changeable in their wills," reinforcing the popular opinion of Othello's otherness (although it is uncertain whether Iago believes this, or is merely using the idea to his own ends). Constantly urging Rodorigo to "put money in thy purse," he claims that he can destroy the "frail vow" between "an erring barbarian and supersubtle Venetian" and promises that Rodorigo will soon "enjoy" Desdemona. His references to money and sex show Iago's preoccupation with the physical rather than spiritual aspects of human existence. He suggests that Rodorigo "cuckold" Othello. They arrange to meet the next day.

Lines 391–412: Alone, Iago reveals his contempt for Rodorigo, commenting: "Thus do I ever make my fool my purse." He reiterates his hatred for Othello and reveals another possible motive: he believes that Othello has slept with his wife, Emilia, although he is not sure. He is willing to act on "mere suspicion," however, suggesting that Iago's desire to destroy Othello is based on something more complex and inherent than simple revenge. Iago outlines his plan to convince Othello that Cassio is having an affair with Desdemona and comments that Othello's "free and open nature" makes him gullible.

ACT 2 SCENE 1

Lines 1–187: In Cyprus, Montano and two gentlemen discuss the storm at sea, a metaphor for the turmoil that Iago is to create. News arrives that the storm has destroyed the Turkish fleet and that Cassio has arrived, but that his ship was parted from Othello's. Cassio arrives and starts to report when cries of "a sail!" are heard. He sends to find out if Othello has arrived and begins to tell Montano of Othello's marriage, clearly showing his admiration for Desdemona, "a maid / that paragons description." Iago enters with Desdemona, Rodorigo, and Emilia, and Cassio immediately kneels before Desdemona, chivalrously greeting her as "The riches of the ship." Desdemona thanks him briefly, but is more concerned for the safety of her husband. As he describes how they were parted, another ship is sighted and Cassio sends once more for news. As they wait, everyone talks lightheartedly. Iago shows his quick wit but, even though the tone is light, his negative, perhaps aggressive, attitude toward women is revealed, particularly his own wife, whom he does not hesitate to criticize in public. Desdemona makes it clear that she is joining in out of politeness and demonstrates her own wit, but her chief concern is Othello. Cassio draws her apart and they talk, observed by Iago. He is pleased at the attention that Cassio pays to Desdemona:

although Cassio is only being courteous, Iago reveals that "with as little a web as this" he will "ensnare as great a fly as Cassio." The use of aside emphasizes the secrecy and deception of his character, and the change in language is also interesting as he shifts into prose. He is interrupted by the trumpet announcing Othello's arrival.

Lines 188–290: Othello and Desdemona are reunited. Othello ironically sends "good Iago" (who is plotting aside how he will destroy their happiness) to oversee the disembarking of his ship. Alone with Rodorigo, Iago tells him directly that Desdemona is in love with Cassio. Again shifting into prose and using coarse sexual imagery, Iago argues that Desdemona is already tiring of "the Moor" and is looking for a younger "second choice" in Cassio. Rodorigo is skeptical at first, but Iago easily convinces him and reveals a plan to destroy Cassio. He tells Rodorigo to find Cassio when he is on watch that night and to "find some occasion to anger" him. He claims that Cassio is "rash" and will "strike at" Rodorigo, which will give Iago the weapon he needs against him.

Lines 291–317: Iago's soliloquy reiterates his hatred for Othello and his suspicions that Othello has slept with Emilia. He declares that he will be revenged, "wife for wife." He also suspects Cassio of sleeping with Emilia, suggesting a jealous and irrational side to his character. He intends to disturb Othello's "peace and quiet / Even to madness."

ACT 2 SCENE 2

The Herald announces a feast in celebration of Othello's marriage.

ACT 2 SCENE 3

Lines 1–152: Othello places Cassio in charge of "the guard" and leads Desdemona away to bed, observing that they have yet to consummate their marriage (a fact that undermines Iago's repeated representations of their relationship as purely sexual). Iago suggests that they drink Othello's health. Cassio is reluctant, explaining that he has "unhappy brains for drinking," but Iago skillfully persuades him and sends Cassio to call in the gallants with the wine. Iago reveals his intention to ply Cassio with alcohol, making him "full of quarrel and offence." He observes that Rodorigo and three other watchers are already very drunk, having been "flustered with flowing cups" by himself. Cassio returns, having been given a drink by Montano. Iago encourages him to have more, feigning cheery drunkenness on his own part. Cassio's increasingly confused speech shows his growing inebriation, as do his repeated, comic denials that he is drunk. He leaves, and Iago observes to Montano that Cassio is a great soldier, but his "vice" of drinking is worrying. Rodorigo arrives, and Iago sends him after Cassio. There is a cry within and Rodorigo rushes back, pursued by an angry Cassio. Montano tries to stop Cassio and tells him that he is drunk. Cassio and Montano begin to fight, and Iago, still in control, sends Rodorigo to "cry a mutiny," before beginning to call out for help.

Lines 153–252: Othello arrives and stops the fight, assisted by Iago who is now playing the role of his loyal follower. Othello asks "Honest Iago" who began the fight, but Iago claims he does not know. Cassio "cannot speak" and Montano claims that he was acting in self-defense. Frustrated, Othello claims that his "blood" begins to "rule" his reason, showing that he can be moved to anger. He demands to know from Iago "who began it." Feigning reluctance and appearing to defend Cassio, Iago blames him. Othello ironically praises Iago's "honesty and love" in defending Cassio and strips Cassio of his officership. Desdemona interrupts them, and Othello's soldierly tone is contrasted with his loving reassurances to his "sweeting" as he leads her back indoors.

Lines 253–375: Iago feigns concern for Cassio, who is devastated at the loss of his "reputation." Ironically reinforcing the distance between appearance and reality, Iago tells Cassio that "Reputation is an idle and most false imposition." He suggests that Cassio appeal to Desdemona to intercede with Othello. Cassio agrees and leaves. Alone, Iago dwells on the subtlety of his plan, pleased that no one could actually say that he "play[s] the villain," as the advice he has given Cassio is good. He adds, however, that "When devils will the blackest sins put on, / They do suggest at first with heavenly shows," reinforcing the black/white and good/evil motifs, as well as the theme of deception. He intends to tell Othello that Desdemona is only pleading for Cassio because she desires him. Rodorigo returns, complaining that he still does not have Desdemona. Iago reassures him and sends him away. Iago decides to get Emilia to persuade Desdemona to plead for Cassio while he sets up Othello to find Cassio "Soliciting" Desdemona.

ACT 3 SCENE 1

Cassio instructs some musicians to play beneath Othello's window. In comic contrast to the events of the previous scene, the Clown engages in a series of bawdy quibbles before Iago interrupts them. Cassio tells him that he has sent to ask Emilia if she can arrange "some access" to "virtuous Desdemona." Iago offers to draw Othello out of the way so Cassio may speak more freely, and Cassio observes how "kind and honest" Iago is. Emilia brings the news that Desdemona has already spoken to Othello about Cassio. Cassio still wishes to speak to Desdemona, however, and Emilia agrees to help him.

ACT 3 SCENE 2

Othello instructs Iago to meet him later.

ACT 3 SCENE 3

Lines 1–99: Desdemona reassures Cassio that she will speak to Othello. Emilia ironically comments that her husband is as grieved by the situation "As if the cause were his," establishing her naïveté. Desdemona vows to "intermingle" everything Othello does with "Cassio's suit" and Cassio leaves. As Othello and Iago approach, Iago suggests that Cassio looked "guilty-like" as he left. Desdemona greets them and says that she has been talking with "a suitor," an unfortunately ambiguous word choice. She urges Othello to call Cassio back, but his replies to her entreaties are brief and distracted, suggesting that Iago has already begun to affect his perception. The women leave.

Lines 100–309: Iago continues to work on Othello, creating jealousy and doubt while appearing supportive and loyal. His techniques are clever and subtle: he never makes any direct statements and is always ambiguous, seeming to praise and deny where he is doing otherwise, and always answering Othello's questions with ones of his own. He ironically warns Othello against "the green-eyed monster" of jealousy, but tells him to watch Desdemona when she is with Cassio. He reminds Othello that Desdemona is capable of deception: she deceived Brabantio to marry him. He begs Othello not to think any more about it, but suggests that if Desdemona pleads on Cassio's behalf "With any strong or vehement importunity, / Much will be seen in that." Othello, filled with pain and anger, gives his first soliloquy of the play (the audience has more access to the inner thoughts of the "villain" of the play than its eponymous "hero"). Even in so short a time, Iago has succeeded in making Othello doubt Desdemona's fidelity. As Desdemona approaches, however, we see that he still loves her, and that he finds it hard to believe that she is false.

Lines 310–528: Desdemona perceives that Othello is "not well." She offers him her handkerchief, but he pushes it away and she drops it. As they leave, Emilia picks up the handkerchief, observing that it was Othello's first gift to Desdemona. She reveals that Iago has repeatedly asked her to steal it, although she does not know why. Iago enters and Emilia gives him the handkerchief, but he will not tell her why he wants it and sends her away. Alone, he reveals his intention to leave it in Cassio's lodging. As he contemplates how he has already changed "the Moor" with his "poison," Othello returns, muttering agitatedly. Iago feigns concern as Othello contemplates Desdemona's supposed betrayal. He angrily demands that Iago prove that Desdemona is "a whore." Iago feigns hurt, ironically observing that to be "direct and honest is not safe." He asks Othello what proof he wants, using increasingly coarse sexual imagery to torture and anger him. Iago claims to have shared a room with Cassio recently and overheard him plotting with Desdemona in his sleep. Othello declares that he will "tear" Desdemona "all to pieces." Iago tells Othello that he has seen Cassio "wipe his beard" with Desdemona's handkerchief. The calm reason we associate with Othello seems to leave him as he calls for "blood, blood, blood!" and swears revenge. He kneels before Iago, emphasizing the shift in power between them. Iago swears allegiance to "wronged Othello" and agrees to kill Cassio.

ACT 3 SCENE 4

Lines 1–104: Desdemona and Emilia search for Cassio's lodgings, accompanied by the Clown, whose bantering creates a contrast with the violent emotions of the previous scene. Desdemona sends him to find Cassio. Emilia denies all knowledge of the lost handkerchief when Desdemona questions her, complicating her characterization with a potential shift from naïveté to deceit. Desdemona is worried that Othello will be put to "ill thinking" by the loss, but reassures herself that he is not a jealous man. Othello arrives and, in an aside that marks his withdrawal from their relationship, comments on how hard it is to "dissemble" as he tries to act normally. Desdemona, unaware, continues to petition for Cassio. Othello asks for her handkerchief and tells her its history: it was given to Othello's mother by an Egyptian "charmer" who told her that "while she kept it" it would "subdue" Othello's father "Entirely to her love." If she lost it, however, Othello's father "should hold her loathèd." Othello warns Desdemona that to lose the handkerchief would mean "perdition" and, noting her distress, demands to see it. Desdemona denies that it is lost and returns to the subject of Cassio. Othello leaves abruptly.

Lines 105–177: Iago urges Cassio to "importune" Desdemona. He does, but a bewildered Desdemona tells him that she has incurred Othello's "displeasure" and that "My lord is not my lord," emphasizing the apparent change in Othello's identity. Iago goes to find Othello. Desdemona convinces herself that Othello is troubled by state business, reasoning that she has never given him "cause" to be jealous. She tells Cassio to wait while she finds Othello.

Lines 178–217: When the women have gone, Cassio is approached by Bianca who flirts with him. He gives her Desdemona's handkerchief and asks her to copy the embroidery. She jealously assumes that it is a "token" from another woman, but he denies this, saying that he does not know whose it is, he just found it in his chamber. He promises to see Bianca soon.

ACT 4 SCENE 1

Lines 1–175: Iago continues to subtly increase Othello's fury through his use of sexual innuendo as he tells Othello that Cassio has the handkerchief and implies that he has confessed to sleeping with Desdemona. Although still uncertain, Othello's disjointed language shows the breakdown of his self-control. He falls down unconscious as Cassio arrives, and Iago claims that Othello has epilepsy, warning that he breaks into "savage madness" if woken from a fit, thus further undermining Othello's reputation. He suggests that Cassio return later. Othello wakes and Iago tells him to hide and listen in while he speaks to Cassio. Othello withdraws and Iago reveals that he is actually going to speak to Cassio about Bianca, knowing that reference to Bianca's love for him will make Cassio laugh. Cassio arrives and, briefly out of Othello's hearing, Iago refers to Bianca, causing Cassio to laugh. Their bawdy conversation continues, observed by Othello, whose asides reveal he believes them to be speaking about Desdemona. Bianca arrives unexpectedly and angrily returns the handkerchief to Cassio, insisting that it must be "some minx's token." She and Cassio leave.

Lines 176–302: Othello is convinced and declares that he will kill Desdemona. Iago urges him to "strangle her in her bed" and promises that he will kill Cassio. Desdemona arrives, bringing Lodovico with news from Venice. Othello appears calm, but Lodovico inquires after Cassio and Desdemona tells him about the "unkind breach" between them, innocently commenting on her own "love" for Cassio. Othello loses control and strikes Desdemona, calling her a "devil." Once Othello has left, Lodovico expresses shock and questions Othello's reputation as the "noble Moor," whose nature "passion could not shake," showing that Iago is managing to destroy Othello publicly as well as personally.

ACT 4 SCENE 2

Lines 1–189: Othello questions Emilia, who says that Desdemona is "honest, chaste and true" and insists that she cannot have been unfaithful. Othello sends her to fetch Desdemona, reflecting that he does not have to believe Emilia as she is "a simple bawd." Emilia shows Desdemona in and Othello tells her to guard the door. Sensing Othello's "fury," Desdemona is confused, especially when he asks her to swear that she is "honest." She begs to be told "what ignorant sin" she has committed, and Othello accuses her of being a "strumpet" and a "whore." Amazed, Desdemona denies this, but Othello is unmoved and leaves. Emilia tries to comfort Desdemona, but she replies distractedly and asks her to fetch Iago. Iago feigns concern and pretends to comfort Desdemona, while Emilia insists ironically that "Some busy and insinuating rogue" must have "devised this slander." Desdemona asks Iago to advise her and kneels before him as Othello did in Act 3 Scene 3, emphasizing his power over them both. Iago reassures her that Othello must be troubled by some "business of state" and sends her and Emilia in to supper.

Lines 190–258: Rodorigo arrives, accusing Iago of not dealing "justly" with him, accurately observing that Iago's "words and performances are no kin together." Despite this, Iago manages to talk him around, promising that he will "enjoy" Desdemona provided that he kills Cassio. He outlines a plan whereby the two of them will attack Cassio as he leaves Bianca's that night. Rodorigo seems unconvinced, and Iago leads him away, promising to explain further.

ACT 4 SCENE 3

Presenting a united front in public, Othello and Desdemona say goodbye to their visitor, Lodovico. Othello offers to escort him out, and tells Desdemona to dismiss Emilia and get to bed "on th' instant." The following scene is a tender exchange between the two women as Emilia prepares Desdemona for bed. Emilia has put Desdemona's wedding sheets on her bed at her request and Desdemona prophetically asks Emilia that, if she should die before her, she will shroud her in them. Desdemona sings the melancholy willow song that she learned from her mother's maid, aptly named "Barbary," who had been forsaken in love. The conversation turns to infidelity and Desdemona swears she would never be unfaithful to Othello, claiming she cannot understand why a woman would cheat on her husband. Showing a more pragmatic attitude, and perhaps advocating a more equal relationship between men and women, Emilia observes that many husbands are unfaithful and that the sexes are judged unequally.

ACT 5 SCENE 1

The setting of darkness means that the characters respond chiefly to what they hear, reflecting the role of rumor in the action of the wider play.

Iago and Rodorigo wait for Cassio. Iago conceals himself as Cassio arrives, and Rodorigo strikes with his sword. His blow fails, but Cassio retaliates, seriously wounding Rodorigo. As he does so, Iago, unseen, stabs Cassio in the leg. Cassio cries out and is heard by Othello, who recognizes his voice and assumes that Iago has killed him as promised. Gloating, he leaves to find Desdemona, promising that her "lust-stained" bed "shall with lust's blood be spotted." Lodovico and Gratiano arrive and, hearing Cassio and Rodorigo's cries, fear for their own safety. Iago enters with light and weapons, pretending that he has come to investigate the noise. Cassio hears Iago's voice and calls out. Feigning shock and concern for Cassio, Iago quickly finds Rodorigo and kills him under cover of the darkness, directly taking action for the first time in the play. He helps Cassio, asking Lodovico and Gratiano to assist him. They are joined by Bianca and then Emilia. As Cassio is carried out, Iago accuses Bianca of being behind the attack, saying that it is "the fruits of whoring." He sends Emilia to tell Othello and Desdemona.

ACT 5 SCENE 2

Lines 1–123: Othello approaches Desdemona's bed, holding a light—a visual symbol of the light/life, darkness/death imagery that runs throughout his soliloquy. He dwells on images of purity, such as alabaster and snow, and images of death, many of which have a sexual connotation, such as the plucked rose. He kisses Desdemona and his resolve almost breaks. She wakes and he tells her that she must pray, as he cannot kill her "unpreparèd spirit." Desdemona pleads with Othello, repeating that she does not love Cassio and did not give him the handkerchief. Othello informs her that Cassio is dead and, misunderstanding her innocent tears at this news, he smothers her. As he does so, Emilia calls for him. His calm certainty breaks down as he fluctuates between Emilia's calls and Desdemona's body. Eventually, he lets Emilia in.

Lines 124–270: Emilia reports that Cassio has killed Rodorigo, and Othello is dismayed to learn that Cassio is not dead. As they talk, Desdemona cries out, and, parting the bed curtains, Emilia finds her. Desdemona claims that she is "guiltless" and, denying Othello's responsibility for her murder, she dies. Othello, however, sees Desdemona's final act as further evidence that Desdemona is "a liar gone to burning hell" and tells Emilia that he killed his wife because "she was a whore." Emilia argues that Desdemona was "heavenly true" and Othello tells her that her own husband told him of Desdemona's affair with Cassio. Emilia is stunned and unable to say anything except "My husband?" for some time, before scornfully telling Othello that Iago lied and that he is a "gull." She calls for help. Montano, Gratiano, and Iago enter, and Emilia tells Iago that he "told a lie, an odious, damnèd lie," a sharp contrast to the label of honesty he has been given throughout the play. She announces that Desdemona is dead and Gratiano and Montano are horrified. Gratiano reveals that Brabantio has died in grief at his daughter's marriage. Othello insists that Desdemona was "foul" and unfaithful, and tells them that she gave Cassio the handkerchief. Despite Iago's threats, Emilia bravely reveals that she found the handkerchief and gave it to him. Othello tries to kill Iago, but Iago stabs Emilia and flees.

Lines 271–416: Emilia asks to be laid by her mistress's side. Montano tells Gratiano to guard "the Moor" while he pursues Iago. Emilia's last words are to assure Othello of Desdemona's innocence and her love for him. As Othello laments Desdemona's death, Lodovico and Montano bring in Iago as a prisoner and the wounded

Cassio. Othello stabs Iago but fails to kill him. With all the remaining characters assembled, the truth is established and evidence produced of Iago's villainy, but he refuses to explain himself and vows "From this time forth I never will speak word." Othello is stripped of his command and Cassio given leadership in Cyprus. As he is to be led away, Othello begs to be remembered as "one that loved not wisely but too well" before stabbing himself. He kisses Desdemona as he dies. Iago's punishment is for Cassio to decide. Lodovico recommends the use of torture while he returns immediately to Venice to report what has happened.

OTHELLO IN PERFORMANCE: THE RSC AND BEYOND

The best way to understand a Shakespeare play is to see it or ideally to participate in it. By examining a range of productions, we may gain a sense of the extraordinary variety of approaches and interpretations that are possible—a variety that gives Shakespeare his unique capacity to be reinvented and made "our contemporary" four centuries after his death.

We begin with a brief overview of the play's theatrical and cinematic life, offering historical perspectives on how it has been performed. We then analyze in more detail a series of productions staged over the last half-century by the Royal Shakespeare Company. The sense of dialogue between productions that can only occur when a company is dedicated to the revival and investigation of the Shakespeare canon over a long period, together with the uniquely comprehensive archival resource of promptbooks, program notes, reviews, and interviews held on behalf of the RSC at the Shakespeare Birthplace Trust in Stratford-upon-Avon, allows an "RSC stage history" to become a crucible in which the chemistry of the play can be explored.

Finally, we go to the horse's mouth. Modern theater is dominated by the figure of the director. He or she must hold together the whole play, whereas the actor must concentrate on his or her part. The director's viewpoint is therefore especially valuable. Shakespeare's plasticity is wonderfully revealed when we hear directors of highly successful productions answering the same questions in very different ways.

FOUR CENTURIES OF *OTHELLO*: AN OVERVIEW

Despite the theatrical challenges it presents, *Othello* has been performed almost continuously since the first recorded performance on

November 1, 1604, at the court of James I. This has resulted in a remarkably full performance history focused historically on the roles of Othello and Iago and, to a lesser extent, Desdemona. The uneven balance between the main parts, with Iago speaking 31 percent of the lines to Othello's 25 percent, has often resulted in a sort of theatrical contest between the two which a number of productions have capitalized on by having actors alternate the roles.

Richard Burbage, the leading tragedian with the King's Men, and the first Othello, was celebrated for his performance, described by an anonymous elegist as "his chiefest part, / Wherein beyond the rest he moved the heart." There is evidence that Iago was played by one of the company comedians, John Lowin.[1] A spectator of the performance by the King's Men at Oxford in 1610 records how the audience was moved "to tears" in the last scene when "that famous Desdemona, killed before us by her husband, although she always acted her whole part supremely well, when she was killed she was even more moving, for when she fell back upon the bed she implored the pity of the spectators by her very face."[2] Interestingly, neither Othello's color nor the fact that Desdemona was played by a boy was considered noteworthy. After Burbage's death, until the closure of the theaters in 1642 Othello was played by Ellyaerdt Swanston with Joseph Taylor as Iago. Since Taylor is also known to have inherited the role of Hamlet, this suggests that it was no longer regarded as a role for a comic actor.

Othello was one of the first plays to be performed after the Restoration and subsequent reopening of the theaters in 1660. It was assigned to the newly formed King's Men under Thomas Killigrew and hence avoided the radical rewriting of William Davenant, although promptbooks that survive for the next two centuries record a tendency to cut lines and sometimes whole scenes (such as Othello's fit and the eavesdropping scene) that came to be regarded as lacking in decorum.[3] Samuel Pepys saw a performance at the Phoenix, recording in his diary how the "very pretty lady that sat by me cried to see Desdemona smothered."[4] The Restoration theater introduced scenery and women actors, but the first recorded instance of a woman performing on the English stage was Margaret Hughes as Desdemona on December 8, 1660, so the production

Pepys saw in October which so moved the "pretty lady" must have been with a boy actor.

Othello was the part in which Thomas Betterton, the leading actor of the early eighteenth century, "excelled himself," according to Colley Cibber.[5] Judging by contemporary accounts, he was able to combine heroic and pathetic aspects of the character. Cibber talks of Betterton's "commanding mien of majesty" and the way in which his voice "gave more spirit to terror than the softer passions," whereas Richard Steele was struck by "the wonderful agony" in which he appeared "when he examined the circumstances of the handkerchief . . . the mixture of love that intruded upon his mind upon the innocent answers Desdemona makes."[6] If Othello was the noble Moor, Iago had to be irredeemably villainous; the actor specializing in such parts who played Iago to Betterton's Othello was Samuel Sandford, described by Cibber as "a low and crooked person" having "such bodily defects" as rendered him unsuitable for "great or amiable characters."[7]

Barton Booth, renowned for noble deportment and dignity, took over the part from Betterton, bringing charm and "manly sweetness" to the role and a grief in which his "tears broke from him."[8] The *Grub Street Journal* complained that Colley Cibber's Iago, by contrast, "shrugs up his shoulders, shakes his noddle, and with a fawning motion of his hands" drawls out his words so that "Othello must be supposed a fool, a stock, if he does not see through him."[9] James Quin, who succeeded Booth, was also noted for his dignity, whereas David Garrick, who revolutionized eighteenth-century acting with his ease and naturalness, failed in the part. His interpretation, described as suggesting rather "a man under the impression of fear, or on whom some bodily torture was inflicting, than one labouring under the emotions of such tumultuous passions,"[10] was clearly in advance of the times.

Contemporary criticism suggests a growing awareness of racial issues. The actor-dramatist Samuel Foote objected to Quin's performance, commenting: "Sure never has there been a character more generally misunderstood, both by audience and actor, than this before us, to mistake the most tender-hearted, compassionate, humane man, for a cruel, bloody, and obdurate savage,"[11] while

Quin in turn criticized Garrick's appearance in the part, for which he wore a turban, asking: "Why does he not bring the tea-kettle and lamp?"[12]—a reference to the "small black boy in a plumed turban holding a kettle in Hogarth's series *A Harlot's Progress*."[13] Garrick was more successful as one of several actors who played Iago to Spranger Barry's handsome, graceful Othello. Barry contrived by all accounts to be even more "sweet" and "comely"[14] than Booth. His performance, characterized by "blended passages of *rage* and *heartfelt affection*,"[15] was perfectly matched by Susanna Cibber's "expression of love, grief, tenderness"[16] as Desdemona.

A translation of the play in 1792 by Jean-François Ducis, in which the great French tragedian Talma played Othello, caught the mood of revolutionary France, coming a year after the successful slave revolt in the French colony of San Domingo (modern-day Haiti). Ducis' version was heavily cut and adapted. There was further cutting of the English text in the late eighteenth and early nineteenth centuries in the interests of propriety, which suited the neoclassical acting of John Philip Kemble, described by Hazlitt as "the very still-life and statuary of the stage."[17] His Othello was "grand and awful and pathetic, . . . European,"[18] despite his Moorish costume. However, Kemble's sister, Sarah Siddons, playing Desdemona, was warmly praised and given credit for a changed appreciation of the role in which she "established an interest and importance to that character which it had never possessed before."[19] Despite the beginnings of a changing critical perspective with regard to Iago, the part was still being played as "a pantomime villain,"[20] although Edmund Kean had given an innovative performance as "a gay, light-hearted monster, a careless, cordial, comfortable villain."[21]

Kean went on to play Othello for many years in a performance Leigh Hunt regarded as "the masterpiece of the living stage."[22] Like Garrick before him, Kean brought passion and naturalism to his roles, triumphing as Othello despite the limitations imposed by his physique.[23] He used relatively light makeup for the part in order for his facial expressions to be more easily visible. Kean's performance developed over the years and he continued to play the part until 1833, when he finally collapsed onstage into the arms of his son

2. "Talk you of killing?" Sarah Siddons as Desdemona at Drury Lane in 1785. Her performance established a new "interest and importance" to the part.

Charles, who was then playing Iago. By the time that William Charles Macready took over the role, there was a growing public debate over Othello's racial origins and the role of sexuality within the play. Macready had played Iago to Kean's Othello, but was "baffled"[24] when he took over the role.

Meanwhile, in New York, leading American tragedian Edwin Forrest played Othello at the Bowery Theater. He was so successful that he continued to play the part for forty years, visiting London with it in 1845. Although it was popular with audiences, many English critics objected to the violence of Forrest's performance. His biographer, William Rounesville Alger, argued for the legitimacy of Forrest's interpretation though, comparing it favorably with his predecessors and contemporaries.[25] There were also notable productions in mainland Europe. French actor Charles Fechter played the part in English at the Princess' Theatre in 1861 to mixed

3. "Were it my cue to fight, I should have known it / Without a prompter." Edmund Kean at Drury Lane Theatre, 1814. His Othello was "the master-piece of the living stage."

reviews. Novelist and critic Henry James greatly admired Tommaso Salvini's Othello, despite the "grotesque, unpardonable, abominable" practice of having him speak in his native Italian while the rest of the cast performed in English. James reflected upon the Italianate nature of Salvini's Othello: "No more complete picture of passion can be given to the stage in our day,— passion beginning in noble repose and spending itself in black insanity . . . Salvini's rendering of the part is the portrait of an African by an Italian; a fact which should give the judicious spectator, in advance, the pitch of the performance." He went on to contrast his performance with that of another notable Italian actor:

> In the Othello . . . of Salvini's distinguished countryman, Ernesto Rossi, there is . . . a kind of bestial fury . . . Rossi gloats in his tenderness and bellows in his pain. Salvini, though the simplicity, credulity, and impulsiveness of his personage are constantly before him, takes a higher line altogether; the personage is intensely human.[26]

While Forrest was playing Othello in the United States and England, the first black Othello, Ira Aldridge, played to packed houses across Europe, having previously played the role to acclaim in the English provinces and, for just two performances in April 1833, on the stage of Covent Garden in London. Touring in the years after the revolutions of 1848, Aldridge's performances were enthusiastically received, although criticism of his "naturalness" often suggests unconsciously racist attitudes: "In the role of Othello Mr Aldridge was extraordinary—he is a genuine tiger and one is terrified for the artists who play Desdemona and Iago, for it seems that actually they will come to harm."[27]

Henry Irving was another actor who found that Othello eluded him. In the 1881 Lyceum production he alternated Othello/Iago with Edwin Booth. Despite their different styles, Booth's traditional, classical style versus Irving's more modern naturalism, both actors won praise as Iago while disappointing as Othello. However, Irving's was recognized as "emphatically a new Iago,"[28] decisively changing attitudes to the role:

Mr. Irving's Iago conceals his inherent vileness and depravity under a frank, soldierly, swaggering manner. His reputation for honesty becomes readily intelligible; it arises from his rude, frank air, now cynical, now convivial, yet always really malevolent and vicious.[29]

The twentieth century confronted many of the play's problematic qualities. Critical attitudes toward Othello were radically revised in the light of T. S. Eliot's and F. R. Leavis' negative assessments of the character as egoistic and self-deluding. This made traditional portrayals of Othello's "nobility" difficult and tended to further accentuate the role of Iago. Race and racism became an issue in casting the play.

The African American singer and actor Paul Robeson played Othello at the Savoy in 1930 in a production hampered by a set and lighting that left the actors upstage and in the dark. Despite Robeson's imposing physical presence, Herbert Farjeon described him as "the under-dog from the start. The cares of 'Old Man River' were still upon him. He was a member of a subject race, still dragging the chains of his ancestors."[30] Peggy Ashcroft as Desdemona and Sybil Thorndike as Emilia were both praised for their performances. When Robeson came to reprise the role with greater success at the Shubert Theater, New York, in 1943 as America's first black Othello, he is reported to have told the director, Margaret Webster, that looking back on the earlier production he had felt so "overwhelmed by the thought of playing Shakespeare at all, especially in London, with his unmistakable American accent, that he never reached the point of looking Othello squarely in the eye."[31] Webster's influential and hugely successful production focused firmly on the issue of race and racism, permanently changing attitudes to the play.

Meanwhile, Tyrone Guthrie cast Ralph Richardson as Othello in his 1938 production at the Old Vic with Laurence Olivier as Iago. Guthrie and Olivier, influenced by Freudian psychology, saw Iago as motivated by repressed homosexual desire. The critics were generally severe:

Mr. Ralph Richardson . . . plays the Moor with skill, dignity and taste. He has a beautiful voice, and speaks his lines with

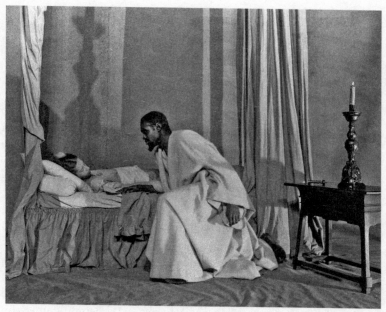

4."It is the cause, it is the cause, my soul": Paul Robeson, the first black actor since Ira Aldridge to play Othello in London, with Peggy Ashcroft at the Savoy, 1930.

understanding. But he fails to be heroic; his Othello inspires no awe; we are sorry for him, but we do not feel the profound pity that should extend from him to the whole condition of man; and the tragedy dwindles into a thriller about a villain who ruins an amiable and well-bred simpleton. The excessive mildness of the Othello is aggravated by the excessive liveliness of the Iago . . . We are shown, not a lion killed by a viper, but a virtuoso toreador playing a bull. And it is his exquisite accomplishment that we concentrate upon, not the blind processes of the victim.[32]

Orson Welles' 1951 production at St James Theatre, in which he starred and directed, attracted equally unflattering reviews. Blacking up by white actors, while not yet regarded as unacceptable, was now a source of humor:

The glad cry "The coalman cometh!" was suppressed with difficulty when Mr Orson Welles came on the stage as Othello, clad in a sooty costume of familiar cut that greatly amplified his already impressive frame . . . Mr. Welles is a stiff actor, apparently limited in gesture and expression, but he has dignity and a commanding voice. The speech to the Senate, spoken very quietly and naturally, is extremely effective and in the early scenes at Cyprus there is no question of Othello's military authority. But when he is on fire with jealousy Mr. Welles can only stand as if stunned, his eyes fixed and glaring. Then he looks lost, passion and poetry missing.[33]

Welles' film of the production the following year won first prize at the Cannes Film Festival.

In 1956 at the Old Vic, John Neville and Richard Burton alternated the roles of Othello and Iago, but neither managed Othello satisfactorily. John Gielgud played the part in Franco Zeffirelli's 1961 Stratford production. Despite the beauty of his vocal delivery, Gielgud was generally considered miscast. Three years later, Laurence Olivier played Othello in John Dexter's production for the National Theatre's inaugural season. Olivier famously did painstaking research on his voice and appearance. The production caused a sensation: "Many loved Olivier's performance. Many loathed it. No one could ignore it."[34] Doubts might be cast upon his preparations but not the power of his performance:

Whether the Negroid physiognomy which Olivier was at such pains to create was necessary to establish this character I take leave to question . . . But of the cathartic power and visible splendor of the performance there can be no doubt whatever.[35]

As another critic put it:

It could have been caricature, an embarrassment. Instead, after the second performance, a well-known Negro actor rose in the stalls bravoeing. For obviously it was done with love; with the main purpose of substituting for the dead grandeur of the Moorish empire one modern audiences could respond to: the grandeur of Africa. He was the continent, like a figure of Rubens' allegory.[36]

Since then, performances of the play with white actors blacking-up have become increasingly problematic. Donald Sinden at Stratford in 1979 and Paul Scofield at the National in 1980 attempted it, but, as Julie Hankey records, both "actually raised laughs at some of Othello's extravagant moments."[37]

In the earliest productions of the play, race does not seem to have figured largely—the main focus was on rank, the undoing of a superior by a malevolent subordinate. Judged in the light of the West's subsequent history of colonialism, it has become increasingly difficult to mount a successful production. The Ghanaian-born actor Hugh Quarshie has argued that the play is in fact inherently racist and that no black actor should attempt Othello.[38] The most successful recent productions have, however, cast black actors. In America, James Earl Jones first played Othello in 1964 at the New York Shakespeare Festival. His lack of classical training was seen as an obstacle that he was able to overcome "in the force and integrity of his delivery."[39] Reprising the role at the 1981 American Shakespeare Festival, Jones had grown in the part, although it was Christopher Plummer's Iago who gained most of the plaudits. Janet Suzman staged a production in apartheid South Africa at the Market Theatre, Johannesburg, in 1985 with John Kani as Othello, Richard Haines as Iago, and Joanna Weinberg as Desdemona as a deliberate challenge to the government's political ideology. It played for six weeks and was hugely successful with black and white audiences alike.

In Terry Hands' 1985 production for the RSC, Ben Kingsley played Othello to David Suchet's sexually ambiguous Iago. Much was made at the time of the rather pale-skinned Kingsley's mixed African-Indian heritage. In 1989 the Jamaican-born operatic bass-baritone Willard White was cast against Ian McKellen as Iago at the RSC's The Other Place. Sam Mendes cast David Harewood as Othello against Simon Russell Beale's Iago at the National Theatre in 1997. Two years later, Michael Attenborough directed Ray Fearon and Richard McCabe in an RSC production. In 2001, Doug Hughes cast

Keith David as Othello and Liev Schreiber as Iago at New York's Joseph Papp Public Theater. In 2004 Gregory Doran directed the black South African Sello Maake Ka-Ncube as Othello, with Antony Sher as Iago. The RSC productions are discussed below in more detail, but it would be fair to say that in all of these Iago was seen as dramatically more successful, begging questions about the balance between the roles in the writing and the policy of color-blind casting that now paradoxically applies to every role except Othello. Othello has become a superb opportunity for black performers, offering a breakthrough role for rising stars (such as Chiwetel Ejiofor in Michael Grandage's Donmar Warehouse production of 2008, with Ewan McGregor as Iago) and a change of direction for established figures (such as Willard White the opera singer and, in 2009, the comedian Lenny Henry, who was directed in the role by Barrie Rutter for Northern Broadsides). But it is, for now, a part from which white actors are barred. Jude Kelly's "photo-negative"Othello in 1997 in Washington, D.C., with Patrick Stewart's Othello as the only white cast member proved an interesting experiment while hardly providing a long-term solution.

Given the increasingly problematic nature of conventional productions, it is not surprising that a number of radical revisions, adaptations, and offshoots have been produced, including Murray Carlin's Not Now, Sweet Desdemona (1969), Jack Good's rock opera Catch My Soul (1970–71); Charles Marowitz's An Othello (1972), Paula Vogel's Desdemona: A Play About a Handkerchief (1979), Djanet Sears' Harlem Duet (1997), Caleen Sinnette Jennings' Casting Othello (1999), Andrew Davies' updated television adaptation Othello (2001), and Tim Blake Nelson's film "O" (2001). The most successful adaptation is undoubtedly Giuseppe Verdi's operatic masterpiece Otello (1887) in a genre which does not pretend to realism.

A wide range of film versions are available, including a fascinating 1922 German silent movie directed by the expatriate Russian Dimitri Buchowetzki, starring Emil Jannings and Werner Krauss. Orson Welles' 1952 film took four years to make owing to financial difficulties; using a heavily cut text and Welles' characteristically adventurous camera work, it was much more successful than the stage version. Russian director Sergei Yuttuvich produced his Russian adaptation in 1955 with Sergei Bondarchuk as Othello. In 1964, Stuart Burge filmed John Dexter's National Theatre production with Laurence Olivier, Frank Finlay, and Maggie Smith. Olivier's performance, while undeniably powerful, is disturbing in its appropriation of the black body[40] and looks dated. Trevor Nunn's (1990) RSC production at The Other Place with Willard White and Ian McKellen, with an American Civil War setting, fares better than Jonathan Miller's for the BBC starring Anthony Hopkins in the same year. Oliver Parker's 1995 film with Laurence Fishburne as Othello and Kenneth Branagh as Iago was highly acclaimed but is problematic in its own way: "Parker configures him [Othello] as a fascinating and useful outsider in Venice, a man whose power carries hints of an eroticism, derived from his arresting physicality . . . less the supreme exemplum of Venice than an exotic misfit within it."[41] However, the film belonged to Branagh. As one critic put it: "Kenneth Branagh doesn't just steal the show; one suspects he might have sat in the director's chair as well."[42]

AT THE RSC

"Haply, for I am black"

The great Irish actor Michéal MacLiammóir called *Othello* the "most passionately human of all Shakespeare plays."[43] Diving into a wealth of painful emotions, Shakespeare offers us an intense exploration of human relationships and frailties. By focusing on a limited number of characters in a claustrophobic setting there is no relief for the audience, who witness helplessly the vile destruction perpetrated by the worst emotional vandal in English literature. When done well, this can be an agonizing and almost unbearable experience in the theater.

Not by accident, Othello has a long history of audience intervention: of performances in which someone, forgetting that it is only a play, has stood up and tried to warn Othello against Iago, or to proclaim Desdemona's innocence.[44]

And yet, Othello has a rather checkered past in performance with very few productions touching that raw nerve, the open wound, that we sense when reading the play. Sexual jealousy was obviously something that Shakespeare understood well: Leontes' perplexing and irrational jealousy in *The Winter's Tale*; the strong emotional evidence we find in the *Sonnets*. There is an extraordinary realism in the behavior and feelings expressed in these works. Onstage, however, the problem lies not with believability, but with the two central characters. It has proved difficult to find two actors of equal strength and a director who can maintain the balance between them. If Iago dominates too easily, it can be detrimental to the actor playing Othello, diminishing the magnificence of the character so the impact of his fall is lessened.

Until recently, the actor playing Othello has had the further barrier of convincingly portraying a man of a different race, blacking up and adopting characteristics that can appear as racial stereotypes. As critic Michael Billington pointed out, this has led to fewer performances and a diminishing of the play's place among the greatest of tragedies:

> Othello has lately become the odd man out among Shakespeare's tragedies. Current racial sensitivity makes it virtually impossible to have a white actor blackening up as the hero.[45]

The RSC has not had a white actor playing Othello since 1979, but opinion is still heavily divided as to whether it would be acceptable at all in the twenty-first century to have an actor blacking up. With theater audiences made up of predominantly white, middle- and upper-class people, Bob Peck, who played Iago in 1979, pointed out that

> The controversial element in the play is the way in which an inter-racial marriage is used to force an audience, whose own prejudices are put into the mouth and actions of a very seductive and persuasive villain, to adopt a moral attitude towards its events.[46]

5. Donald Sinden blacked up for the role of Othello in the RSC's 1979 production directed by Ronald Eyre.

Writing a year later, this production's Othello, Donald Sinden, was sometimes alarmed by audience reaction:

> We tell ourselves it is usually those who are not very bright who feel it but I wonder . . . you felt sympathy going to Iago, you were fighting to keep that sympathy. They were nearly cheering him, egging him on, go on there, get the black man, like goading a bull. It was really sinister. All that talk of majesty and dignity in Othello meant nothing right here in Britain in 1980. They thought "He's black and a bloody fool to try and make it anyway."[47]

6. Sello Maake Ka-Ncube as Othello in the RSC's 2004 production directed by Gregory Doran capitalized on his African cultural heritage and the experience of growing up under apartheid in South Africa.

In 2004, Gregory Doran chose two South African actors who had been brought up under apartheid to play Othello and Iago, Sello Maake Ka-Ncube and Antony Sher.

Their experiences of living under a racist regime informed their performances, as Ka-Ncube explained:

> Certainly the play has powerful resonances for me as someone who grew up under Apartheid, but being an artist is always about taking risks and being black—whether you grew up in South Africa under Apartheid or in Manchester or as an African American—is about being at risk all the time. That's something you live with in a world that is defined by white men's standards.[48]

Reviewers picked up on this in his performance:

> . . . Ka-Ncube's Othello . . . wears an African beaded necklace under his jacket and, even before you glimpse that, you sense a

trace of cultural uncertainty beneath his proud, assured air. Though he doesn't flinch when his enraged new father-in-law accuses him of bewitching Desdemona, his abstemiously blank expression—eyes front—suggests this is not the first time he has taken racist flak. His own references to his unpolished speech sound genuinely self-deprecating, making his susceptibility the more credible when he is encouraged to doubt Desdemona's love.[49]

Sher used genuine examples of racist behavior he witnessed in his past:

> [something] we both use, which perhaps would not have come to us if we were not both South Africans, is when you really start to blow, when you say: "Arise, black vengeance." I remember, in rehearsals, you began reverting to an almost tribal ancestral behaviour, as if you were summoning the ancestors, which you do with stamping. That allows me, when you have your epileptic fit and are unconscious at my feet, to mimic and mock your tribal behaviour. That again, to me, feels very much from the South Africa of our youth, where white people would mock black people, or would simply not take you seriously, but would see something clown-like or apelike in that behaviour.[50]

The understanding that these two actors had of living in an overtly racist society obviously benefited them when tackling the play, producing powerful performances. However, most actors who have played Othello, black and white, don't consider the play a "tragedy of racism"—crimes of passion, after all, are committed by all races. Nevertheless, it is Othello's "otherness," the fact that he is an outsider, which gives Iago the advantage when working on his insecurities.

Ray Fearon, who played Othello in 1999, believed that the issue of race is essential but that having an actor of power was the most important thing:

> I don't believe in giving black actors the role. You give it to actors who are credible. You get someone of quality. But

Othello says, "I am Black." You can't get round that. He's black in a world of white people, insecure, other, paranoid. Only his blackness makes sense of the play. Because I'm black, I know how he feels. When I wear a pea cap and trainers, people just see me as a stereotypical black man. That attitude is going to take a long time to go away.[51]

Fearon being much younger than the traditional Othello, lines had to be cut with reference to age, but the sexual chemistry between Othello and Desdemona was much more pronounced:

Fearon is not the most profound of Othellos, but, thanks also to Waites's unaffected warmth, he is one of the most touching. I have seen more distraught Moors, but few who wailed and gasped and touched their Desdemonas with more feeling. It is not just a case of killing the thing he loves, but of hardly being able to let her out of his arms. And he compensates for his lack of weight by growing in charisma and fire. The man who half-drowns Iago in a ewer, or follows his furious yell of "goats and monkeys" with a torrent of spit directed at the wife he has just whacked round the chops, is not to be fooled with.[52]

The physicality of the play in its displays of affection and violence also makes it practical to have a black actor in the part of Othello, as Trevor Nunn, who directed a production for the RSC in 1989, pointed out:

Not only for political reasons, but for reasons of integrity to the play, and sheer theatrical practicality. A play that's so over-whelmingly about male-female relationships needs a physical relationship between Othello and Desdemona. And with a white actor in black make-up that's the one thing you can't have. If they touch each other, Othello comes off on Desdemona.[53]

In Nunn's production Othello's vocal control set him apart as much as his color:

Willard White, the black opera bass cast as Othello, often seems to be the only person on stage speaking verse, his utterances as rhythmically distinctive as his rich, dark vocal register. He gives life to the old cliché about "the Othello music": this towering, Negro general is as alien to the Venetians in his speech as in his physical appearance.[54]

In 1985, Ben Kingsley was the first non-Caucasian actor to play Othello at Stratford since Paul Robeson in 1959. Playing opposite David Suchet, the two actors were physically similar, dark-eyed and bearded, causing many critics to comment on the fact. Kingsley himself felt that "Othello and Iago are almost two faces of the same man . . . They are both suffering from the same psychological disturbance"[55]—hence Iago's ability to manipulate someone whom he understands completely. Although the set was abstract in design the costuming went for authenticity:

Terry Hands's production, and especially its costumes . . . reflect an Elizabethan society that used violence to achieve its ends and heroes to spearhead its conquests . . . The starting point for Kingsley's preparation was indeed a Moor and more particularly the portrait of the Moorish Ambassador to the court of Queen Elizabeth I.[56]

All reviewers mentioned the impressive impact of Kingsley's first entrance as an Arab Moor:

On to the stage of midnight black, with everyone on it wearing black, steps a strange aloof figure in a dazzling white robe. A grey bearded ancient, mysteriously smiling, he might be some grave Indian mystic on a visit to an unknown planet.[57]

He enters with solemn tread, wins the Senate over with humor (even clicking his teeth as he talks of "the cannibals that each other eat") and dotes crazily on his Desdemona. This is a man, ageing and ringlet-locked, who has invested all his happiness in a young bride . . . and who is thrown into chaos by doubt.[58]

A Military Life

> From a technical viewpoint, *Othello* makes no special demands in staging. The emotions tapped in the play—love, hate, jealousy, envy—are so elemental that elaborate settings may actually detract from the bare display of them. Scene changes are likely . . . to break the momentum . . . The realism of the play lies in its emotional development, not in scenery.[59]

This statement was proved when in 1961 Franco Zeffirelli staged *Othello* in full Venetian splendor. Elaborate sets with massive scene changes may have given the stage the genuine look of Renaissance Italy, but killed the sense of claustrophobia and unstoppable momentum, and completely dwarfed the actors' performances.

One of the major difficulties has been to balance the play's public dimension with the personal space of private emotion:

> The gradual narrowing of the play's locales is but one contributor to the play's remorseless focusing on the personal lives of the main characters: life in the great Mediterranean city contracts to a beleaguered island and its frightened populace, then to the rooms in Othello's headquarters, and then to the marriage bed round which the curtains are finally drawn to shut out the sight of the pain that can ultimately be only personal.[60]

Ralph Koltai, designer of Terry Hands' 1985 production, went for a minimalist interpretation. The characters were in Elizabethan dress, but the setting consisted of a black stage with "smoked-perspex screens edged with gold,"[61] behind which sat "sculptural emblems of a Cypriot crucifix later replaced by a dangerously resting gold lion,"[62] an emblem of Venetian imperialism.

> There is little stage furniture, scarcely any attempt at social realism. A few flickers of light on the back wall suggest Venice; the storm that marks Othello's arrival at Cyprus, brilliantly taking its cue in a welcome suggestion of diabolism from Iago's "Hell and night / Must bring this monstrous birth to the world's light," is the only big production number: lights blindingly

flash, the noises of thunder are theatrical rather than natural. The overall effect of the design . . . is to release the play from local associations and to put the focus very much on the actors, who perform urgently, with a high degree of psychological realism.[63]

Starting with John Barton in 1971, most recent productions have emphasized the military setting of the play. Thus the public element remains without taking away from the intimacy of the action. With this genuine sense of army life we get important distinctions in rank from costume, rules of conduct influencing characters' behavior, and the isolating effect of the army barracks on Desdemona.

Julia Trevelyan Oman, designer of the 1971 production set in the nineteenth century, was influenced by early war photographs from the Crimea and American Civil War:

> They represent the past, but the near past, and the uniforms and background details still have a poignant reality and emotional appeal for us . . . I see Cyprus as a remote dusty army outpost cut off from civilisation, and Othello himself as a soldier as different in manner and dress from the other professionals in his army as Napoleon or Rommel from theirs.[64]

> In this barrack atmosphere, heavy with the celibate fantasies of men herded together in heat, it's easy to understand why Othello should trust his senior NCO more than his new bride from home; how jealousy might crackle through his imagination like fire through a dry thorn-bush. Meaning is restored to the play's talk of honour, reputation. Where else, today, but in the Army could we accept a drunken fight spelling disgrace for Cassio or a man regarding his wife's infidelity as the ruin of his career?[65]

Michael Attenborough's 1999 production used an Edwardian militaristic world with special attention paid to the inevitable tensions and jealousies of army life:

> Cyprus feels like a British colonial outpost with soldiers in red tunics, Desdemona in a muslin dress and army bands playing in the distance: as in *Much Ado*, it strikes me that Shakespeare

understood the peculiar danger of the aftermath of conflict
when leisure afternoons are filled with malice and mischief . . .
it is the military context that gives resonance to [Richard]
McCabe's wonderfully observed Iago . . . When Cassio taunts
him with the fact that the lieutenant must be saved before the
ensign, you see a look of pure hate, quickly masked, flash
across McCabe's eyes. . . . [66]

Stephen Brimson Lewis' set in 2004 intensified the sense of claustrophobia in the play by having "a framework of rusting, corrugated
iron and a wire fence, [which] vividly suggests a decaying end of
empire location, a military stockade behind which Othello and his
men retreat."[67]

The army barracks become a microcosm of Venetian life isolated
within enemy territory. Trevor Nunn's production in 1989 also
hinted at the tensions outside the barrack walls:

. . . costumed by Bob Crowley in a style suggestive of Chekhov
crossed with the American Civil War . . . Watch-dogs bark,
clocks chime, while in Cyprus—a place, we are reminded, with
larger racial tensions of its own—the cicadas are periodically
silenced not only by distant church music, but the muezzin's
call to prayer.[68]

The influence of the military on personality was vividly demon-
strated in Trevor Nunn's 1989 production, performed in the inten-
sity of a studio theater, The Other Place:

Cyprus is clearly defined as a simmering colonial outpost
where the women fuss over the barley-water while the men get
on with post-war admin . . . [Ian] McKellen [as Iago] is the
absolute embodiment of the professional soldier: every detail is
correct down to the little baccy-tin for half-smoked cheroots
and the obsessive way he tidies his barrack-room blankets.[69]

McKellen's performance in 1989 was noted for this fastidiousness
born out of army life:

Psychotically unable to tolerate disorder, Iago is perpetually
tidying up the barracks, righting overturned chairs, pouncing
on the litter. For this "model" NCO, the marriage of Desdemona and black Othello, an even more conspicuous irregular-
ity in his world, naturally demands eradicating too . . .
Unsmiling, the least jocular of Iagos, McKellen establishes no
rapport with the audience—something of a feat in The Other
Place—let alone the usual sense of complicity. In this terrifying performance, asides, like soliloquies, are private, echoing
inside the desert of his head.[70]

This militarism and precision of Iago's devices is what makes the
man so chilling. In 2004, Antony Sher's

knowing, nudging, darkly funny performance invites us to
appreciate the intricate mechanics of destruction. And in his
modern khaki his Iago looks like a chunky, florid blend of an
Afrikaner cop and the moustached Hitler; but nobody could
more subtly use concern, helpfulness, moral indignation and
blunt soldierly decency to lure a man and a marriage on to the
rocks. It's awful and it's impressive.[71]

A Woman's Place

In a military world the role of women is marginalized, although
clearly defined. As in John Barton's 1971 production, the effect is to

isolate and make Desdemona more vulnerable, and the innate
brutality of the play more obviously naturalistic.[72]

The daily life of an army on active service is as foreign and
exotic to Desdemona as is her new-made lord. Any support
from family, friends and the only society she has known as a
gently-nurtured aristocratic girl is removed from her by her
voyage to Cyprus, leaving her with only the intimacy of Emilia,
whose allegiance is at least partially to her husband. Of course,
to Othello the camp has always been the centre of his exis-

tence; but this particular camp environment is rendered unfamiliar by the presence of a wife.[73]

Women are by definition excluded from the battlefield and barracks. Kept in the bedroom and at the dinner table, they share neither the same experiences nor the same intimacies. No wonder the husbands . . . relate more intensely to their fellows than to their wives.[74]

In 2004, Greg Doran created

a predominantly male, militaristic society in which women are either romanticised or treated as whores. Lisa Dillon's fragile, loyal, indisputably loving Desdemona wanders into this world like a rose waiting to be crushed. And Amanda Harris's Emilia . . . is a perfect portrayal of the hardened service wife who has long learned to adjust to this brutal male ethos.[75]

The attitude toward women was portrayed as disturbingly misogynist:

The Venetian soldiers . . . are so sloppily dressed they look as if they'd have trouble controlling Mykonos, let alone Cyprus; but they're a nasty lot, who punch Nathalie Armin's harmless Bianca and push around the Islamic women who gather on cushions at the front of the stage or lurk behind steel netting at its rear.[76]

This issue of Iago's repulsion toward physical contact with his wife has been played as disgust at her supposed infidelity, and as a homosexual leaning, but is also indicative of the redundancy of these women in a man's world. Michael Attenborough's attention to this fact was highly praised when he directed Othello in 1999:

The virtue of this production is that it creates a militaristic world where women's needs and desires go unrecognised: the drinking-scene, in particular, is beautifully staged with the

men engaging in bizarre quasi-homosexual rituals. And part
of Iago's tragedy is that he is so much a creature of this world
that he sees women as little more than sexual objects waiting
to be crushed.[77]

Of course, Iago is severely psychologically twisted; his view of everyone, but especially women, rancid with images of bestiality. One
instantly pities Emilia. In 2004, what incited Antony Sher's Iago was

a disgusted fascination with sex. Amanda Harris's excellent
Emilia, his embittered wife, repels him so much that his fingers
move into strangling mode before they readjust into shoulder
massage.[78]

His jealousy of Emilia is only proprietorial. Here . . . Harris's
performance brilliantly fills in the picture. She is tense and
tired, smokes nervously, takes the odd tipple and is clearly
bored to the gills with Iago's wise-guy joviality and heavy-
handed sex jokes. In this marriage, she is an object, but a dangerous object: at the end Iago stabs her in the genitals.[79]

In 1985:

The Emilia of Janet Dale is a marvellous study in rejected sexuality, canoodling her way for a fleet moment into Iago's favour
with the procured handkerchief only to find herself spun from
the embrace in a premonition of [Ben] Kingsley's "turn, turn,
turn" humiliation of Desdemona which leads to a truly shocking slap on the face.[80]

At the beginning of the play, Othello's demonstrative affection for his
new bride distinctly marks out his behavior as different from the rest
of his command. In 1999:

Military discipline and ceremonial are the façade cracked open
by Othello's infatuation with Desdemona. The obliviousness of
Fearon's Othello to the embarrassment of Lieutenant Cassio

(Henry Ian Cusick) at his hungry fondlings of Desdemona on the quayside makes it more than usually credible that he should be so blind to Iago.[81]

As Iago's poison works on Othello we see his behavior and language toward women change. Othello physically demonstrates the bestial behavior which Iago only thinks and talks about. They become two sides of the same jealous monster. In 1979:

> Sinden conveys the ecstasy of jealousy with splendid conviction. At one point he is reduced to emptying his wife's laundry basket and sniffing the sheets for evidence of copulation. And he carries the humiliation of Desdemona further than I have ever seen by threatening to tup her in front of Emilia and by hurling her contemptuously to the ground in front of the Venetian visitors.[82]

Shakespeare presents us with two women at either end of the scale, one who has suffered at the hands of a brute, and is worldly-wise through her experiences as both abused and army wife, and one new to that lifestyle and marriage. Imogen Stubbs as Desdemona in Trevor Nunn's production was very girlish in nature:

> There is an apt sense of Desdemona the daughter about this interpretation. Her teasing and cajoling manner is that of a favourite young girl playing up to her daddy. As well as emphasising the generation gap, it helps Iago when he opportunistically reminds Othello how she was false to her father in Venice in order to get away from his arms.[83]

> hurling herself prematurely into an adult world, [Desdemona] is fragile, lovely, spoilt, manipulatively aware of her charm, and very young . . . On the quayside, waiting for Othello, her flippant exchanges with Iago reveal a deep uncertainty as to how a married woman ought to behave under such circumstance, and end in tears.[84]

The development of the relationship between Desdemona and Zoë Wanamaker's Emilia in this production was given an added depth, poignancy, and focus. Traditionally, she is portrayed as the "warm, motherly Emilia,"[85] but more recent productions have cast women with less of an age difference in the two roles. In 1989, the two women started out as strangers, Emilia being reluctantly assigned to the task of companion-cum-maid. This made better sense of the fact that Emilia doesn't admit to Desdemona that the handkerchief has been taken:

> [She] seemed to be jealous of a relationship which made her acutely aware of the inadequacy of her own marriage. When Emilia denies to Desdemona any knowledge of what has happened to the handkerchief, it can be an uncomfortable moment inconsistent with loyal friendship, but for Zoë Wanamaker it read powerfully as a moment in which she was prepared to have Desdemona suffer a little of the marital disharmony that for Emilia was habitual.[86]

The willow song scene acted as a breaking down of the divisions between the two women. At first reluctant to emotionally engage with this inexperienced girl, even pushing her arms from her when Desdemona hugs her for comfort, their shared experience betrayed a developing bond. In a clever piece of directing, the two women were linked in the final scenes by combining their voices. After smothering Desdemona with his hand, Willard White's Othello lay back on the bed, distraught. Outside Emilia was heard calling gently "My lord, my lord." In a voice almost spectral in its urgency and tone, Othello believed that he was hearing Desdemona's voice, took the pillow and then smothered her again. As Desdemona struggled to utter her last words, Emilia helped her by completing her sentences.[87]

> She berates Othello and as her own culpability is revealed she displays remarkable courage and moral strength. For Zoë Wanamaker, this was all the more powerful because of the absence of any easy sentimentality in her earlier relationship with Desdemona.[88]

Significantly, Emilia was left dead on the floor, ignored by those present, with no word of her sacrifice.

A Mind Diseased

On playing the role of Iago, David Suchet commented:

> Actors seem to have latched on to one quality and played that—the smiling villain, the devil's agent, the latent homosexual. Or you get the cold, objective playwright Iago, the one who creates the action. One thing I have discovered this first week is that any of those interpretations will work—up to a certain point. Then it would be a struggle to maintain it for the rest of the play. Studying the text very carefully one notices that Shakespeare himself has not got a clear line on Iago. If he had, it would be clear.[89]

Shakespeare endows Iago with a psychological condition beyond most people's understanding. He gives no clear line with him because there *is* no clear line with a self-absorbed psychotic. The audience is taken on a disturbing journey into the mind of someone suffering a mental disturbance, and is left with the realization that the only genuine reason for his behavior lies in his own twisted nature, which is unfathomable. Actors playing Iago have picked up on certain elements of character that are evident in the text to give themselves an accessible psychological route into this dark void of a man.

Like many real-life serial killers, he shows one face to the world while being a completely different character underneath. He wishes to tear apart all that is beautiful, pure, and honorable. Bob Peck, who played the part in 1979, stated that Iago, completely aware of his own corruption,

> seems to me to be a man whose life of deception and fraud is so repugnant to him that he can't bear to see virtue, compassion, love or anything of positive moral good in others.[90]

Iago is a man who has structured his life on the principle that human beings are merely animals. For him, words like "nobility," "honour," "self-sacrifice" and "love" are shams . . . And yet Iago is not quite secure in his cynicism. Styles of life which argue against him constitute a personal affront. In order to preserve his own self-respect, to avoid becoming ugly even in his own eyes, he must either prove that they are hypocritical, or else destroy them. This is why he needs to turn Desdemona's virtue into pitch, to make Cassio drunk, and to drag Othello down until he is speaking Iago's characteristic language of "goats and monkeys" instead of his own.[91]

Bob Peck's performance had picked up on the image of the tough, reliable, and jovial NCO. Like most modern Iagos, he spoke with a regional accent to indicate his class—and another reason for hatred:

> Far from being an incarnation of motiveless malice, he is intensely jealous, crudely ambitious and utterly callous, a hate machine created by the slow, dehumanising process of professional warfare.[92]

He played the part with far more humor than usual, involving the audience and chuckling over his achievements, setting himself up from the start as the arch manipulator:

> During Iago's first major soliloquy, the one where he sets up the plan to destroy Othello and his rather shaky alibi for so doing, [Ronald] Eyre has the other four principals concerned. Emilia, Desdemona, Cassio and the Moor himself line up silently on stage behind him, so that Iago may view them almost as if they were waxworks before arranging them into his evil patterns.[93]

Iagos have varied enormously, but they remain constant in their emphasis on one thing—sexual jealousy. Richard McCabe pointed out:

> Iago's psychosis runs far deeper than mere ambition . . . Here is a man consumed by professional and personal jealousy to the point of destruction.[94]

When comforting Desdemona in Act 4 Scene 2, McCabe's Iago held her in his arms:

> the more I played the sympathetic uncle figure, the more repulsive it became . . . The effect on my Iago, though, was devastating . . . Many killers prefer not to think of their victims as real human beings as this can trigger a moral sense within them. So I let out a gasp, contorted my body from its customary ramrod erectness, and turned upstage as if to hide the effect my internal conflict was revealing . . . [95]

Similarly, in 1989, Ian McKellen rocked Desdemona gently in his arms and stroked her hair as if taking some perverse sexual pleasure from touching the wife of his enemy.

In 2004, Antony Sher's Iago,

> when briefly alone in Desdemona's dressing room . . . stealthily kisses a dress hanging in her wardrobe trunk. Women and their sexuality are fascinating, but alien and threatening . . . [96]

Conversely, in 1985, David Suchet followed

> a Freudian line by implying Iago is deeply in love with Othello and manically jealous of Desdemona. Instead of gloating over the pole-axed, epileptic hero, he stands over him stroking his hair and urging him on to virile revenge . . . giving us a deeply masculine homosexual prone to sudden, terrifying glimpses into his own iniquity: when he cries "Men should be what they seem / Or those that be not, would they might seem none" he stops short like a man who has peered into the abyss.[97]

He suggested

> a deep vein of fellow feeling with his commander, as if he sought to educate him in manly detachment. It is a deeply human reading of a deeply inhuman character.[98]

at the death of Othello he makes a last impulsive gesture to embrace the corpse before letting his head fall, as though his own life has now run out . . . the Satanic element has been suppressed in pursuit of an explanation not really supplied by the text.[99]

Suchet here again broke with tradition, surprising his audience who expected to see the stony-faced or gloating Iago at the end of the play, demonstrating no remorse or regret, unreadable to the last. In 1989 the effect of Iago's final stare left the audience chilled with the conviction that they were in the company of a complete sociopath:

here is an arresting final image of the pinioned Iago gazing down on the death-loaded bed, not with any hint of snickering triumph but with a blank astonishment at the havoc he has created. There is no hint of pity. Instead Ian McKellen's countenance suggests the inhuman detachment and moral vacuum of the murderer surveying his victims.[100]

THE DIRECTOR'S CUT: INTERVIEWS WITH TREVOR NUNN AND MICHAEL ATTENBOROUGH

Sir Trevor Nunn is the most successful and one of the most highly regarded of modern British theater directors. Born in 1940, he was a brilliant student at Cambridge, strongly influenced by the literary close reading of Dr. F. R. Leavis. At the age of just twenty-eight he succeeded Peter Hall as artistic director of the RSC, where he remained until 1978. He greatly expanded the range of the company's work and its ambition in terms of venues and touring. He also achieved huge success in musical theater and subsequently became artistic director of the National Theatre in London. His productions are always full of textual insights, while being clean and elegant in design. Among his most admired Shakespearean work has been a series of tragedies with Ian McKellen in leading roles: *Macbeth* (1976, with Judi Dench, in the dark, intimate space of The Other Place), *Othello* (1989, with McKellen as Iago and Imogen Stubbs as Desdemona), discussed here, and *King Lear* (2007, in the

Stratford Complete Works Festival, on world tour, and then in London).

Michael Attenborough, born in 1950 to a distinguished theatrical family, graduated from Sussex University in 1972 and worked as associate director at the Mercury Theatre, Colchester, from 1972 to 1974. He was artistic director of the Leeds (now West Yorkshire) Playhouse from 1974 to 1979, associate director of the Young Vic from 1979 to 1980, artistic director of the Palace Theatre, Watford, from 1980 to 1983, and director of the Hampstead Theatre from 1984 to 1989, which won twenty-three awards during his tenure. In 1989 he was appointed artistic director of the Turnstyle Group in the West End and then, in 1990, resident director and executive producer of the Royal Shakespeare Company, becoming principal associate director in 1996. In July 2002 he was appointed artistic director of London's Almeida Theatre. He is also joint vice-chairman of the Royal Academy of Dramatic Art and an honorary associate artist of the RSC. Originally seen as specializing in directing new writing, he rapidly established himself as a sensual, non-flashy director of Shakespeare's plays. He directed *Othello* for the RSC in 1999 with Ray Fearon as Othello, Richard McCabe as Iago, and Zoë Waites as Desdemona.

Does Iago lie to the audience? Are we really supposed to believe his accusations about both Othello and Cassio cuckolding him? Also with regard to Iago: his language is full of sexual imagery throughout the play. How much of a clue to his character does that give you?

TN: The question of yours I feel impelled to start with is whether or not we are "supposed to believe" Iago's accusations about being cuckolded by Othello and Cassio; in my view, this question comes closest to discovering and defining what Shakespeare is exploring. Shakespeare frequently chose a "theme" on and around which he would compose a complex dramatic debate, after having selected a "story" which could provide him with his necessary range of opportunities. So *Romeo and Juliet* is his play about "Love," which involves Shakespeare in an equal and necessary exploration of "Hate" and the interconnection of these feelings. *Hamlet* is his play about

"Death"—from a ghost returning to address the living, to a bourn from which no traveler returns, to suicide, to a grave littered with decomposing skulls—but it's a discussion which involves Shakespeare in an exploration too of the will to live, and resolutions of how to live with the knowledge of mortality.

In this way, *Othello* is self-evidently Shakespeare's play about "Jealousy" but that subject draws him to an equal and necessary investigation of the concept of "Trust." "Honest" Iago is trusted by his commander, his colleagues, by Rodorigo, by Desdemona and, with misgivings, by Emilia. Iago's scheme is to stir Othello into jealousy, to increase that jealousy to such an extreme that there can only be violent consequences. But in Shakespeare's play about jealousy, the most jealous character is not Othello, but Iago.

"Honest" Iago is jealous of the Moor, jealous of Cassio for achieving the promotion Iago hoped for, and jealous of the physical sublimation that marriage has given Desdemona and Othello. His jealousy finds expression in suspicion, bile, and contempt, and accordingly he plays with the idea that both the men he hates have slept with his wife.

Very early on in his writing career, Shakespeare discovered the energy and frisson that derives from a character intent on wickedness, sharing his (or her) intentions directly with the audience. Aaron and Tamora share with us their hidden malevolence, Richard III lets us delightedly into his darkly comic view of life, and so on throughout the canon until *King Lear*, where Edmund capitalizes on engaging our sympathy and support for "bastards." But the most daring and outrageous use of this device is in the writing of Iago; Shakespeare invites us to see the surrounding world through Iago's eyes, and therefore to find his willingness to confide in us alluring, funny, and a kind of privilege. We are aware that we are in a dangerous relationship, that we are spending time with somebody whose magnetism is thrilling but who is requiring us to compromise our sense of morality, increasingly with each implicating soliloquy.

MA: Well, he puts both those accusations of cuckoldry as *possibilities*. I don't think he swears that it's happened. It is conjecture, and even if they haven't, it suits him to believe that they have. So, no, I don't think he lies to the audience. I think what he reveals to the audience is the scale of his insecurity. I think it's obvious neither of those things has happened, but it's not obvious to *him*. It is an imagined truth, but to the paranoid person there's no difference between imagination and truth. I don't think he's lying, I think it suits his paranoia.

The sexual imagery is probably the biggest clue of all. The play is about Iago's jealousy. Like poison poured in the ear, he poisons Othello with language, with persuasion. He's so clever with language, and it's fascinating that as Othello turns, he starts talking like Iago: "goats and monkeys" and in the "brothel scene" [Act 4 Scene 2] when he talks about "a cistern for foul toads," it could be Iago talking.

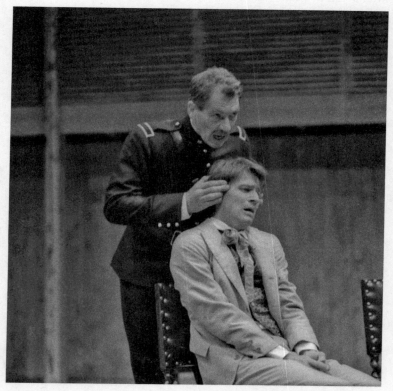

7. Ian McKellen as "Honest Iago" in Trevor Nunn's 1989 production at The Other Place with Michael Grandage as Rodorigo.

But the reason I say that it is the most important clue is that I suspect Iago's biggest insecurity is sexual, even bigger than his professional insecurity. Shakespeare couldn't be clearer; we get the biggest, clearest window into his personality from Emilia. When she talks very emotionally in that key speech in Act 4 Scene 3 it's clearly all about her relationship with Iago. We get a picture of a man who knocks her around, who's cruel, who's staggeringly jealous, and who is promiscuous with whores. In a way, he has the same kind of emotional immaturity as Othello, but he's twenty times cleverer, more devious and more malicious. But the nature of jealousy, the springboard, the flower bed from which jealousy happens is clearly insecurity. We would know that. We become jealous in our own relationships because we're insecure about ourselves. I think Iago's sexual insecurity is absolutely huge. What his language portrays is a fascination with sex, but also disgust. He never talks about it beautifully. He talks about it in ugly, animalistic, bestial, purely sexual terms—he *never* talks about love. And that's why I think it's the biggest clue of all.

Since Paul Robeson played the part of Othello, race has been a big issue for the play, in terms of both casting and interpretation. Where did you stand on this?

TN: Ours was the first RSC production, and possibly the first in England since Paul Robeson at Stratford, to cast a black artist in the title role. As director, I could not possibly have gone ahead with the production if I had failed to find the casting of an artist of color to play the central role. The days of the acceptability of white actors wearing black makeup had gone by the end of the 1970s, even though there were few candidates in those days who were qualified by experience or training to provide the authenticity that roles like Aaron and Othello so clearly demanded.

I was very fortunate to encounter the magnificent Jamaican-born opera singer Willard White at Glyndebourne, when we worked together on Gershwin's epoch-making and culture-defining *Porgy and Bess*. It was clear to me that Willard was as much an extraordinarily imaginative and daring actor as he was a uniquely mellifluous bass-baritone. So, yes, Paul Robeson revisited, though it wasn't until after we had opened *Othello* that I realized that Robeson had actually been the last black artist to play the part in England. I reasoned with Willard that if he was ever to play Othello, it would have to be in the theater because Verdi's account of the role makes him (unaccountably) a tenor, and Willard, as I said, is a glorious bass-baritone.

MA: One of the things that I profoundly disagree with is Coleridge's statement about Iago's "*motiveless* malignity." I think what Shakespeare actually does is to provide so many motives—some of them fantastical, some of them made up, some of them paranoid, some of them real (like, for example, Cassio's promotion)—that race becomes one of a number of factors. I think the play is not about Othello's jealousy, but about Iago's jealousy; the fact that this black chap has succeeded both sexually and professionally faster than he has is simply another element of that. Yes, Iago is a racist. Yes, Brabantio turns out to be a racist, having sat around the fireside happily with Desdemona and Othello. But it's clearly not a fully racist society in Venice: they're very proud of Othello. I suspect there's a degree of making a virtue of necessity: he's clearly the most able soldier and therefore they have to accept him, but there's no sense of an incipient racism there; nor indeed from any of the other characters like Rodorigo or Cassio. I think the point about racism is how it fits with Iago's make-up, personality, neuroses. One of the extraordinary things about Shakespeare's writing is that he managed to grasp hold of several stereotypes—which we still wrestle with four hundred years later—and render them human. The Jew in Shylock, color in Othello, and indeed women; he expands and humanizes the whole notion of being a Shrew. And so while he does grasp the issue of racism, I don't think it's a play *about* racism.

Historically, Desdemona has traditionally been represented in terms of innocence and victimhood, but in more recent times more attention has perhaps been paid to her independence of spirit and adventurousness—she rebels against her father and insists on going to Cyprus. Was yours a spunky Desdemona?

TN: How Desdemona came to be seen and presented—as in Verdi's *Otello*—as a creature of angelic innocence is bewildering when so much evidence points in a different direction. Certainly in our production, we stressed that it was Brabantio's trust in Desdemona that had been betrayed, that she had colluded to the full in the elopement, both out of her independence and a sense of adventure, and indeed out of passionate feelings of love in anticipation of sexual and sensual fulfillment.

We explored how different the reality of Cyprus was for Desdemona, compared with her imaginings. In our production, she found herself in a military fort on the edge of civilization, surrounded entirely by sex-starved men in uniform who were, almost without exception, undressing her with their eyes whenever she appeared, and making her the subject of ribald fantasy. In this world of sexual tension, Emilia represents a haven, and Cassio appears to be a mild-mannered articulate young man (obviously with no head for alcohol) who is something of an exception to the rule.

MA: Yes. It was one of the reasons why I wanted to do the play. Zoë Waites had been a very spirited Juliet. I think Juliet is much more intelligent and imaginative than Romeo, and I wanted the same scale of pluck, intelligence, imagination, independence, and sheer bloody fight. Desdemona is the victim of the play, but she's not to be played as a victim. She, also, is blinkered; she's blinkered because even in the scene with Emilia she still religiously believes in Othello, despite the fact that he's attacked her. But, that aside, she's a very bright kid. One of the genius moments in the writing, and genius moments from Iago, is when he says to Othello in Act 3 Scene 3, "She deceived her father brilliantly, why do you think she couldn't deceive you?" He turns her intelligence, her sophistication, and her ability against Othello. Iago has spotted that Desdemona is shrewd and bright and no fool at all. It seems to me to dilute and weaken the play if she's played in any way as passive.

In the "brothel scene" I did something which I would never have done with two actors whom I didn't know very well. We were only in the second week of rehearsals; we had a rough physical shape for the scene and we knew what we wanted it to be about—Othello torn between love and hate. It was fundamentally a scene about him punishing her, but then finding at least half a dozen moments where his whole stomach turns over and he thinks, "Oh my God, you're beautiful," or "Oh my God, I love you so much." The truth of the situation just wells up in his stomach and grabs him by the throat. The actors were still on the book and I said (and it's about as complicated a scene as there is in the play), "Look, let's just throw ourselves at it." It was one of the most astonishing things I have ever seen in a rehearsal room. It just blew the top of your head off. I was crying, the stage manager was crying, it was astonishing. And the reason for that was that those two actors had no problem with being completely vulnerable. And yet they were very specific with the text, it wasn't just generalized emotion. That version of the scene never really changed. We refined it, but that sense of these huge surges of love, anger, and terror never really altered. There would have been no point in rehearsing that way if Desdemona wasn't, at one level or other, Othello's equal.

How important do you see the age gap between Othello and Desdemona, and how did that affect your casting of the roles?

TN: I had a rarely advantageous situation to build upon then, an actor to play Othello of magnificent handsome appearance, with a voice that stopped all other conversation the moment he entered a room, a man of international expertise and indomitable courage as he had conquered opera audiences around the globe.

He was twenty or so years older than his Desdemona, an age differential that I think is absolutely fundamental to the play. The fact that Othello describes himself as "declined / Into the vale of years" reveals that he is conscious of being no longer young, having won a bride who is still very young and who, therefore, may have a ready disposition to exchange him for younger company. When he secretly marries Desdemona, Othello is already a national hero, famous, celebrated, a giant among pygmies. I have seen versions of the play where Othello is dashing, youthful, up and coming, and I have felt that what Iago does to him is of less consequence than the play requires, because the edifice that came crashing down was just not big enough, the destruction wrought was just not sufficiently *impossible*.

MA: I'd just done *Romeo and Juliet* with Ray Fearon and Zoë Waites and they were absolutely breathtaking. Towards the end of our international tour I remember getting the two of them together in a hotel in Belgium and saying, "Would you like to play Othello and Desdemona?" And they both said, instantly, "Yes." So the casting arose out of the fact that I'd got two really talented young actors who had this incredible chemistry. The big issue for Ray was his age [he was thirty-two at the time of the production]. To age his appearance he shaved his hair and grew a beard, and I did actually have to cut a line: "declined / Into the vale of years."

Some people commented on the fact he was too young. I think that's just because they had inside knowledge that that is how the play is written. There is absolutely no evidence in the rest of the play that his age makes any difference at all. In fact, quite the reverse. I would say a younger man helps in terms of explaining his promotion and his leadership, and their effect on Iago, so I deliberately cast an Iago [Richard McCabe] who was older than Othello; it's usually the other way around.

But also Ray's age undermined the conventional view of Othello as "Oh, he's an old man, he can't get it up and that's why he's vulnerable to Cassio." There is no evidence for that. What I think is a much more interesting story to tell is that Othello is an emotional virgin. This is why I believe the question of color is less interesting. He's a soldier, a raconteur, but he has never engaged in emotional relationships. Whereas an older man would have experience of this, a younger man would possess a certain naïveté; I think that's what makes him so vulnerable to Iago's plotting. So not only was I not making an excuse for Ray's youth, I felt it was a positive advantage. I thought it made the audience examine the nature of his vulnerability beyond simply being an old man. Our Othello was virile and beautiful, very sexy, and he had a very physical relationship with Desdemona. Interestingly, whereas a lot of reviewers in Stratford said he was too young, several of them openly, clearly recanted when we came to London. Initially, they just couldn't see beyond his appearance. Indeed, the London reviews were terrific.

Did you and your actors make any unexpected discoveries about Cassio and/or Rodorigo?

MA: I didn't really have expectations so I couldn't tell you what was expected or unexpected. But I think that it's true to say that I was quite shocked by how stupid Rodorigo was! A lot of the men in the play are totally governed by obsession. I think, for example, that Othello becomes addicted to jealousy. At one point he says, "Give me proof that she's unfaithful." He doesn't say, "Please find out that she's not." It's as if he *wants* this torment. "It is the green-eyed monster which doth mock / The meat it feeds on." Rodorigo suffers from the same kind of obsession, which turns him into an idiot. When the truth is staring him in the face, Othello still can't see it. When you

8. Richard McCabe's Iago was deliberately cast to be older than Ray Fearon's relatively young Othello in Michael Attenborough's 1999 RSC production.

think Othello or Rodorigo are so gullible as to believe Iago, you have to see it in the context of men who simply can't see the world beyond Desdemona.

I don't think Cassio contained any surprises. I wanted him to be a different social class from Iago. I wanted him to be much more beautiful than Iago but still a soldier. There are images that echo each other through the play; this is another very emotionally immature person. His only relationship is with a whore whom he doesn't visit very often. These aren't grown-ups! Arguably the only real grown-up in the play is Emilia. Everybody else's lives are very blinkered. I rather liked Cassio—I grew to like him more and more. There's so much said about him, and actually working on him and rehearsing him you really felt sorry for him. But he is quite naive. There's a lot of naïveté within the play, and a lack of sophistication.

What is revealed by Emilia's speech at the end of Act 4 Scene 3 about how women as well as men have affections, desires for sport, and frailty?

MA: I think it's a speech about Emilia's own relationship. It's a desperately sad scene because they are just missing each other in the dark. Desdemona is being very selective with what she hears, and Emilia, who is a woman of the world, has seen it all in all its horror, is in a way warning her. And Desdemona is sort of sticking her fingers in her ears and going "La, la, la, I can't hear you!" That's the tragedy of that scene. I think it's there because Iago is never going to tell you the truth about himself, but Emilia does. She doesn't talk about other relationships. In fact what she says, rather as Shylock does, is "Do we not have affections too? Just because we're put upon, it doesn't make us insensible." It's the best statement about women in the past five hundred years! The scene's prime function is to show us two very different female views of the world, and to give us insight into the Iago–Emilia marriage.

Critics worry about the play's "double-time" scheme: looked at one way, the events are compressed over just three nights (with a gap for the sea voyage after the first act), but for Iago's plot to

make sense, a much longer span of time must pass. Why does this not seem such a problem in the theater?

TN: Shakespeare uses the device of "double-time" scheme in many of the great plays. It's not a mistake, it's an intention, and it's intended for theater performance, not for the scholar's study. He creates an illusion of scale, distance, and the elapse of time suggesting epic, life-changing events, but in performance there must always be a sense of a narrative urgently moving on at a speed which can neither be controlled nor contained by the protagonists. Shakespeare also uses anachronism as a device, so that his plays can be set in an ancient and contemporary world at one and the same time. Cleopatra playing "billiards" in ancient Egypt, Gloucester not needing "spectacles" in ancient Britain are not oversights but, like the street talk and slang abounding in the plays, spurts of contemporary energy for an audience engaged in the here and now of the drama.

MA: I strongly suspect Shakespeare didn't think about it very much. What he obviously did want to do was compress the timescale, so that in the three hours in the theater you are *shocked* by the speed at which things happen. If he were to give naturalistic explanations for events he would have to stretch it out and therefore the whole thing would be less shocking. It's the shock of the speed and scale of Othello's decline that creates the effect.

How did you and your designer set about creating the contrasting worlds of Venice and Cyprus, and of public versus private life?

TN: *Othello* is the most domestic of the tragedies. We divided the play at a point where the handkerchief is dropped. As the second part begins, any one of four characters might have picked it up before, almost randomly, Emilia noticed it. A negligible small square of fabric becomes the deciding factor in a catastrophe of multiple deaths, terror, and the furthest extremes of emotional suffering. Shakespeare couldn't be clearer. The climax of the play takes place in a *bedroom*. I was so glad, therefore, to be doing a small theater intimate-scale production, where the bedroom could be the size of a bedroom, and not, as we have often seen, a palatial space the size of two tennis courts, robbing Shakespeare of his messy, muddled, up-close revelation of what happens behind the locked doors of a marriage gone wrong.

MA: One of the challenging elements in designing Shakespeare is that he wrote for a nonscenic theater, and therefore saw sequences following quickly, one after the other, changing location very swiftly. I remember Cicely Berry saying once, "There's no pause in Shakespeare until the end of the play." We tried very hard to keep the flow of things, so both Venice and Cyprus were quite spare; consequently, if you introduced an item of scenery it really had an effect.

For Venice I wanted something quite magisterial and formal, not particularly decorative. I wasn't concerned with a literal representation of Venice so it wasn't very beautiful; rather it was elegant and spare. If I were to put another adjective to it, it would be masculine. The scene where Othello persuades the Duke and the Senators to accept the marriage was very formal. We chose early twentieth-century costumes because, like Trevor [Nunn], I felt that the military context was very important. The Duke and Brabantio were like the formal elders of Venice, in frock coats and in an elegant, very male setting, with a big long table, inkwells, and blotters: quite starchy.

In Cyprus, although the setting is an army camp, it is much more sensual. So we wanted heat and light as opposed to coolness and elegance. I wanted something that evoked a camp, so there was no architecture. Robert Jones [the designer] had these canvas panels that came in and out so that you could completely shutter off the upstage area, or open the whole stage up. It could configure into different arrangements that would give you different locations. The great benefits of what he did were twofold. One, it was in quite a gentle, warm color that made it feel very sensual. If you backlit it you could perform shadow-play behind it. The other thing was that it seemed to me that there are several stunning moments in the play where you go from an incredibly intense and intimate scene into one where suddenly everyone is present: for example, Act 4 Scene 1, which begins with Othello and Iago, where Othello is absolutely losing his mind. Lodovico arrives with news from Venice and suddenly the stage is flooded with soldiers. It's the scene in which he eventually slaps Desdemona. So from that intimate, awful, ferocious, locking-antlers quality which Othello and Iago have, suddenly everything flew out and we were in a public place and Othello was on public show; he was the army commander, and he was expected to act in a particular way and yet he was clearly cracking up. This places the audience in the position of being in on a secret about Othello's internal life which the other characters aren't aware of. That feeling of being able to go from a two-handed scene to a twelve- or fifteen-handed scene, at the click of a light switch, was really important.

I also felt it was important that you got a strong sense of Emilia and, particularly, Desdemona being fishes out of water in Cyprus; that they shouldn't, strictly speaking, really be there. So, for example, when Desdemona landed in Cyprus, she arrived with half a dozen hatboxes. She was an elegant, urban girl with a lot of money. It's hot; there are a lot of soldiers, with sweat under their arms, and this girl arrives as if she's gone to the Mediterranean on holiday! I wanted the increasing feeling that she didn't know what to do with herself at the formal arrival in Cyprus. Should she join the parade? Should she watch the parade? During that wonderful scene where there's the riot in the middle of the night, we played it that Othello and Desdemona were trying to consummate their marriage and are interrupted and he has to get up. He arrives bare-chested, holding a sword, and he's clearly been disturbed from his love life. And she comes on covered by a sheet and all the men suddenly become aware that there's a half-naked woman there. She was out of place. So although it was a very sensual place it was not there to accommodate sophisticated, well-dressed, wealthy, urban girls.

T. S. Eliot famously read Othello's farewell speech ("Soft you; a word . . .") as a deluded man cheering himself up. That's a bit harsh, isn't it? But on the other hand, there is an element of Othello, after having been stripped bare ("goats and monkeys," "that common whore of Venice," and all that), now protecting his image once again with the carapace of his poetic music?

MA: I think that's actually a half-truth. Yes, there's no question that his assessment of what has happened is going to be different from ours. We wouldn't appraise it in the same way. But I don't think that necessarily means he is twisting the truth in a cynical or manipulative way. If you feel life draining out of you then you will say things that aren't necessarily going to be gospel truth. But I do think that a lot of what he says in that last speech is true. In a way, what is awful about it is not the reconstruction of his image, but his bewilderment as his mind races. Othello actually says very little in that last scene. He is like a spectator. Now he has learned what really happened, he has to reassess reality. So the scale of what's happening in his head when his life is draining away is colossal. I don't think it's anything manipulative or vain. I think it's a man in a state of complete incomprehension and bewilderment. Like centuries of people since, he's trying to work out *why* it happened. And Iago gives nothing away; he takes his secret to the grave. It's a very hard speech to generalize about. It's actually a man trying to find truth.

ANTONY SHER ON PLAYING IAGO

Sir Antony Sher was born in Cape Town in 1949. After compulsory military service in South Africa, he traveled to London to train as an actor. He joined the Liverpool Everyman Theatre in the 1970s, working with a group of gifted young actors and writers that included Willy Russell, Alan Bleasdale, Julie Walters, Trevor Eve, and Jonathan Pryce, playing Ringo in Willy Russell's *John, Paul, George, Ringo . . . & Bert*. He joined the RSC in 1982 and played the title role in *Tartuffe* and the Fool in *King Lear*. In 1984 he won the prestigious Laurence Olivier Award for his performance in the RSC's *Richard III*. Since then he has played numerous leading roles in the theater as well as on film and television, including *Tamburlaine*, *Cyrano de Bergerac*, and *Macbeth*, as well as Shylock in *The Merchant of Venice* and Iago in the RSC's 2004 *Othello* at the Swan Theatre directed by Gregory Doran, which he discusses here. He also writes books and plays, including the theatrical memoirs *Year of the King* (1985) and *Woza Shakespeare: Titus Andronicus in South Africa* (1997, cowritten with his partner Gregory Doran).

The play is called *Othello* and yet Iago's is the largest part. Does that somehow make the role different from Macbeth or Richard III

or Hamlet or Lear, where the journey of the lead actor and that of the play are the same?

I don't think it matters that the play is called *Othello*, yet Iago is the larger role—the piece is structured as a thrilling combat between two heavyweights. Iago may be the instigator of the fight, and Othello the victim, yet the two men become locked together in a deadly hold, dragging each other down to destruction. And so they share, equally, the journey of the play.

Unlike most of the big Shakespearean roles, Iago's contains a large measure of prose as opposed to verse: is there something distinctive about inhabiting a prose mind?

The fact that a large amount of Iago's dialogue is written in prose became very useful to our setting of the play, which was a military base on Cyprus, mid-twentieth century. In this context Iago was a recognizably modern NCO figure—a rough-talking square-basher, a master of barrack-room banter, and one who knows when to break open the bottles and start the songs, a veteran serviceman, immensely popular with the troops, and, to the rest of the world, just "honest Iago." This interpretation was much more available in prose than it would've been in verse.

Iago's language is full of sexual imagery throughout the play. How much of a clue to his character does that give you?

Iago can't seem to open his mouth without some sexual allusion spilling out. You could argue that this is just the way soldiers talk, but there's something odder, more perverse in Iago's language. To him, having sexual intercourse is "making the beast with two backs." Why this savage image? Perhaps a clue comes in his speech about Desdemona: "Now, I do love her too, / Not out of absolute lust—though peradventure / I stand accountant for as great a sin." Why does Iago have to reassure us that he could be lustful if he chose? We wouldn't expect anything less of this supremely macho man. Is it that he's impotent, and physically incapable of making the "beast with two backs"? Or is he sterile? Could these things account for his strange energy, his appetite for chaos, his nihilism? I'm not sure. I certainly based my portrayal on the idea of a man with a severe sexual hang-up, though I rather liked leaving this undefined.

Does Iago lie to the audience? Are we really supposed to believe his accusations about both Othello and Cassio cuckolding him?

I don't believe that Iago lies to the audience in his soliloquies. When he suggests that both Othello and Cassio have slept with his wife, Emilia, he thinks it's true, so it's no more like lying than Leontes' accusations about Hermione's fidelity in *The Winter's Tale*. In fact, having previously played Leontes, I believe he and Iago are suffering from the same condition; medically it's known as morbid or sexual jealousy, when someone becomes convinced, falsely, that their partner is betraying them. This possibility was enhanced in our production by Amanda Harris playing Emilia as a boozy, flirty army wife.

9. Antony Sher as a morbidly "jealous" Iago with Amanda Harris playing Emilia as a "boozy, flirty army wife" in Gregory Doran's RSC production at the Swan Theatre in 2004.

We all felt that although the play is famously about one man con-
sumed with jealousy, it's actually about two. Iago seems as much
under the spell of the "green-eyed monster" as is the Moor. I think
the reason that Iago is so successful at duping Othello is that Iago
knows about jealousy from deep within. "O, beware, my lord, of jealousy," he says with real feeling. Earlier, talking of his suspicion that
Othello has slept with Emilia, he says "the thought whereof / Doth—
like a poisonous mineral—gnaw my inwards." Iago is like a man
with a highly contagious disease, who is determined to pass on the
germs. This aspect of Iago was crucial to my interpretation. I totally
reject Samuel Taylor Coleridge's reading of the role, where Iago is
simply possessed by some kind of "motiveless malignity."

**Some have found a homoerotic strain in the play—or at the very
least a sharp contrast between the intense all-male world of the
army and the domestic/feminine sphere introduced by Desdemona. Was this a productive approach for you?**

As a gay man I've never found any homoerotic strain in the play. I
suppose the theory comes from the sequence when Iago tells of
sleeping next to Cassio one night, and Cassio becoming aroused, and
kissing Iago. I think this is just Iago in rabid, tabloid-journalist mode,
trying to paint Cassio in the most salacious colors imaginable. I also
wonder if the Iago-as-gay idea comes from a time when gay equaled
evil. Hollywood did this for a while: the bad guy was always some
twisted faggot. (Now it's changed: the bad guy is just played by a
British actor.)

**What are your recollections of working on the great "temptation"
scene in the middle of the play, where Iago seems to infect
Othello with his language, as if transferring the "monster" in his
own mind into Othello's?**

One of the greatest episodes in all of Shakespeare is Act 3 Scene 3:
the so-called "jealousy scene," when Iago convinces Othello of Desdemona's unfaithfulness. Apart from brief appearances by Desdemona and Emilia, it is a colossal two-hander (in playing time, it lasts
about half an hour), during which both the characters and the

actors have to slug it out tirelessly, in an extremely explosive situation. It would only take one wrong move from Iago, or someone to overhear and expose his lies, and the whole maneuver would backfire, and lead Othello to make a murderous attack on Iago rather than Desdemona. Or what if Desdemona didn't drop her handkerchief halfway through, providing Iago with the one piece of visual evidence which will, eventually, in Othello's eyes, clinch the case? One of Greg Doran's preoccupations as a director is to constantly seek out what he calls "the crossroads"—those moments when the action might suddenly go a different way. He wants the audience to sit up sharply, wondering if this story is as familiar as they thought. You can't act tension or danger onstage without providing some of the real thing, in terms of spontaneity and invention. The great South African actor Sello Maake Ka-Ncube (Othello) and I played the Act 3 Scene 3 crossroads for all they were worth, and each night it felt like a wild rollercoaster ride, without either of us quite knowing who would reach the other end safely or in command.

What do you make of Iago's refusal to speak at the end?

Iago's vow of silence at the end is, I think, a very simple matter. Arising from a very complex one. He himself can't explain what happened; any more than a psychopath can say, "I did it because of that." Whatever it is that Iago suffers from—let psychiatrists call it "sexual jealousy" or Coleridge "motiveless malignity"— the man has been on a tremendous drug rush, fueled by weird chemicals in his own brain, and now it's over. The only appropriate response is his final statement: "what you know, you know: / From this time forth I never will speak word." Shakespeare leaves a powerful mystery there, like he does in all his best plays—questions, not answers, about human behavior.

SHAKESPEARE'S CAREER
IN THE THEATER

BEGINNINGS

William Shakespeare was an extraordinarily intelligent man who was born and died in an ordinary market town in the English Midlands. He lived an uneventful life in an eventful age. Born in April 1564, he was the eldest son of John Shakespeare, a glove-maker who was prominent on the town council until he fell into financial difficulties. Young William was educated at the local grammar in Stratford-upon-Avon, Warwickshire, where he gained a thorough grounding in the Latin language, the art of rhetoric, and classical poetry. He married Ann Hathaway and had three children (Susanna, then the twins Hamnet and Judith) before his twenty-first birthday: an exceptionally young age for the period. We do not know how he supported his family in the mid-1580s.

Like many clever country boys, he moved to the city in order to make his way in the world. Like many creative people, he found a career in the entertainment business. Public playhouses and professional full-time acting companies reliant on the market for their income were born in Shakespeare's childhood. When he arrived in London as a man, sometime in the late 1580s, a new phenomenon was in the making: the actor who is so successful that he becomes a "star." The word did not exist in its modern sense, but the pattern is recognizable: audiences went to the theater not so much to see a particular show as to witness the comedian Richard Tarlton or the dramatic actor Edward Alleyn.

Shakespeare was an actor before he was a writer. It appears not to have been long before he realized that he was never going to grow into a great comedian like Tarlton or a great tragedian like Alleyn. Instead, he found a role within his company as the man who patched up old plays, breathing new life, new dramatic twists, into tired repertory pieces. He paid close attention to the work of the university-educated dramatists who were writing history plays and tragedies for the public stage in a style more ambitious, sweeping, and poetically grand than anything that had been seen before. But he may also have noted that what his friend and rival Ben Jonson would call "Marlowe's mighty line" sometimes faltered in the mode of comedy. Going to university, as Christopher Marlowe did, was all well and good for honing the arts of rhetorical elaboration and classical allusion, but it could lead to a loss of the common touch. To stay close to a large segment of the potential audience for public theater, it was necessary to write for clowns as well as kings and to intersperse the flights of poetry with the humor of the tavern, the privy, and the brothel: Shakespeare was the first to establish himself early in his career as an equal master of tragedy, comedy, and history. He realized that theater could be the medium to make the national past available to a wider audience than the elite who could afford to read large history books: his signature early works include not only the classical tragedy *Titus Andronicus* but also the sequence of English historical plays on the Wars of the Roses.

He also invented a new role for himself, that of in-house company dramatist. Where his peers and predecessors had to sell their plays to the theater managers on a poorly paid piecework basis, Shakespeare took a percentage of the box-office income. The Lord Chamberlain's Men constituted themselves in 1594 as a joint stock company, with the profits being distributed among the core actors who had invested as sharers. Shakespeare acted himself—he appears in the cast lists of some of Ben Jonson's plays as well as the list of actors' names at the beginning of his own collected works—but his principal duty was to write two or three plays a year for the company. By holding shares, he was effectively earning himself a royalty on his work, something no author had ever done before in England. When the Lord Chamberlain's Men collected their fee for performance at court in the Christmas season of 1594, three of them went along to the Treasurer of the Chamber: not just Richard Burbage the tragedian and Will Kempe the clown, but also Shakespeare the scriptwriter. That was something new.

The next four years were the golden period in Shakespeare's

career, though overshadowed by the death of his only son Hamnet, aged eleven, in 1596. In his early thirties and in full command of both his poetic and his theatrical medium, he perfected his art of comedy, while also developing his tragic and historical writing in new ways. In 1598, Francis Meres, a Cambridge University graduate with his finger on the pulse of the London literary world, praised Shakespeare for his excellence across the genres:

> As Plautus and Seneca are accounted the best for comedy and tragedy among the Latins, so Shakespeare among the English is the most excellent in both kinds for the stage; for comedy, witness his *Gentlemen of Verona*, his *Errors*, his *Love Labours Lost*, his *Love Labours Won*, his *Midsummer Night Dream* and his *Merchant of Venice*: for tragedy his *Richard the 2*, *Richard the 3*, *Henry the 4*, *King John*, *Titus Andronicus* and his *Romeo and Juliet*.

For Meres, as for the many writers who praised the "honey-flowing vein" of *Venus and Adonis* and *Lucrece*, narrative poems written when the theaters were closed due to plague in 1593–94, Shakespeare was marked above all by his linguistic skill, by the gift of turning elegant poetic phrases.

PLAYHOUSES

Elizabethan playhouses were "thrust" or "one-room" theaters. To understand Shakespeare's original theatrical life, we have to forget about the indoor theater of later times, with its proscenium arch and curtain that would be opened at the beginning and closed at the end of each act. In the proscenium arch theater, stage and auditorium are effectively two separate rooms: the audience looks from one world into another as if through the imaginary "fourth wall" framed by the proscenium. The picture-frame stage, together with the elabo-rate scenic effects and backdrops beyond it, created the illusion of a self-contained world—especially once nineteenth-century develop-ments in the control of artificial lighting meant that the auditorium could be darkened and the spectators made to focus on the lighted stage. Shakespeare, by contrast, wrote for a bare platform stage with a standing audience gathered around it in a courtyard in full daylight. The audience members were always conscious of themselves and their fellow spectators, and they shared the same "room" as the actors. A sense of immediate presence and the creation of rapport with the audience were all-important. The actor could not afford to imagine he was in a closed world, with silent witnesses dutifully observing him from the darkness.

Shakespeare's theatrical career began at the Rose Theatre in Southwark. The stage was wide and shallow, trapezoid in shape, like a lozenge. This design had a great deal of potential for the theatrical equivalent of cinematic split-screen effects, whereby one group of characters would enter at the door at one end of the tiring-house wall at the back of the stage and another group through the door at the other end, thus creating two rival tableaux. Many of the battle-heavy and faction-filled plays that premiered at the Rose have scenes of just this sort.

At the rear of the Rose stage, there were three capacious exits, each over ten feet wide. Unfortunately, the very limited excavation of a fragmentary portion of the original Globe site, in 1989, revealed nothing about the stage. The first Globe was built in 1599 with similar proportions to those of another theater, the Fortune, albeit that the former was polygonal and looked circular, whereas the latter was rectangular. The building contract for the Fortune survives and allows us to infer that the stage of the Globe was probably substantially wider than it was deep (perhaps forty-three feet wide and twenty-seven feet deep). It may well have been tapered at the front, like that of the Rose.

The capacity of the Globe was said to have been enormous, perhaps in excess of three thousand. It has been conjectured that about eight hundred people may have stood in the yard, with two thousand or more in the three layers of covered galleries. The other "public" playhouses were also of large capacity, whereas the indoor Blackfriars theater that Shakespeare's company began using in 1608—the former refectory of a monastery—had overall internal dimensions of a mere forty-six by sixty feet. It would have made for a much more intimate theatrical experience and had a much smaller capacity, probably of about six hundred people. Since they paid at least six-pence a head, the Blackfriars attracted a more select or "private" audience. The atmosphere would have been closer to that of an indoor performance before the court in the Whitehall Palace or at Richmond. That Shakespeare always wrote for indoor production at court as well as outdoor performance in the public theater should make us cautious about inferring, as some scholars have, that the opportunity provided by the intimacy of the Blackfriars led to a significant change toward a "chamber" style in his last plays—which, besides, were performed at both the Globe and the Blackfriars. After the occupation of the Blackfriars a five-act structure seems to have become more important to Shakespeare. That was because of artificial lighting: there were musical interludes between the acts, while the candles were trimmed and replaced. Again, though, something similar must have been necessary for indoor court performances throughout his career.

Front of house there were the "gatherers" who collected the money from audience members: a penny to stand in the open-air yard, another penny for a place in the covered galleries, sixpence for the prominent "lord's rooms" to the side of the stage. In the indoor "private" theaters, gallants from the audience who fancied making themselves part of the spectacle sat on stools on the edge of the stage itself. Scholars debate as to how widespread this practice was in the public theaters such as the Globe. Once the audience were in place and the money counted, the gatherers were available to be extras onstage. That is one reason why battles and crowd scenes often come later rather than early in Shakespeare's plays. There was no formal prohibition upon performance by women, and there certainly were women among the gatherers, so it is not beyond the bounds of possibility that female crowd members were played by females.

The play began at two o'clock in the afternoon and the theater had to be cleared by five. After the main show, there would be a jig—which consisted not only of dancing, but also of knockabout comedy (it is the origin of the farcical "afterpiece" in the eighteenth-century theater). So the time available for a Shakespeare play was about two and a half hours, somewhere between the "two hours' traffic" mentioned in the prologue to *Romeo and Juliet* and the "three hours' spectacle" referred to in the preface to the 1647 Folio of Beaumont and Fletcher's plays. The prologue to a play by Thomas Middleton refers to a thousand lines as "one hour's words," so the likelihood is that about two and a half thousand, or a maximum of three thousand lines, made up the performed text. This is indeed the length of most of Shakespeare's comedies, whereas many of his tragedies and histories are much longer, raising the possibility that he wrote full scripts, possibly with eventual publication in mind, in the full knowledge that the stage version would be heavily cut. The short Quarto texts published in his lifetime—they used to be called "Bad" Quartos—provide fascinating evidence as to the kind of cutting that probably took place. So, for instance, the First Quarto of *Hamlet* neatly merges two occasions when Hamlet is overheard, the "Fishmonger" and the "nunnery" scenes.

The social composition of the audience was mixed. The poet Sir John Davies wrote of "A thousand townsmen, gentlemen and whores, / Porters and servingmen" who would "together throng" at the public playhouses. Though moralists associated female play-going with adultery and the sex trade, many perfectly respectable citizens' wives were regular attendees. Some, no doubt, resembled the modern groupie: a story attested in two different sources has one citizen's wife making a post-show assignation with Richard Burbage and ending up in bed with Shakespeare—supposedly eliciting from the latter the quip that William the Conqueror was before Richard III. Defenders of theater liked to say that by witnessing the comeuppance of villains on the stage, audience members would repent of their own wrongdoings, but the reality is that most people went to the theater then, as they do now, for entertainment more than moral edification. Besides, it would be foolish to suppose that audiences behaved in a homogeneous way: a pamphlet of the 1630s tells of how two men went to see *Pericles* and one of them laughed while the other wept. Bishop John Hall complained that people went to church for the same reasons that they went to the theater: "for company, for custom, for recreation . . . to feed his eyes or his ears . . . or perhaps for sleep."

Men-about-town and clever young lawyers went to be seen as much as to see. In the modern popular imagination, shaped not least by *Shakespeare in Love* and the opening sequence of Laurence

Olivier's *Henry V* film, the penny-paying groundlings stand in the yard hurling abuse or encouragement and hazelnuts or orange peel at the actors, while the sophisticates in the covered galleries appreciate Shakespeare's soaring poetry. The reality was probably the other way around. A "groundling" was a kind of fish, so the nickname suggests the penny audience standing below the level of the stage and gazing in silent open-mouthed wonder at the spectacle unfolding above them. The more difficult audience members, who kept up a running commentary of clever remarks on the performance and who occasionally got into quarrels with players, were the gallants. Like Hollywood movies in modern times, Elizabethan and Jacobean plays exercised a powerful influence on the fashion and behavior of the young. John Marston mocks the lawyers who would open their lips, perhaps to court a girl, and out would "flow / Naught but pure Juliet and Romeo."

THE ENSEMBLE AT WORK

In the absence of typewriters and photocopying machines, reading aloud would have been the means by which the company got to know a new play. The tradition of the playwright reading his complete script to the assembled company endured for generations. A copy would then have been taken to the Master of the Revels for licensing. The theater book-holder or prompter would then have copied the parts for distribution to the actors. A partbook consisted of the character's lines, with each speech preceded by the last three or four words of the speech before, the so-called "cue." These would have been taken away and studied or "conned." During this period of learning the parts, an actor might have had some one-to-one instruction, perhaps from the dramatist, perhaps from a senior actor who had played the same part before, and, in the case of an apprentice, from his master. A high percentage of Desdemona's lines occur in dialogue with Othello, of Lady Macbeth's with Macbeth, Cleopatra's with Antony, and Volumnia's with Coriolanus. The roles would almost certainly have been taken by the apprentice of the lead actor, usually Burbage, who delivers the majority of the cues. Given that apprentices lodged with their masters, there would have been ample

10. Hypothetical reconstruction of the interior of an Elizabethan playhouse during a performance.

opportunity for personal instruction, which may be what made it possible for young men to play such demanding parts.

After the parts were learned, there may have been no more than a single rehearsal before the first performance. With six different plays to be put on every week, there was no time for more. Actors, then, would go into a show with a very limited sense of the whole. The notion of a collective rehearsal process that is itself a process of discovery for the actors is wholly modern and would have been incomprehensible to Shakespeare and his original ensemble. Given the number of parts an actor had to hold in his memory, the forgetting of lines was probably more frequent than in the modern theater. The book-holder was on hand to prompt.

Backstage personnel included the property man, the tire-man who oversaw the costumes, call boys, attendants, and the musicians, who might play at various times from the main stage, the rooms above, and within the tiring-house. Scriptwriters sometimes made a nuisance of themselves backstage. There was often tension between the acting companies and the freelance playwrights from whom they purchased scripts: it was a smart move on the part of Shakespeare and the Lord Chamberlain's Men to bring the writing process in-house.

Scenery was limited, though sometimes set pieces were brought on (a bank of flowers, a bed, the mouth of hell). The trapdoor from below, the gallery stage above, and the curtained discovery-space at the back allowed for an array of special effects: the rising of ghosts and appari-tions, the descent of gods, dialogue between a character at a window and another at ground level, the revelation of a statue or a pair of lovers playing at chess. Ingenious use could be made of props, as with the ass's head in *A Midsummer Night's Dream*. In a theater that does not clutter the stage with the material paraphernalia of everyday life, those objects that are deployed may take on powerful symbolic weight, as when Shylock bears his weighing scales in one hand and knife in the other, thus becoming a parody of the figure of Justice who traditionally bears a sword and a balance. Among the more signifi-cant items in the property cupboard of Shakespeare's company, there would have been a throne (the "chair of state"), joint stools, books, bottles, coins, purses, letters (which are brought onstage, read or referred to on about eighty occasions in the complete works), maps, gloves, a set of stocks (in which Kent is put in *King Lear*), rings, rapiers, daggers, broadswords, staves, pistols, masks and vizards, heads and skulls, torches and tapers and lanterns which served to signal night scenes on the daylit stage, a buck's head, an ass's head, animal cos-tumes. Live animals also put in appearances, most notably the dog Crab in *The Two Gentlemen of Verona* and possibly a young polar bear in *The Winter's Tale*.

The costumes were the most important visual dimension of the play. Playwrights were paid between £2 and £6 per script, whereas Alleyn was not averse to paying £20 for "a black velvet cloak with sleeves embroidered all with silver and gold." No matter the period of the play, actors always wore contemporary costume. The excitement for the audience came not from any impression of historical accu-racy, but from the richness of the attire and perhaps the transgres-sive thrill of the knowledge that here were commoners like themselves strutting in the costumes of courtiers in effective defiance of the strict sumptuary laws whereby in real life people had to wear the clothes that befitted their social station.

To an even greater degree than props, costumes could carry symbolic importance. Racial characteristics could be suggested: a breastplate and helmet for a Roman soldier, a turban for a Turk, long robes for exotic characters such as Moors, a gabardine for a Jew. The figure of Time, as in *The Winter's Tale*, would be equipped with hourglass, scythe and wings; Rumour, who speaks the prologue of *2 Henry IV*, wore a costume adorned with a thousand tongues. The wardrobe in the tiring-house of the Globe would have contained much of the same stock as that of rival manager Philip Henslowe at the Rose: green gowns for outlaws and foresters, black for melancholy men such as Jaques and people in mourning such as the Countess in *All's Well That Ends Well* (at the beginning of *Hamlet*, the prince is still in mourning black when everyone else is in festive garb for the wedding of the new king), a gown and hood for a friar (or a feigned friar like the duke in *Measure for Measure*), blue coats and tawny to distinguish the followers of rival factions, a leather apron and ruler for a carpenter (as in the opening scene of *Julius Caesar*—and in *A Midsummer Night's Dream*, where this is the only sign that Peter Quince is a carpenter), a cockle hat with staff and a pair of sandals for a pilgrim or palmer (the disguise assumed by Helen in *All's Well*), bodices and kirtles with farthingales beneath for the boys who are to be dressed as girls. A gender switch such as that of Rosalind or Jessica seems to have taken between fifty and eighty lines of dialogue—Viola does not resume her "maiden weeds," but remains in her boy's costume to the end of *Twelfth Night* because a change would have slowed down the action at just the moment it was speeding to a climax. Henslowe's inventory also included "a robe for to go invisible": Oberon, Puck, and Ariel must have had something similar.

As the costumes appealed to the eyes, so there was music for the ears. Comedies included many songs. Desdemona's willow song, perhaps a late addition to the text, is a rare and thus exceptionally poignant example from tragedy. Trumpets and tuckets sounded for ceremonial entrances, drums denoted an army on the march. Background music could create atmosphere, as at the beginning of *Twelfth Night*, during the lovers' dialogue near the end of *The Mer-*

chant of Venice, when the statue seemingly comes to life in *The Winter's Tale*, and for the revival of Pericles and of Lear (in the Quarto text, but not the Folio). The haunting sound of the hautboy suggested a realm beyond the human, as when the god Hercules is imagined deserting Mark Antony. Dances symbolized the harmony of the end of a comedy—though in Shakespeare's world of mingled joy and sorrow, someone is usually left out of the circle.

The most important resource was, of course, the actors themselves. They needed many skills: in the words of one contemporary commentator, "dancing, activity, music, song, elocution, ability of body, memory, skill of weapon, pregnancy of wit." Their bodies were as significant as their voices. Hamlet tells the player to "suit the action to the word, the word to the action": moments of strong emotion, known as "passions," relied on a repertoire of dramatic gestures as well as a modulation of the voice. When Titus Andronicus has had his hand chopped off, he asks "How can I grace my talk, / Wanting a hand to give it action?" A pen portrait of "The Character of an Excellent Actor" by the dramatist John Webster is almost certainly based on his impression of Shakespeare's leading man, Richard Burbage: "By a full and significant action of body, he charms our attention: sit in a full theatre, and you will think you see so many lines drawn from the circumference of so many ears, whiles the actor is the centre. . . ."

Though Burbage was admired above all others, praise was also heaped upon the apprentice players whose alto voices fitted them for the parts of women. A spectator at Oxford in 1610 records how the audience was reduced to tears by the pathos of Desdemona's death. The puritans who fumed about the biblical prohibition upon cross-dressing and the encouragement to sodomy constituted by the sight of an adult male kissing a teenage boy onstage were a small minority. Little is known, however, about the characteristics of the leading apprentices in Shakespeare's company. It may perhaps be inferred that one was a lot taller than the other, since Shakespeare often wrote for a pair of female friends, one tall and fair, the other short and dark (Helena and Hermia, Rosalind and Celia, Beatrice and Hero).

We know little about Shakespeare's own acting roles—an early allusion indicates that he often took royal parts, and a venerable tradition gives him old Adam in *As You Like It* and the ghost of old King Hamlet. Save for Burbage's lead roles and the generic part of the clown, all such castings are mere speculation. We do not even know for sure whether the original Falstaff was Will Kempe or another actor who specialized in comic roles, Thomas Pope.

Kempe left the company in early 1599. Tradition has it that he fell out with Shakespeare over the matter of excessive improvisation. He was replaced by Robert Armin, who was less of a clown and more of a cerebral wit: this explains the difference between such parts as Lancelet Gobbo and Dogberry, which were written for Kempe, and the more verbally sophisticated Feste and Lear's Fool, which were written for Armin.

One thing that is clear from surviving "plots" or storyboards of plays from the period is that a degree of doubling was necessary. *2 Henry VI* has over sixty speaking parts, but more than half of the characters appear only in a single scene and most scenes have only six to eight speakers. At a stretch, the play could be performed by thirteen actors. When Thomas Platter saw *Julius Caesar* at the Globe in 1599, he noted that there were about fifteen. Why doesn't Paris go to the Capulet ball in *Romeo and Juliet*? Perhaps because he was doubled with Mercutio, who does. In *The Winter's Tale*, Mamillius might have come back as Perdita and Antigonus been doubled by Camillo, making the partnership with Paulina at the end a very neat touch. Titania and Oberon are often played by the same pair as Hippolyta and Theseus, suggesting a symbolic matching of the rulers of the worlds of night and day, but it is questionable whether there would have been time for the necessary costume changes. As so often, one is left in a realm of tantalizing speculation.

THE KING'S MAN

On Queen Elizabeth's death in 1603, the new king, James I, who had held the Scottish throne as James VI since he had been an infant, immediately took the Lord Chamberlain's Men under his direct patronage. Henceforth they would be the King's Men, and for the rest of Shakespeare's career they were favored with far more court performances than any of their rivals. There even seem to have been rumors early in the reign that Shakespeare and Burbage were being considered for knighthoods, an unprecedented honor for mere actors—and one that in the event was not accorded to a member of the profession for nearly three hundred years, when the title was bestowed upon Henry Irving, the leading Shakespearean actor of Queen Victoria's reign.

Shakespeare's productivity rate slowed in the Jacobean years, not because of age or some personal trauma, but because there were frequent outbreaks of plague, causing the theaters to be closed for long periods. The King's Men were forced to spend many months on the road. Between November 1603 and 1608, they were to be found at various towns in the south and Midlands, though Shakespeare probably did not tour with them by this time. He had bought a large house back home in Stratford and was accumulating other property. He may indeed have stopped acting soon after the new king took the throne. With the London theaters closed so much of the time and a large repertoire on the stocks, Shakespeare seems to have focused his energies on writing a few long and complex tragedies that could have been played on demand at court: *Othello*, *King Lear*, *Antony and Cleopatra*, *Coriolanus*, and *Cymbeline* are among his longest and poetically grandest plays. *Macbeth* only survives in a shorter text, which shows signs of adaptation after Shakespeare's death. The bitterly satirical *Timon of Athens*, apparently a collaboration with Thomas Middleton that may have failed on the stage, also belongs to this period. In comedy, too, he wrote longer and morally darker works than in the Elizabethan period, pushing at the very bounds of the form in *Measure for Measure* and *All's Well That Ends Well*.

From 1608 onward, when the King's Men began occupying the indoor Blackfriars playhouse (as a winter house, meaning that they only used the outdoor Globe in summer?), Shakespeare turned to a more romantic style. His company had a great success with a revived and altered version of an old pastoral play called *Mucedorus*. It even featured a bear. The younger dramatist John Fletcher, meanwhile, sometimes working in collaboration with Francis Beaumont, was pioneering a new style of tragicomedy, a mix of romance and royalism laced with intrigue and pastoral excursions. Shakespeare experimented with this idiom in *Cymbeline* and it was presumably with his blessing that Fletcher eventually took over as the King's Men's company dramatist. The two writers apparently collaborated on three plays in the years 1612–14: a lost romance called *Cardenio* (based on the love-madness of a character in Cervantes' *Don Quixote*), *Henry VIII* (originally staged with the title "All Is True"), and *The Two Noble Kinsmen*, a dramatization of Chaucer's "Knight's Tale." These were written after Shakespeare's two final solo-authored plays, *The Winter's Tale*, a self-consciously old-fashioned work dramatizing the pastoral romance of his old enemy Robert Greene, and *The Tempest*, which at one and the same time drew together multiple theatrical traditions, diverse reading, and contemporary interest in the fate of a ship that had been wrecked on the way to the New World.

The collaborations with Fletcher suggest that Shakespeare's career ended with a slow fade rather than the sudden retirement supposed by the nineteenth-century Romantic critics who read Prospero's epilogue to *The Tempest* as Shakespeare's personal farewell to his art. In the last few years of his life Shakespeare certainly spent more of his time in Stratford-upon-Avon, where he became further involved in property dealing and litigation. But his London life also continued. In 1613 he made his first major London property purchase: a freehold house in the Blackfriars district, close to his company's indoor theater. *The Two Noble Kinsmen* may have been written as late as 1614, and Shakespeare was in London on business a little over a year before he died of an unknown cause at home in Stratford-upon-Avon in 1616, probably on his fifty-second birthday.

About half the sum of his works were published in his lifetime, in texts of variable quality. A few years after his death, his fellow actors began putting together an authorized edition of his complete *Comedies, Histories and Tragedies*. It appeared in 1623, in large "Folio" format. This collection of thirty-six plays gave Shakespeare his immortality. In the words of his fellow dramatist Ben Jonson, who contributed two poems of praise at the start of the Folio, the body of his work made him "a monument without a tomb":

> And art alive still while thy book doth live
> And we have wits to read and praise to give . . .
> He was not of an age, but for all time!

SHAKESPEARE'S WORKS:
A CHRONOLOGY

1589–91	*? Arden of Faversham* (possible part authorship)
1589–92	*The Taming of the Shrew*
1589–92	*? Edward the Third* (possible part authorship)
1591	*The Second Part of Henry the Sixth*, originally called *The First Part of the Contention betwixt the Two Famous Houses of York and Lancaster* (element of co-authorship possible)
1591	*The Third Part of Henry the Sixth*, originally called *The True Tragedy of Richard Duke of York* (element of co-authorship probable)
1591–92	*The Two Gentlemen of Verona*
1591–92; perhaps revised 1594	*The Lamentable Tragedy of Titus Andronicus* (probably cowritten with, or revising an earlier version by, George Peele)
1592	*The First Part of Henry the Sixth*, probably with Thomas Nashe and others
1592/94	*King Richard the Third*
1593	*Venus and Adonis* (poem)
1593–94	*The Rape of Lucrece* (poem)
1593–1608	*Sonnets* (154 poems, published 1609 with *A Lover's Complaint*, a poem of disputed authorship)
1592–94/ 1600–03	*Sir Thomas More* (a single scene for a play originally by Anthony Munday, with other revisions by Henry Chettle, Thomas Dekker, and Thomas Heywood)
1594	*The Comedy of Errors*
1595	*Love's Labour's Lost*

1595–97	*Love's Labour's Won* (a lost play, unless the original title for another comedy)
1595–96	*A Midsummer Night's Dream*
1595–96	*The Tragedy of Romeo and Juliet*
1595–96	*King Richard the Second*
1595–97	*The Life and Death of King John* (possibly earlier)
1596–97	*The Merchant of Venice*
1596–97	*The First Part of Henry the Fourth*
1597–98	*The Second Part of Henry the Fourth*
1598	*Much Ado About Nothing*
1598–99	*The Passionate Pilgrim* (20 poems, some not by Shakespeare)
1599	*The Life of Henry the Fifth*
1599	"To the Queen" (epilogue for a court performance)
1599	*As You Like It*
1599	*The Tragedy of Julius Caesar*
1600–01	*The Tragedy of Hamlet, Prince of Denmark* (perhaps revising an earlier version)
1600–01	*The Merry Wives of Windsor* (perhaps revising version of 1597–99)
1601	"Let the Bird of Loudest Lay" (poem, known since 1807 as "The Phoenix and Turtle" [turtledove])
1601	*Twelfth Night, or What You Will*
1601–02	*The Tragedy of Troilus and Cressida*
1604	*The Tragedy of Othello, the Moor of Venice*
1604	*Measure for Measure*
1605	*All's Well That Ends Well*
1605	*The Life of Timon of Athens*, with Thomas Middleton
1605–06	*The Tragedy of King Lear*
1605–08	? contribution to *The Four Plays in One* (lost, except for *A Yorkshire Tragedy*, mostly by Thomas Middleton)

1606	*The Tragedy of Macbeth* (surviving text has additional scenes by Thomas Middleton)
1606–07	*The Tragedy of Antony and Cleopatra*
1608	*The Tragedy of Coriolanus*
1608	*Pericles, Prince of Tyre*, with George Wilkins
1610	*The Tragedy of Cymbeline*
1611	*The Winter's Tale*
1611	*The Tempest*
1612–13	*Cardenio*, with John Fletcher (survives only in later adaptation called *Double Falsehood* by Lewis Theobald)
1613	*Henry VIII (All Is True)*, with John Fletcher
1613–14	*The Two Noble Kinsmen*, with John Fletcher

THE HISTORY BEHIND THE TRAGEDIES: A CHRONOLOGY

Era/Date	Event	Location	Play
Greek myth	Trojan War	Troy	*Troilus and Cressida*
Greek myth	Theseus King of Athens	Athens	*The Two Noble Kinsmen*
c. tenth–ninth century BC?	Leir King of Britain (legendary)	Britain	*King Lear*
535–510 BC	Tarquin II King of Rome	Rome	*The Rape of Lucrece*
493 BC	Caius Martius captures Corioli	Italy	*Coriolanus*
431–404 BC	Peloponnesian War	Greece	*Timon of Athens*
17 Mar 45 BC	Battle of Munda: Caesar's victory over Pompey's sons	Munda, Spain	*Julius Caesar*
Oct 45 BC	Caesar returns to Rome for triumph	Rome	*Julius Caesar*
15 Mar 44 BC	Assassination of Caesar	Rome	*Julius Caesar*
27 Nov 43 BC	Formation of Second Triumvirate	Rome	*Julius Caesar*
Oct 42 BC	Battle of Philippi	Philippi, Macedonia	*Julius Caesar*
Winter 41–40 BC	Antony visits Cleopatra	Egypt	*Antony and Cleopatra*
Oct 40 BC	Pact of Brundisium; marriage of Antony and Octavia	Italy	*Antony and Cleopatra*
39 BC	Pact of Misenum between Pompey and the triumvirs	Campania, Italy	*Antony and Cleopatra*

39–38 BC	Ventidius defeats the Parthians in a series of engagements	Syria	*Antony and Cleopatra*
34 BC	Cleopatra and her children proclaimed rulers of the eastern Mediterranean	Alexandria	*Antony and Cleopatra*
2 Sep 31 BC	Battle of Actium	On the coast of western Greece	*Antony and Cleopatra*
Aug 30 BC	Death of Antony	Alexandria	*Antony and Cleopatra*
12 Aug 30 BC	Death of Cleopatra	Alexandria	*Antony and Cleopatra*
Early first century AD	Cunobelinus/ Cymbeline rules Britain (and dies before AD 43)	Britain	*Cymbeline*
During the reign of a fictional (late?) Roman emperor		Rome	*Titus Andronicus*
c. ninth–tenth century AD	Existence of legendary Amleth?	Denmark	*Hamlet*
15 Aug 1040	Death of Duncan I of Scotland	Bothnguane, Scotland	*Macbeth*
1053	Malcolm invades Scotland	Scotland	*Macbeth*
15 Aug 1057	Death of Macbeth	Lumphanan, Scotland	*Macbeth*
7 Oct 1571	Naval battle of Lepanto between Christians and Turks	The Mediterranean, off the coast of Greece	A context for *Othello*

FURTHER READING AND VIEWING

CRITICAL APPROACHES

Calderwood, James L., *The Properties of Othello* (1989). Theoretically informed account using the concept of "property" to explore different aspects of the play including historical, psychological, and linguistic.

Erickson, Peter, and Maurice Hunt, eds., *Approaches to Teaching Shakespeare's Othello* (2005). Useful review of resources and discussion of varied approaches.

Heilman, Robert, *Magic in the Web: Action and Language in Othello* (1956). Excellent analysis of patterns of imagery.

Honigmann, E. A. J., *The Texts of "Othello" and Shakespearian Revision* (1996). Detailed account of the relationship between Folio and Quarto texts.

Loomba, Ania, *Shakespeare, Race, and Colonialism* (2002). Postcolonial reading on race and history of imperialism, includes excellent essay on *Othello*.

Muir, Kenneth, and Philip Edwards, eds., *Aspects of Othello* (1977). Useful selection of articles reprinted from *Shakespeare Survey*.

Nostbakken, Faith, *Understanding Othello* (2000). Useful student casebook covering drama, context, and performance.

Orlin, Lena Cowen, ed., *Othello*, New Casebook Series (2004). Useful selection of recent critical essays.

Pechter, Edward, *Othello and the Interpretive Traditions* (1999). Overview of critical approaches.

Potter, Nicholas, ed., *William Shakespeare: Othello* (2000). Columbia Critical Guides series. Useful, detailed account of critical history.

Spivack, Bernard, *Shakespeare and the Allegory of Evil* (1958). Relates the role of Iago to the figure of Vice in medieval morality plays.

Vaughan, Virginia Mason, *Othello: A Contextual History* (1994).

Excellent on play's Jacobean contexts in Part I; Part II considers a range of historical performances.

Vaughan, Virginia Mason, and Kent Cartwright, eds., *Othello: New Perspectives* (1991). Useful collection of varied essays on text, performance, and contemporary critical approaches.

Wain, John, ed., *Shakespeare: Othello: A Casebook* (1971, revised 1994). Useful collection including important early essays.

THE PLAY IN PERFORMANCE

Cook, Judith, *Women in Shakespeare* (1980). Useful chapter on tragic heroines includes Desdemona.

———, *Shakespeare's Players* (1983). Chapter on "jealousy" includes discussion of Othello and Iago.

Hankey, Julie, ed., *Othello: William Shakespeare*, Plays in Performance series (2005). Excellent detailed stage history with annotated play text.

Jackson, Russell, and Robert Smallwood, eds., *Players of Shakespeare 2* (1988). Includes Ben Kingsley on Othello and David Suchet on Iago.

Parsons, Keith, and Pamela Mason, *Shakespeare in Performance* (1995). Useful overview of stage history and important historical productions.

Potter, Lois, *Othello, Shakespeare in Performance* (2002). Sophisticated account of stage history, including film versions.

Rosenberg, Marvin, *The Masks of Othello* (1961). Fascinating and detailed chronological account of the play in performance.

Sales, Roger, ed., "Bob Peck on Playing Iago," *Shakespeare in Perspective, Volume Two* (1985).

Smallwood, Robert, ed., *Players of Shakespeare 5* (2003). Includes Richard McCabe on playing Iago.

Tynan, Kenneth, ed., *Othello, by William Shakespeare: The National Theatre Production* (1966). Detailed account of John Dexter's 1964 National Theatre production with Laurence Olivier as Othello.

Vaughan, Virginia Mason, *Othello: A Contextual History* (1994). Part II considers a range of historical performances.

Vaughan, Virginia Mason, and Kent Cartwright, eds., *Othello: New Perspectives* (1991). Useful collection of varied essays on text, performance, and contemporary critical approaches.

Wine, Martin, *Othello: Text and Performance* (1984). Basic overview of text with detailed account of important twentieth-century performances in Part 2.

AVAILABLE ON DVD

Othello directed by Dmitri Buchowetzki (1922, DVD 2001). Interesting German silent film version with contrasting performance styles of Emil Jannings (Othello) and Werner Krauss (Iago).

A Double Life directed by George Cukor (1947, DVD 2003). Adaptation updated to postwar New York with Ronald Colman, winner of Best Actor award for performance; Signe Hasso, Edmund O'Brien, Shelly Winters.

Othello directed by Orson Welles (1952, DVD 1999). Bold, award-winning version with Welles himself as Othello, Michéal MacLiammoir as Iago, and Susan Cloutier as Desdemona, with typically adventurous cinematography. Welles made a film about the production, *Filming Othello* (1978).

Othello directed by Sergei Yutkevich (1955, VHS 1992). Stunning Russian version—cast includes Sergei Bondarchuk (Othello), Irina Skobtseva (Desdemona), and Andrei Popov (Iago). Yutkevich won Best Director award at Cannes in 1956.

All Night Long directed by Michael Relph, Basil Deardon (1961, DVD 2004). Adaptation described as "a wildly enjoyable 1961 British jazz version . . . that even considerately throws in that happy ending that Shakespeare forgot."

Othello directed by Stuart Burge (1965, DVD 2003). Film of John Dexter's National Theatre production starring Laurence Olivier (Othello), Maggie Smith (Desdemona), Frank Finlay (Iago), and Joyce Redman (Emilia). Powerful: divided views about Olivier's performance.

Othello directed by Franklin Melton (1981, DVD 2001). Film of traditional stage version with Ron Moody (Iago), Jenny Agutter (Desdemona), and William Marshall (Othello).

Otello directed by Franco Zeffirelli (1986, DVD 2005). Based on Giuseppe Verdi's opera with Plácido Domingo as Otello, Katia Ricciarelli as Desdemona, and Justino Díaz as Jago—described as "powerful and full-blooded."

Othello directed by Janet Suzman (1988, DVD 2006). Filmed version of celebrated South African production staged at the Market Theatre, Johannesburg, with John Kani, Richard Haines, and Joanna Weinberg.

Othello directed by Trevor Nunn (1990, DVD 2003). Film of RSC production with Ian McKellen (Iago), Imogen Stubbs (Desdemona), Willard White (Othello), and Zoë Wanamaker (Emilia).

Shakespeare: The Animated Tales directed by Aida Ziablikova (1992, DVD 2005). *Othello* voiced by Alec McCowan, Michael Kitchen, Suzanne Burden; inventive 27-minute animated British/Russian coproduction with script by Leon Garfield, using a combination of Shakespeare's text and narration.

Othello directed by Oliver Parker (1995, DVD 2000). Overtly sexual production with Laurence Fishburne (Othello), Kenneth Branagh (Iago), and Irene Jacob (Desdemona); Branagh dominates as Iago.

"O" directed by Tim Blake Nelson (2000, DVD 2002). A "clever and serious" adaptation set in an American high school with Mekhi Phifer and Julia Stiles.

Othello directed by Geoffrey Sax (2001, DVD 2002). Updated TV version by Andrew Davies with John Othello as the first black commissioner of the Metropolitan Police with fine performances from Eamonn Walker (John Othello), Keeley Hawes (Dessie), and Christopher Eccleston (Ben Jago).

REFERENCES

1. Thomas Baldwin, *The Organization and Personnel of the Shakespearean Company* (1961), p. 248.
2. Henry Jackson, a member of Corpus Christi College, Oxford, in a letter originally in Latin dated September 1610 (Ms ccc 304ff 83v and 84r), in *Eyewitnesses of Shakespeare: First Hand Accounts of Performances 1590–1890*, ed. Gamini Salgado (1975), p. 30.
3. Marvin Rosenberg, *The Masks of Othello: The Search for the Identity of Othello, Iago, and Desdemona by Three Centuries of Actors and Critics* (1961), pp. 20–7.
4. Samuel Pepys, Diary entry, 11 October 1660.
5. Colley Cibber, *An Apology for His Life* (1914), p. 69.
6. Richard Steele, *The Tatler*, No. 167, 2 May 1710.
7. Cibber, *Apology*, p. 77.
8. Theophilus Cibber, "Barton Booth," in *The Lives and Characters of the Most Eminent Actors and Actresses of Great Britain and Ireland* (1753), pp. 45–50.
9. *Grub Street Journal*, 31 October 1734.
10. Henry Aston in James Boaden (ed.), *The Private Correspondence of David Garrick, with the Most Celebrated Persons of His Time*, Volume I (1831–32), p. 30.
11. Samuel Foote, *A Treatise on the Passions, so Far as They Regard the Stage: With a Critical Enquiry into the Theatrical Merit of Mr. G—k, Mr. Q—n, and Mr. B—y the First Considered in the Part of Lear, the Two Last Opposed in Othello* (1976), pp. 33–4.
12. Arthur Murphy, *The Life of David Garrick, Esq* (1801), p. 70.
13. Julie Hankey (ed.), *Shakespeare in Production: Othello* (2005), p. 24.
14. Thomas Davies, *Memoirs of the Life of David Garrick* (1780), Volume II (1972), p. 240.
15. William Cooke, *Memoirs of Charles Macklin: Comedian* (1804), p. 158.
16. Davies, *Memoirs of the Life of David Garrick*, Volume II, p. 241.
17. William Hazlitt, *The Complete Works of William Hazlitt*, ed. P. P. Howe after the edition of A. R. Waller and Arnold Glover, Volume 5, *Lectures on the English Poets and a View of the English Stage* (1930), p. 304.
18. James Boaden, *Memoirs of the Life of John Philip Kemble, Esq: Including*

a History of the Stage from the Time of Garrick to the Present Period, Volume I (1825), p. 256.

19. *London Magazine*, March 1785.
20. Hankey, *Othello*, p. 35.
21. William Hazlitt, "Mr Kean's Iago," in his *A View of the English Stage; or, a Series of Dramatic Criticisms*, edited by W. Spencer Jackson (1906), pp. 19–20.
22. Leigh Hunt, review of *Othello* in *The Examiner*, No. 562, October 5, 1818, p. 632.
23. Henry Crabb Robinson, diary entry for 19 May 1814, in *The London Theatre, 1811–1866: Selections from the Diary of Henry Crabb Robinson*, ed. Eluned Brown (1966), pp. 57–8.
24. John Forster Kirk, "Shakespeare's Tragedies," quoted in Hankey, *Othello*, p. 46.
25. William Rounesville Alger, "Othello," in his *Life of Edwin Forrest: The American Tragedian*, Volume II (1877), pp. 768–80.
26. Henry James, "Tommaso Salvini: In Boston (1883)," in *The Scenic Art: Notes on Acting & the Drama, 1872–1901*, ed. Allan Wade (1948), pp. 168–85.
27. Quoted in Hankey, *Othello*, p. 55.
28. Clement Scott, "*Othello*: Irving as Iago," in *The Bells to King Arthur* (1896), pp. 207–9.
29. Dutton Cook, "*Othello* at the Lyceum," in *The Academy*, Volume XIX, No. 470, 7 May 1881, pp. 344–5.
30. Herbert Farjeon, "A Back-Stage Tragedy," in his *The Shakespearean Scene: Dramatic Criticisms* (1949), pp. 165–7.
31. Margaret Webster, *Don't Put Your Daughter on the Stage* (1972), pp. 106–7.
32. Raymond Mortimer, "*Othello* at the Old Vic," *The New Statesman & Nation*, Volume XV, No. 365, 19 February 1938, p. 287.
33. Eric Keown, review of *Othello*, *Punch*, Volume CCXXI, No. 5792, 31 October 1951, p. 500.
34. John Cottrell, "Acting for Acting's Sake," in his *Laurence Olivier* (1975), pp. 336–47.
35. Robert Speaight, "Shakespeare in Britain," *Shakespeare Quarterly*, Volume XV, No. 4, 1964, pp. 377–89.
36. Ronald Bryden, "Olivier's Moor," *New Statesman*, Volume LXVII, No. 1729, 1 May 1964, p. 696.
37. Hankey, *Othello*, p. 89.
38. Hugh Quarshie, *Second Thoughts About Othello*, International Shakespeare Association, Occasional Paper 7, 1999.

39. Howard Taubman, "James Earl Jones is Cast as the Moor," *The New York Times*, 15 July 1964, p. L29.

40. Barbara Hodgdon, "Race-ing Othello," in *The Shakespeare Trade: Performances and Appropriations* (1998), p. 26.

41. Judith Buchanan, "Virgin and Ape, Venetian and Infidel: Labellings of Otherness in Oliver Parker's *Othello*," in *Shakespeare, Film Fin de Siècle*, ed. Mark Thornton Burnett and Ramona Wray (2000), pp. 179–202.

42. Rita Kempley, review in *Washington Post*, 29 December 1995.

43. *Observer*, 12 April 1959 (MacLiammóir played Iago to Orson Welles' Othello in the 1952 film of the play).

44. Anne Barton, "Hell and Night," *Othello* RSC programme, 1979.

45. Michael Billington, *Guardian*, 26 August 1989.

46. Bob Peck, *Othello*, in Roger Sales (ed.), *Shakespeare in Perspective*, Volume Two, 1985.

47. Donald Sinden on playing Othello, in Judith Cook, *Shakespeare's Players*, 1983.

48. Sello Maake Ka-Ncube on playing Othello, RSC Online Playguide, 2004.

49. Kate Bassett, *Independent on Sunday*, 22 February 2004.

50. Antony Sher and Sello Maake Ka-Ncube discuss acting in *Othello*, *Guardian*, 25 May 2004.

51. Ray Fearon in interview with Nicci Gerrard, *Observer Magazine*, 25 April 1999.

52. Benedict Nightingale, *The Times*, 23 April 1999.

53. Trevor Nunn in interview, *Independent*, 17 August 1989.

54. Anne Barton, *Times Literary Supplement*, 8 September 1989.

55. Ben Kingsley and David Suchet in interview with Lesley Thornton, *Observer Colour Magazine*, 22 September 1985.

56. John Higgins, *The Times*, 21 September 1985 (this portrait was used on the program cover).

57. John Barber, *Daily Telegraph*, 26 September 1985.

58. Michael Billington, *Guardian*, 26 September 1985.

59. Martin Wine, *Othello: Text and Performance*, 1984.

60. Norman Sanders note, *Othello* RSC program, 1989.

61. Billington, *Guardian*, 26 September 1985.

62. Michael Coveney, *Financial Times*, 26 September 1985.

63. Stanley Wells, *Times Higher Educational Supplement*, 4 October 1985.

64. Julia Trevelyan Oman, "The Design," *Othello* RSC program, 1971.

65. Ronald Bryden, *Observer*, 12 September 1971.

66. Michael Billington, *Guardian*, 23 April 1999.

67. Nicholas de Jongh, *Evening Standard*, 19 February 2004.
68. Barton, *Times Literary Supplement*, 8 September 1989.
69. Michael Billington, *Guardian*, 26 August 1989.
70. Anne Barton, *Times Literary Supplement*, 8 September 1989.
71. Benedict Nightingale, *Times*, 20 February 2004.
72. Gareth Lloyd Evans, *Guardian*, 10 January 1971.
73. Norman Sanders, note, *Othello* RSC program, 1989.
74. Virginia Mason Vaughan, *Othello: A Contextual History*, 1994.
75. Michael Billington, *Guardian*, 20 February 2004.
76. Benedict Nightingale, *The Times*, 20 February 2004.
77. Michael Billington, *Guardian*, 23 April 1999.
78. Nightingale, *The Times*, 20 February 2004.
79. John Peter, *Sunday Times*, 29 February 2004.
80. Coveney, *Financial Times*, 26.September 1985.
81. Patrick Carnegy, *Spectator*, 1 May 1999.
82. Michael Billington, *Guardian*, 8 August 1979.
83. Christopher Edwards, *Spectator*, 2 September 1989.
84. Barton, *Times Literary Supplement*, 8 September 1989.
85. Frank Marcus, *Sunday Telegraph*, 12 September 1971 (his description of Elizabeth Spriggs' performance).
86. "Othello," in Keith Parsons and Pamela Mason, *Shakespeare in Performance*, 1995.
87. The promptbook notes: NB Emilia says Desdemona's lines as she mouths them.
88. Parsons and Mason, *Shakespeare in Performance*.
89. Ben Kingsley and David Suchet in interview with Lesley Thornton, *Observer Colour Magazine*, 22 September 1985.
90. Bob Peck, *Othello*, in Roger Sales (ed.), *Shakespeare in Perspective*, Volume Two.
91. Barton, "Hell and Night."
92. Steve Grant, *Observer*, 12 August 1979.
93. Sheridan Morley, *Punch*, 22 August 1979.
94. Richard McCabe, "Iago in *Othello*," in Robert Smallwood (ed.), *Players of Shakespeare* 5, 2003.
95. Ibid.
96. John Peter, *Sunday Times*, 29 February 2004.
97. Billington, *Guardian*, 26 September 1985.
98. Wells, *Times Higher Educational Supplement*, 4 October 1985.
99. Irving Wardle, *The Times*, 25 September 1985.
100. Michael Billington, *Country Life*, 7 September 1989.

ACKNOWLEDGMENTS AND PICTURE CREDITS

Preparation of "*Othello* in Performance" was assisted by a generous grant from the CAPITAL Centre (Creativity and Performance in Teaching and Learning) of the University of Warwick for research in the RSC archive at the Shakespeare Birthplace Trust. The Arts and Humanities Research Council (AHRC) funded a term's research leave that enabled Jonathan Bate to work on "The Director's Cut."

Picture research by Michelle Morton. Grateful acknowledgment is made to the Shakespeare Birthplace Trust for assistance with picture research (special thanks to Helen Hargest) and reproduction fees.

Images of RSC productions are supplied by the Shakespeare Centre Library and Archive, Stratford-upon-Avon. This Library, maintained by the Shakespeare Birthplace Trust, holds the most important collection of Shakespeare material in the UK, including the Royal Shakespeare Company's official archive. It is open to the public free of charge.

For more information see www.shakespeare.org.uk.

5. Directed by Ronald Eyre (1979) Joe Cocks Studio Collection © Shakespeare Birthplace Trust
6. Directed by Gregory Doran (2004) Manuel Harlan © Royal Shakespeare Company
7. Directed by Trevor Nunn (1989) Joe Cocks Studio Collection © Shakespeare Birthplace Trust
8. Directed by Michael Attenborough (1999) Malcolm Davies © Shakespeare Birthplace Trust
9. Directed by Gregory Doran (2004) © Stewart Hemley
10. Reconstructed Elizabethan playhouse © Charcoalblue

With new commentary, as well as definitive text and cutting-edge notes from the RSC's *William Shakespeare: Complete Works,* the first authoritative, modernized edition of Shakespeare's First Folio in more than 300 years.

Hamlet

Love's Labour's Lost

A Midsummer Night's Dream

Richard III

The Tempest

Also available in hardcover
William Shakespeare: Complete Works

"Timely, original, and beautifully conceived . . . a remarkable edition."
—James Shapiro, professor, Columbia University, bestselling author of *A Year in the Life of Shakespeare: 1599*